THE NEW
MACDESIGNER'S
HANDBOOK

THE *NEW* MACDESIGNER'S HANDBOOK

ALASTAIR CAMPBELL

REVISED BY
ROGER PRING

RUNNING PRESS
PHILADELPHIA · LONDON

A QUARTO BOOK

Copyright © 1992, 1997 Quarto Inc.

All rights reserved under the Pan American and International Copyright Conventions

First published in the United States of America in 1992 by Running Press Book Publishers. Second edition 1997

9 8 7 6 5 4 3 2 1
Digit on the right indicates the number of this printing

ISBN 0-7624-0206-7

Library of Congress Cataloging-in-Publication Number 96-72482

This book was designed and produced by Quarto Publishing plc
The Old Brewery
6 Blundell Street
London N7 9BH

Editor Cathy Marriott

Assistant Editor Judith Evans

Text Editors Roger Hearn, Carey Denton

Designer Alastair Campbell

Illustrators Alastair Campbell, Dave Kemp

Studio Manager Dave Kemp

Art Director Moira Clinch

Editorial Director Pippa Rubinstein

This book contains examples of computer software and graphic design work. These examples are included for the purposes of criticism and review.

Manufactured in Hong Kong by
Regent Publishing Services Ltd
Printed in China by
Leefung Asco Printers Ltd

This book may be ordered by mail from the publisher. Please include $2.50 for postage and handling. *But try your bookstore first!*

Running Press Book Publishers
125 South Twenty-second Street
Philadelphia, Pennsylvania 19103-4399

Trademarks
Trademarked names are used throughout this book. We are using the names only
to describe, inform and advise you about various aspects of computer products and to the
benefit of the trademark owner, with no intention of infringement of the trademark.

6 CONTENTS

INTRODUCTION

Talent notwithstanding, all you need to be a graphic designer is an organized mind, a layout pad, some color markers, and the ability to stick small pieces of paper onto larger ones. Or so it was until a mere eight or so years ago, when the only computer to be seen in a design office was used for accounting. At that time, young designers could get jobs without even knowing how to switch on a computer, let alone use one.

Then suddenly our drawing boards became "desktops," layout pads "application software," and the vernacular of scissors and paste changed to "megabytes" and "file output" – the computer had arrived, and the graphic arts revolution had begun.

When I originally wrote this book, the Macintosh computer – then only seven years old – had just begun to appear in the design office as a credible tool, bringing with it all the inherent confusion a revolutionary tool brings. Until that time the function of the graphic designer had been purely to communicate, and, while knowledge of technical processes was important, it was always the *creative* part of the communication chain which was regarded as paramount – technicalities were generally left to technicians. Six years later and it's all changed; designers have, by necessity, become technicians. Perhaps regrettably, but that would ignore the tremendous power that has been put into the hands of the designer, not just in the way it has brought so much of the design process, particularly typography, within his or her control, but also because of the myriad new creative opportunities which have opened up – for example, the Internet and multimedia. Fortunately, the turmoil created by the advent of the computer has begun to settle – areas of expertise are now becoming more clearly defined, and creative flair is once again being given its proper place at the top of the list of preferred graphic design skills.

Of course, change for the better must be applauded, but, in the meantime, the instability it generates also creates the risk of undermining the very core of those industries – the places where design and graphic arts are taught: the schools and colleges. Typography, graphic design, and printing have always been evolving crafts, but hitherto at a pace that allowed the technology to be absorbed and understood as much by those teaching it as by those learning it.

The Swiss writer Max Frisch once wrote that technology is "…the knack of so arranging the world that we don't have to experience it." In the context of graphic design, it would seem that the opposite is true – technology, in making everything accessible to all, has given people the power to arrange the world in a way we have no choice *but* to experience it. Examples of this all too frequently spew forth from the world of "desktop publishing" (the means of producing printed matter literally from the desktop), which provided the catalyst for the revolutionary change that has occurred across all the graphic arts industries. Computers are not by any means new to these industries – computerized laser scanners have been around for more than twenty-five years, while computers have been used in typesetting for some thirty-five. But desktop publishing, user-friendly machines that anyone can operate, has brought about a radical redefinition of the entire graphic arts industries, the secrets and tricks of which are now available to the masses – with predictable aesthetic travesties.

Yet travesties of graphic design are perpetrated not only by desktop publishers but also by many so-called "designers" who use the computer as a subterfuge for their creative inadequacies. Look around and you see the clichés of computer-generated graphics assaulting you from everywhere – pixelated images, distorted type, every font on the menu, dreadful kerning, appalling justification values – and so on.

On the positive side, the computer is a wonderful means not only of extending and enhancing the creative options available, but also of providing the designer with the potential for total control over every stage and aspect of the design process – something that has hitherto not been possible.

But it is as well to remember that just as desktop publishing is not graphic design, so graphic design does not necessarily need to involve computers. Graphic design is the manifestation of a creative solution to a given problem. A computer may give its owner the means to produce graphics, but then so does a pencil and a piece of paper. A computer enables you to render Times Bold but, as many people have discovered, it doesn't tell you what color and size it should be or how to arrange it. No matter what you use the Mac for – type design, illustration, or whatever – nothing can replace the thought process in your head and your ability to transfer those thoughts into a visual statement.

Never before has the responsibility been bestowed so

firmly on the shoulders of the design profession to police the revolution and re-establish and uphold standards which have been steadily eroded in the face of a tidal wave of amateurism brought about by the "progress" of technology.

At the core of the desktop publishing revolution is the way in which the user enters instructions into a computer and the way the computer, in turn, displays those instructions – the "user interface." All computers, by virtue of the fact that they must be given instructions, interface with their users. But the *real* change was the way in which the interface of the new computers began to simulate a desktop by using graphic symbols and a "pointer," controlled by means of a "mouse." This concept, pioneered by Xerox Corporation's Palo Alto Research Center (PARC), became known as a "graphical user interface" (GUI) and was adopted by Apple for its unsuccessful Apple Lisa computer, which was the precursor of the Macintosh.

The Macintosh, by using graphics for its interface, allowed the concept of graphic display to be exploited – and desktop publishing was born.

There *are* other computers which utilize a GUI, notably Microsoft's Windows program, which has given the world of IBM-compatible personal computers (PCs) – which dominate the business world – a GUI which is now closer to that of the Macintosh than it has ever been. With graphics software which had previously been only available for Macs now available for Windows, the choice between a computer running the Macintosh "Operating System" and one running Windows may not seem clear cut. Yet the edge which the Macintosh computer has gained on its competition has enabled it to establish a stronghold in the graphic arts industries, and, although availability of graphics software for Windows-based computers has increased, the Macintosh is still dominant in the graphics field. However, if you need any other reason for choosing a Macintosh, ask a service bureau which computer operating system gives less trouble when outputting designs to final film. In any case, since most designers use Macs – and this will run against the grain of most design thinking (originality rules) – why be different?

So what, then, will a Macintosh do for you? Its benefits are numerous: it will enable you to transform ideas speedily into a more finished state; further down the line, it will eliminate the quaint part of the design process that once required you to stick small pieces of paper onto larger ones; and it will give you the opportunity to enhance and control all those tasks which had hitherto either been difficult to control, laborious, time-consuming or costly.

The aim of this book is to give you a complete overview of every aspect of choosing and using a Macintosh for graphic design. So much of what is written in books and maga-

zines is aimed at the general Macintosh enthusiast, corporate desktop publisher or other business user and thus leans
towards all-embracing, highly-detailed technical information, making it extremely difficult for the novice design user
to beat a straight path through a jungle of irrelevant information and advice.

In planning the book, I decided that it should fulfill three
basic functions: the text serves as general introduction to
Macintosh computers for the designer, whether he or she be
a novice or a seasoned professional. It is deliberately written
to help them overcome any fears they may have of computers. It is also designed to provide instant reference for the
experienced computer user – in the form of tracking and
justification examples, color correction examples, rule
thicknesses and so on. Finally, I hope it provides insights
into some aspects of using computers in design that readers
may not previously have considered.

Chapter One is a simple explanation of the Macintosh
"environment," concerned only with what the graphic
designer really needs to know: what "system software" is
and what it does; the difference between memory and storage; what "RAM" and "ROM" do; how the "desktop" works;
files and folders; and so on.

Chapter Two is concerned with the choice of hardware for
graphic design. It describes the different functions of hardware with an explanation of what each element of the setup does, from the computer itself through to scanners and
graphics tablets.

Chapter Three is a survey of suitable software for the
graphic designer – what different types of applications are
for and what they do, as opposed to how to use them. Applications are grouped according to their function: page makeup, drawing, painting, etc. Choosing an application is one of
the most difficult decisions confronting the Mac graphic
designer. Many applications, particularly those for drawing,
may offer very similar features and ease of use, so your final
choice may ultimately depend simply on the recommenda-
tion of others.

I have tried to avoid voicing too many of my own preferences, since your requirements will quite probably be different from mine. The exception is page makeup, and I refer
consistently throughout the book more to QuarkXPress than
to any other application. This is not to say that QuarkXPress
is necessarily *better* than its competitors; it's just that the
Mac-based graphic arts industry as a whole has adopted it
as its favored layout program on the basis that, as the result
of it being seemingly the most geared toward professional
output, it is the most widely used by professionals. This
chapter also includes material on those huge new areas of
design opportunity – namely, multimedia and the Internet.

Chapter Four examines what is probably the most important, and also the most difficult aspect of the computer for the graphic designer to grasp – typography and the Mac.

Chapter Five looks at appropriate hardware and software configurations and describes the experiences of a design practice and a freelance illustrator who "went Mac" almost at the dawn of the Macintosh age.

Chapter Six looks at how to input text and handle corrections, how to organize images and your work, suggests back-up strategies and looks at working with service bureaus.

Chapter Seven explains pre-press and printing activities – once the preserve of specialist technicians – from imageset-ter output to color separation and correction right through to digitally controlled color printing.

Chapter Eight is an anti-panic, quick-reference trouble-shooting guide to all the problems that a designer is most likely to encounter on the Macintosh: system crashes; memory problems; disk management problems; printing problems and fending off viruses. I have also suggested some titles for further reading.

Chapter Nine, a combined Glossary and Index, explains over 2000 terms, many of them already familiar to the graphic designer, but here applied in a Macintosh context.

This book was written, designed, illustrated, typeset, color separated and output to final film on Apple Macintosh computers. When preparing the first edition, I used a Macintosh IIfx with 8Mb RAM and a 185Mb hard disk, a 19-inch color monitor, and two 44Mb removable hard disk drives. Of course, things have moved on, and this edition was prepared on Power Macs with up to 125Mb RAM and several gigabytes of hard disk space, with recordable CD-ROMs being the preferred method of archiving. Most of the images in the book were scanned on a LinoColor system and film was output on Linotronic imagesetters.

Regarding the production process: I started first by writing the glossary. For this I used Microsoft Word, both because of its sorting feature and so that edits could be made directly to disk in the publisher's offices. This was output as laser-printed galleys set in 12pt Helvetica Condensed, double-spaced (editing 7½pt Univers Light Condensed – the final size and font – would have been impractical). The edited version was then copied and pasted into QuarkXPress, where it was formatted. I wrote the main text directly in QuarkXPress, outputting galleys in its final typeface and size (9pt Walbaum), but with double leading to make the editor's job more comfortable. I laid out the book in QuarkXPress once edited galleys had been returned. I then prepared the illustrations using FreeHand, from which EPS files were exported for incorporating into the QuarkXPress layouts. I wrote the captions in position and laser page proofs of the layouts were printed for editing and proof correction. Revisions to the text for this edition were made directly to the final page files, which had been archived on removable hard disks. The illustrations of the various applications featured in the book were set up on screen using, of course, the applications themselves, from which screen captures were taken with the utility Captivate. The screen captures were separated into process colors using Photoshop. The resulting EPS files were then taken into QuarkXPress, from which final separated film was output. Scanned images were also separated in Photoshop and output via QuarkXPress. The files for film output were transported to the bureau on removable hard disks (the total combined size of just the files used to output this book was 69Mb). The total time taken to output film was approximately 24 hours.

Many people helped me with information, products, and advice during the original preparation of this book, and I am grateful to all of them. I am particularly indebted to Roger Pring, who is responsible for this revision. He was helped by his partner at Cooper Dale, Roger Hearn, who sadly passed away during the preparation of the book, and to him it is dedicated. I would also like to thank the following: Andrew Wakelin, David Porthouse and the staff of Thumb Design Partnership; Steve Caplin; Peter Hince; Trevor Bounford of Chapman/Bounford & Associates; Nick Souter; Anthea Backwell; Alan Coul of Amtech; Dave Taylor of Letraset; Fiona Cochrane of Adobe Systems; Dan Rampé of Claris; Bill Allen of Gomark; David Broad; Judy Martin; finally my wife and kids for putting up with my hermit-like existence while I worked on this book (beware – computers do that to you).

Alastair Campbell

Alastair Campbell graduated from London's Chelsea School of Art in 1969. In 1972 he co-founded the design group QED, with which he won a number of awards for design and illustration – among them a Designer's and Art Directors Association Silver Award – and had work exhibited throughout Europe. He went on to help build up one of the world's largest producers of illustrated books where he was creative director responsible for a long list of titles including a wide range of art and design books. Several of his titles received awards, including The Times Educational Supplement's Information Book Award and The Glenfiddich Award. In 1984 Campbell wrote The Designer's Handbook (revised 1993), which has been adopted as required reading in many design colleges throughout the world. In addition, he has sat on judging panels for various annual design and illustration exhibitions and has lectured extensively throughout Europe on various aspects of design, typography, and illustration. Since 1989, when he bought his first Macintosh computer, Campbell worked as a freelance design consultant with clients both in the United States and in Europe. He now heads Digital Wisdom Publishing Ltd., and was awarded the 1996 MacUser "Eddy" award for Best New Graphics Resource (Mountain High Maps 2.1). He lives near Cambridge with his wife and children.

1
UNDERSTANDING THE MAC
BITS AND BYTES/THE OPERATING SYSTEM/
THE DESKTOP/THE FINDER/ICONS/THE POINTER/
MENUS/WINDOWS/INTERFACE/APPLICATIONS/
FILES/MEMORY/STORAGE

This chapter is an introduction to the Macintosh environment rather than instructions on how to use a Mac – that
is covered by the manuals that come with the computer. It's
not important that you know exactly how a computer
works: a lot of what goes on inside a Mac will seem like
magic and for peace of mind it's probably best left that way.
However, there are a few basic features of computers – or
at least Macintosh computers – that you will need to know a
little about even before you buy one. (You can assume
throughout this book that comments about "the Mac" and
"Macintosh" apply equally to the wide range of Macintosh
"clones" from manufacturers other than Apple.)

Most Macs consist of four items of apparatus (hardware): a keyboard; a mouse (a palm-sized plastic box with
a button on top and a small ball protruding from its underside); something that looks like a television – this is the
monitor; and a box with sockets and slots, which is the
actual computer.

When you connect these together and switch on the
power, you may be surprised, after a few seconds, to hear a
musical tone; this confirms the Mac has tested its own internal systems and is ready to go to work. In these first few
moments, a great deal has happened. This equipment is not
just a collection of dumb electronic devices – it has already
been programed to respond to your commands.

BITS AND BYTES The basis of any computer program is
the idea of instructions set to be "on" as opposed to "off."

The computer consists of millions of tiny interconnected
circuits and switches which, as with any other kind of
switch (a light switch, for instance), need to be moved into a
position that contributes toward forming a circuit or "path."
This is achieved by giving a set of instructions to the computer – not in a way that makes sense to you, but in the only
way the computer can recognize: in the form of a code
which instructs the switches to turn on or off. The on-and-
off pairing can be represented in many ways – it can be a

positive (on) or negative (off) electric charge; it can be something or nothing – an electric current, for instance, which may flow (on) or not (off); or a light, which may shine (on) or be extinguished (off) – it may be something large (on) or small (off); it may be a magnetically charged particle with north (on) or south (off) polarity; or it may even be yes (on) or no (off). When written down, "on" is represented by a "1," and "off" by a "0." (You will find that the power switches on many electrical appliances use the symbols "1" and "0" to denote on and off). This coding is known as the "binary" system (binary meaning dual, in pairs) and a single unit (1 or 0) is called a "binary digit" – or to use its more common short form, a "bit."

However, one bit on its own doesn't contain any real information, and it is only when several bits are strung together that the computer can do anything meaningful. Two bits, for instance, can be paired to give four separate on/off instructions: 00, 11, 10 and 01. So that you can enter words into the computer, and your computer can show you its response in a way that you can understand, words, and therefore individual letters and numbers, must be represented by a code. This means that, by the time all the lower-case letters, capital letters, numbers, punctuation marks, accents and other symbols have been identified, more than 200 separate pieces of information are required

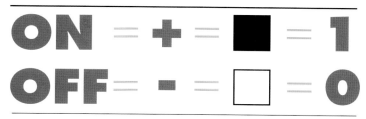

ON	=	**+**	=	■	=	**1**
OFF	=	**-**	=	□	=	**0**

A computer carries out instructions by responding to an electric circuit, which is either complete or broken (on or off). The state of the circuit is represented by a 1 (positive, or on) and a 0 (negative, or off), called binary digits, or bits, each of which signify something or nothing, black or white, etc. (**above**). Two bits can be written in four different combinations and can thus only give four instructions, such as four shades of gray (**above right**). However, eight bits can be written in 256 combinations, each representing a single character. 24 bits can give 16.7 million combinations.

2-bit instructions

00
01
10
11

=

8-bit instructions

01000001 = A
01100001 = a
01000010 = B
01100010 = b
00110001 = 1
00110010
01000011

to represent even one of the simpler alphabets. To have that many individual codes, programmers need a total resource of 256, which is the maximum number of different combinations that eight 0s or 1s can make. Each character is therefore represented by an 8-bit code number. The letter "H," for example, is recognized by your computer as "01001000," whereas a lower-case "h" has to be represented by a different code. Eight bits like this are called a "byte," representing a single character.

If this is beginning to sound complex, don't panic – to use a Mac, you don't need to know any more about binary code than this – actually, you don't need to know *anything* about binary code to use a Mac, but you will probably feel more at ease if you know what constitutes bits and bytes.

THE OPERATING SYSTEM Computer code takes two forms. The first is the pre-written code used, for example, to make the computer start up. The same sort of code forms the basis of the various programs ("applications") you will use to produce work on the Mac. The second type of code automatically translates your contribution – typing words or drawing shapes on screen, into "data" code, or just "data." To you, however, it appears in plain English if you are typing, or as shapes if you are drawing.

The Macintosh operating system is provided in two forms – the first is permanently embedded in a microchip inside the computer and is unalterable. The second is system software – generally already loaded by the manufacturer. You will be able to update this second component, taking advantage of new developments as they arise, simply by copying new software via a floppy disk or CD-ROM (see p.36-9).

THE DESKTOP When you switch on the Mac, the monitor screen shows two little symbols or pictures in the top right and bottom right corners. Along the top of the gray area is a narrow white strip containing a few words and more symbols. This is your first view of the Macintosh working environment, and what is displayed is called the "desktop." The picture symbols are called "icons," and the white strip is the "menu bar." The analogy with a desktop is deliberate, and the analogy follows, as far as is practical, that of your real desk, with folders, files and even a trash can for throwing things away. You can customize your desktop so that it suits the way you work – you can choose to have the pointer move fast or slow, adjust the loudspeaker volume, change the desktop background pattern, and so on.

THE FINDER The program that provides the Mac's operating system is called simply the "System." However, the desktop described above is actually provided by another, separate, program called the "Finder." The Finder program provides the icons, menus and windows that are the tools on your desktop and that enable you to organize your work

Below To operate a computer, you give it instructions ("input") via a keyboard (**1**). The computer (**3**) converts your instructions into data that it can understand (but which you cannot) and which enables it to carry out its tasks. In order that you can see what you are doing and what the computer is doing, your input and the results of anything you have asked the computer to do are converted back into a form that you can understand. This is done by means of displaying characters and

words ("output"), on a monitor screen (**4**). The relationship between your input and computer output is called the "user interface." The Macintosh utilizes a variety of graphic devices which have been designed to make the computer easier to use. These devices, called

"WIMPs," comprise "windows" (**5**), "icons" (**6**), "menus" (**7**) and a "pointer" (**8**) which you can move around the screen by means of a device called a "mouse" (**2**). The use of WIMPs is known as a "graphical user interface" (GUI).

From bits to gigabytes

8 bits = 1 byte
1024 bytes = 1 kilobyte (K)
1024 kilobytes = 1 megabyte (Mb) (1,048,576 bytes)
1024 megabytes = 1 gigabyte (gig) (1,073,741,824 bytes)

Strictly speaking, "kilo" means one thousand, but because computers use a binary system (pairs of numbers) each number is doubled: 2; 4; 8; 16; 32; 64; 128; 256; 512; 1,024.

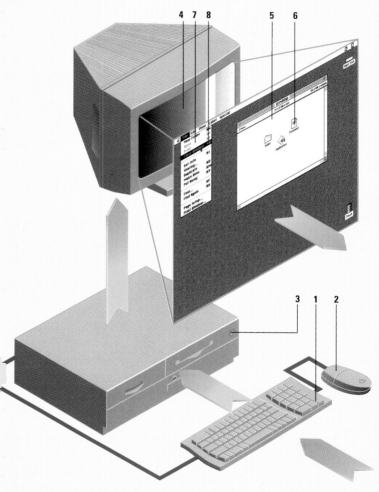

both on the desktop and in folders. The System and the Finder are inseparable – for a Mac to run, both programs must be present.

ICONS An icon is a pictorial representation of a collection of data such as a file or a disk. As far as is possible, the picture on the icon depicts the type of file it represents – a document is usually represented by a rectangle with a turned over corner, while an application icon will depict a hand holding a pen, or some other image that symbolizes the purpose of the application. System file icons sometimes resemble the Mac itself.

THE POINTER You will also see on the screen a small, left-leaning arrow, called the "pointer." When you move the mouse on a flat surface, the pointer responds accordingly by moving around the screen. If you position the pointer over an icon and press the button on top of the mouse (this is called "clicking" the mouse), the icon changes color – it becomes highlighted, indicating that it is "selected." You cannot achieve anything on a Mac unless you select something first – an icon, a command or a piece of text, for example. The shape of the pointer may change from an arrow to a symbol of something else – an "I-beam" or "cursor," for example, if you are editing text, or a wristwatch if your Mac requires you to wait while it performs a task.

MENUS The icon at top right of the desktop represents the machine's internal "hard disk," which is the place where all your work and everything else that you work with will be stored – the "drawers" of the desk, if you like. Just as the drawers in your desk can be opened, so can your hard disk. You do this by selecting the icon as described above, then moving the pointer to the word "File" in the menu bar and clicking the mouse. A list will instantly appear, or "pop down," and will remain visible as long as you keep the mouse button pressed. This list is called a "menu," and the items listed on it are called "commands." By choosing a command on the menu, you are telling your Mac to do something. On the menu you have chosen are several commands. Keeping the mouse button pressed, move the pointer down the list until it reaches "Open." Each command is highlighted as the pointer crosses it. Releasing the mouse button on a highlighted item selects it.

WINDOWS Having selected "Open" from the "File" menu, a white, framed panel containing more icons zooms into view. This panel is called a "window," and the contents of every icon you open in this manner will be displayed in a similar way. In practice, you'll find it quicker to open an icon by pointing at it with the mouse and "double-clicking" – clicking twice in rapid succession on the mouse button.

INTERFACE When you press a key on the keyboard, you enter ("input") something into the computer – you either type words or tell the computer to do something (you give it a command). So that you can keep track of what you are doing, your actions are displayed on the monitor screen. Likewise, if the computer wants to ask or tell you something, it will also do so on the screen, or make a sound indicating that you have requested it to perform a task which it cannot do. This relationship between you and the computer is called the "user interface" ("interface" describes the method by which a computer interacts with a person or some other device such as a printer). The combination of *W*indows, *I*cons, *M*enus (or *M*ouse) and *P*ointer is sometimes referred to as a "WIMPs" computer interface, but this use of graphic devices which interact with each other is more commonly called a "graphical user interface" (GUI).

APPLICATIONS Using the Finder is fine for moving icons around the desktop, opening folders, and so on, but it doesn't enable you to create anything. To produce something useful, you must use another set of program instructions, written to perform specific tasks. Programs that do this are variously called "application software," "application programs," or just "applications." Your Mac may arrive with a selection of such programs already installed and you will certainly be adding new ones via CD-ROM or floppy disk.

When you open an application, you are effectively opening up a box of tools, complete with its own drawing or writing pad, and putting it onto the desktop. With this application you write, draw, paint, or do whatever the application is designed for. Most of the work you do – and certainly everything you actually create – will be done while working with an application (see p.50). It may seem, then, that the applications you use are more important than the computer. But what gives the Macintosh its unique edge over other computers (even those imitating it) is not just the way that it presents a user-friendly environment even without any applications running, but the way in which Apple tries to promote the same user-friendliness within applications written by other software developers (the use of consistent vocabulary across applications – commands and menus, for example). Apple lays down guidelines for developers to follow when writing Mac applications and, although these guidelines often involve areas which are invisible ("transparent") to the user, they are fundamental to the way in which that application conforms to the ease-of-use ethos of the Mac environment.

FILES A file is a collection of data to which a name has been given so that it can be used or stored either by you or by your computer. Every icon you see on your desktop (even a hard or floppy disk icon) represents a file of one kind or another. There are also some invisible files not represented by icons: for example, the desktop itself has an invisible file which records its overall status – a kind of electronic housekeeping. The files which concern you as the user fall into

When a Macintosh computer has finished its startup sequence, the monitor will display the "desktop" (**1**). The white strip at the top is the "menu bar" (**2**), and the words within it "menu titles" (**3**). Although represented pictorially, the icons in the menu bar are menu titles for the "Apple menu" (**4**), the "Help menu" (**5**) and the "Application menu" (**6**). When a menu title is "selected" with the pointer (**7**), a panel, called a "menu," drops down (**8**). The items listed in the menu are called "commands" (**9**). On the desktop are at least two icons: a hard disk icon (**10**), representing the contents of the computer's hard disk, and an icon of a garbage can, called the "trash," where you "throw away" things you no longer need. To see what's "inside" an icon, it must be "opened" by selecting the icon with the pointer (it becomes highlighted) and then choosing the "Open" command from the "File" menu. This produces a panel called a "window" (**11**), which displays the contents of the icon. A window comprises a "Title bar" (**12**),

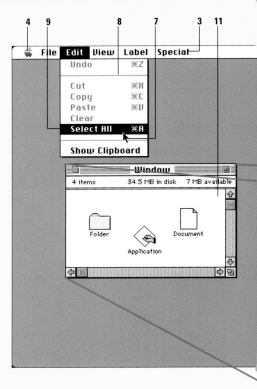

FLOPPY DISK 1

FLOPPY DISK 2

FLOPPY DISK 3

FLOPPY DISK 4

Icons Icons represent disks in, or attached to, a Macintosh computer and the folders and files stored on them. An icon will generally depict, as closely as possible given its small size, the item it represents. The color of the icon indicates its current state, for instance, the icons (**left**) represent an unopen floppy disk (**1**), a selected floppy disk (**2**), an open floppy disk (**3**) and an ejected floppy disk (**4**). The icons (**right**) depict a folder in its unopen (**5**), selected (**6**), and open state (**7**). The trash icon (**8**) is where you delete files you no longer require. The icon bulges when something is placed in the trash (**9**). Just as with a folder, the trash can be

FOLDER ICON 5

FOLDER ICON 6

FOLDER ICON 7

opened and its contents viewed.

a "Close box" (**13**) for closing the window, a "Zoom box" (**14**) for opening up the window to full size, a "Size box" (**15**) for altering the size of the window, and "Scroll arrows" (**16**) for viewing items hidden beyond the edges of the window. The relative position of the visible portion of the

window is indicated by the "Scroll box" (**17**) in the "Scroll bar" (**18**). The icons displayed in the window represent "Files" (**19**) or "Folders" (**20**). The latter may contain other folders or files.

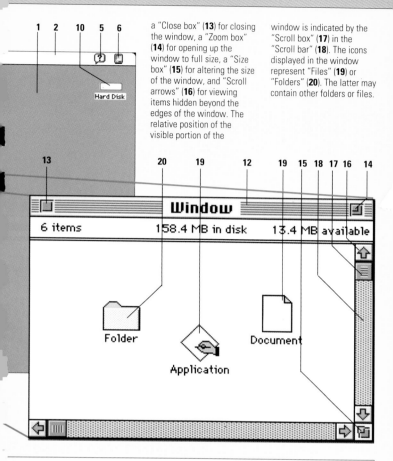

Hard Disk

Folders depicting other icons on the front will either be the system folder (**10**) or a folder within it (**11**).

The basic Macintosh application file icon depicts a hand holding a pen over a piece of paper (**12**) to reflect the productive purpose of an application. Other application icons usually

symbolize the purpose of the application, such as page make-up (QuarkXPress, **13**) or drawing (FreeHand, **14**). Documents are the files you generate within an application. The "generic" document icon depicts a piece of paper with a turned-over corner (**15**). Documents created in applications also retain the identity of their application icons (QuarkXPress, **16**, and FreeHand, **17**, **18**). System

files are often represented by a Mac icon, such as with the Finder (**19**) and the System file itself (**20**).

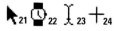

The mouse is represented on screen by the "pointer" icon (**21**) which assumes different shapes for different tasks. The wristwatch (**22**) means "wait," while the "I-beam" (**23**) is used for text, and the cross-hair pointer (**24**) for drawing shapes.

four main groups: system files, application files, document files, and the folders into which the various files can be grouped.

System files These are all the files that form part of the Mac's operating system, including the System and Finder files. They also include files that you may have added to enhance the system, such as fonts (typefaces). The picture depicted by a system file icon will vary depending on the function it performs, but those that form the basis of the operating system generally display a symbol of a Macintosh computer (the System file itself shows a Mac on the side of a folder). System files are always kept in the System folder either inside other subsidiary folders or loose (not in another folder).

Application files This refers to all files belonging to an application, including the application itself. Many larger applications come with a number of subsidiary files. Since the correct location of these subsidiary files is crucial to the operation of the main application, the whole collection of files is copied on to your Mac by an associated "installer" application. When you open ("run") the installer, it places all the files in appropriate places, also creating new folders if necessary. "Help," "Data," "Preferences," and "Defaults" are all typical application files. The application itself is usually identifiable by the full name of the application; for example, the QuarkXPress page layout application is labeled "QuarkXPress®" beneath its icon, whereas subsidiary application files used by QuarkXPress are given names such as "XPress Help" and have their own icons.

Documents A document is any file that you create or modify with an application – a page layout or a letter, for example. The application will ask you to "save" your work by giving it a title and choosing a place on the hard disk in which to store it: at this point the file gains an identity.

Folders These are easy to identify – their icons look just like a closed folder. Strictly speaking, folders are not data files in themselves, but places where you keep data files – you use folders to organize everything on your Mac by putting documents and applications inside. Folders, like documents, have names. The way you name and organize folders is entirely for you to choose – you can put folders within other folders and those folders inside yet other folders (see p.120). The files which comprise your Mac's operating system are located in the System folder – easily identified because it is the only folder icon showing a picture of a Mac – and are best left undisturbed until you are completely familiar with the way the system operates.

MEMORY In order for both you and the computer to manage your work, the computer must keep track of what you are doing at any given moment as well as keeping a record so that you can retrieve your work at a later session.

Using your own memory as an analogy, just as you record your memories by writing them down – in a diary, say – so a computer must transfer data from temporary memory to storage of a more permanent kind.

To achieve both things, the computer uses two kinds of memory – one temporary, the other permanent. Temporary memory is called "random access memory," or "RAM." Confusingly, RAM is also commonly referred to as just "memory." Permanent memory is generally called "storage." Even experienced users sometimes misunderstand the difference between memory and storage. To confuse things even further, there is a third kind of memory called "read-only memory," or "ROM," and I'll deal with that first.

You will frequently come across references to "memory"; the confusion between the ideas of microchip and storage memory is partly due to the fact that they are both measured in "megabytes" (see p.17).

ROM As described earlier in this chapter, the Macintosh operating system is provided in two parts – one as software on its hard disk, the other embedded in a microchip. This microchip stores memory called "read-only memory" (ROM), the contents of which can only be read, not added to or altered. These ROM chips have their information installed at the time of their manufacture and, once the chip is plugged into the Mac, the information cannot be changed except by replacing the chip.

The information in ROM is always available and, unlike RAM, is not erased when you switch off your Mac. The part of the system software that resides in ROM is called the "toolbox," and this contains the pre-installed permanent software that provides information ("routines") about windows, menus, dialog boxes etc., that programmers use when they create applications to make them consistent with the Mac environment. The ROM provides diagnostic routines that test certain hardware functions every time the Mac is switched on.

RAM Just as your memories are erased forever when you die, so "random access memory" (RAM) is lost when the computer is switched off. In the same way that you need energy to live, RAM needs power (in the form of an electric current) to retain the information stored within it. RAM is used by applications to enable you, in turn, to use the application – when you open an application, you are effectively copying part of it from the place where it is stored into RAM. The application itself remains stored, though other parts of it may be copied and put into RAM as and when required. When you use an application – when you type words or draw shapes, for instance – you are doing so in RAM, and the work that you do on screen has no permanence until you store it somewhere (i.e. "save" it to disk, see below). If your electrical supply suddenly fails, for example, you will

Memory and storage
While you work on a computer, you work with data held in its memory, called "random access memory" (RAM). Some of the data may be generated by you, and some put there by the computer's "central processing unit" (CPU) on instructions from you or from the software you are using. The CPU acts as a switch that routes data from one place to another. The CPU retrieves permanently stored data from a medium such as a disk and puts it into the computer's memory

(**1**). From here the data is used for display on a monitor (**2**). Data that you generate is temporarily stored in RAM (**3**) and lasts only for as long as power is supplied to its microchips; thus everything in RAM is lost when you turn the computer off. So that you do not lose your work, it must be "written" to a suitable storage medium (**4**). Another kind of memory, called "read only memory" (ROM), contains permanently stored data that the computer needs in order to operate (**5**).

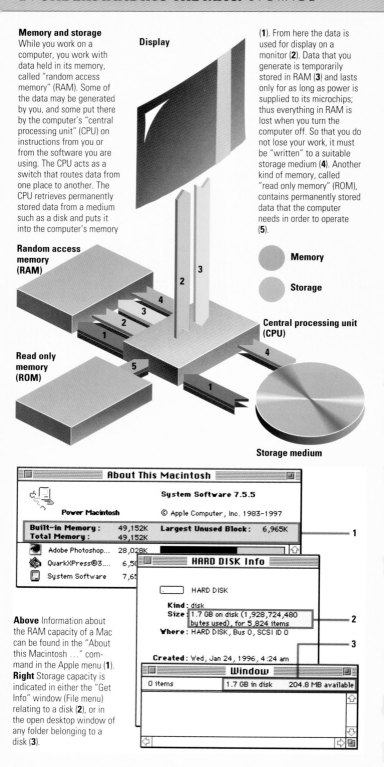

Display

Random access memory (RAM)

Read only memory (ROM)

Memory

Storage

Central processing unit (CPU)

Storage medium

About This Macintosh

System Software 7.5.5

Power Macintosh   © Apple Computer, Inc. 1983-1997

| Built-in Memory : | 49,152K | Largest Unused Block : | 6,965K |
| Total Memory : | 49,152K | | |

- Adobe Photoshop...   28,028K
- QuarkXPress®3....   6,50
- System Software   7,65

HARD DISK Info

HARD DISK

Kind : disk
Size : 1.7 GB on disk (1,928,724,480 bytes used), for 5,824 items
Where : HARD DISK, Bus 0, SCSI ID 0

Created : Wed, Jan 24, 1996, 4:24 am

Window

0 items   1.7 GB in disk   204.8 MB available

Above Information about the RAM capacity of a Mac can be found in the "About this Macintosh ..." command in the Apple menu (**1**).
Right Storage capacity is indicated in either the "Get Info" window (File menu) relating to a disk (**2**), or in the open desktop window of any folder belonging to a disk (**3**).

lose all your on-screen work, though the Mac and anything already saved on to your hard disk will be fine once the power comes on again. This is the most unstable aspect of using a computer, and it is essential to get into the habit of saving your work at frequent intervals – the more frequent, the better.

RAM, like ROM, resides in microchips. The greater number and the capacity of your RAM chips, the more you can achieve in RAM – you can use more fonts (a font only uses RAM when active and usable on your system) – have more applications open at a time (an application only uses RAM when it is open) – and you can work on large, complex layouts or illustrations (as with applications, documents only require RAM when they are open). Different applications occupy different amounts of RAM; a simple word-processing application works happily with less than 1Mb, whereas a professional page layout application may demand 4Mb or more just to start up. New releases and upgrades add more features at the cost of even greater appetite for RAM. You have some control via the "Info" box of each application, but you cannot go below the "preferred" setting.

Parameter RAM (PRAM) Pronounced "pee-ram," this is where settings such as the time and date are stored. Unlike RAM, this information is not erased when you turn off your Mac because it is powered by its own battery (if you removed the battery, you would lose the settings).

Virtual memory The Macintosh is able to supplement its built-in ("installed") RAM by tricking the system into thinking that part of the unoccupied space on the hard disk is RAM, thereby increasing the amount of RAM available for you to work with. This type of RAM is called "virtual memory" and is slower than "real" RAM. Other third-party software offers similar increases in apparent power by subtly changing the way the Mac allocates RAM to applications as you open and close them.

Memory To save your work permanently, you copy it from RAM to one of a variety of storage media. Your storage medium could be a hard or floppy disk, tape or CD-ROM, or a combination. Unlike RAM, which you cannot actually see, storage media are represented on the desktop by icons, each separate storage device having its own icon (you can have several hard disks or "drives" attached to, or in some cases, built into, your Mac – see p.30). Copying your work from RAM to disk is called saving it, and is done by using the Save command from the File menu in the menu bar. This command will only be present in a menu when you are using an application – there is no Save command in the Finder because you don't create anything there – any changes you make to the desktop are automatically recorded in the invisible desktop file.

2
HARDWARE

Perversely, given that they are such capable design tools, computers themselves are usually no more than bland, even ugly boxes, distinguishable to the novice only by the number of twinkling colored lights – the more there are (surely?), the more desirable it must be.

The criteria for choosing a computer system depend not on esthetics but upon its intended use. You may be forgiven for thinking that, when it comes to computers, the needs of all graphic designers are more or less the same, regardless of what specific activity they may be engaged in. Fortunately, one of the outstanding features of the Mac is that it seems to be virtually limitless in its adaptability to different design disciplines. Obviously, cost will rate high on your list of considerations. Don't be under any misapprehension: this is not a once-only capital purchase – you will inevitably find yourself spending money on a more-or-less continuous basis on such things as service agreements, performance enhancements, add-on hardware, new software, upgrades and so on. Of course, the extent to which you continue to shell out depends not only on your relationship with your bank, but also upon your own self-discipline – be warned, you may often find it difficult to resist the many temptations floated in front of you by competing marketeers.

THE MACINTOSH The Macintosh box is often referred to as the "CPU" (central processing unit), even though this term really applies to the microprocessor within it. Of all the hardware that you will buy, one of the most straightforward items to choose is probably the Macintosh computer itself, simply because there are a limited number of models available to choose from, even though there may be many configurations within each model. There are three basic types of Mac: those which incorporate a screen as part of the body of the computer ("compact" Macs); those which don't ("modular" Macs); and battery-powered portable Macs ("PowerBooks"), which incorporate the CPU and screen in a folding case. The screens of early compact Macs were small – only 9in diagonal – and therefore very hard to use for serious design work. Current compacts feature screens of at least 15in that are adequate for all but the most ambitious page design and illustration. The traveling designer might also consider the various models of MessagePad, offering handwriting recognition and wireless links for downloading work to static Macs.

THE MICROPROCESSOR This chip, the central processing unit, represents the brain of the computer. Early Macintosh computers were equipped with CPUs of the Motorola 68000 series. If you are considering economizing by buying this kind of first-generation equipment, bear in mind that only the later 68030 and 68040 chips incorporate a "paged memory-management unit" (PMMU) which, among other things, allows you to take advantage of "virtual memory" (see p.25). Some working designers manage to resist the attractions of the latest models, but in a competitive market they pay an increasing price in terms of lack of processing speed and, more important, the gradual erosion of their ability to run up-to-date software. Seek out such a pioneer and you will hear 50 reasons why none of the above matters more than a very small hill of beans, but the range of Macs on offer now have facilities far in advance of those early models; it is now common, for example, to find machines with multiple processors inside, and speeds hiked to previously unimaginable levels.

SPEED Theoretically, a computer's speed is related to the number of times per second that a quartz crystal inside it pulsates, which, in turn, determines the speed of such things as the time it takes for the screen to redraw or how frequently the CPU needs to access PRAM. These pulses are measured in megahertz (MHz), one MHz representing one million cycles, or instructions, per second, and is referred to as "clock speed." However, technology has advanced, starting with the ability to handle greater amounts of data simultaneously and the development of a CPU with integrated coprocessors and memory. In the first edition of this book we marveled at the blindingly-fast 25MHz clock speed of the then top-of-the-line Quadra 900. Just look in a current Macintosh product list to see how quaint that now appears.

Of all the considerations when buying a Mac for professional use, speed is one of the most important. If you have read any Macintosh magazines, you may have noticed the preponderance of ads for all manner of speed-related enhancements; if you buy a slow machine, you will discover, the hard way, why there are so many.

Of course, speed, like so many things, is relative; and for the first few months of learning to use the Mac, it may not seem a priority. However, as you become more proficient, you may also become increasingly frustrated by the time it takes for commands to be implemented, which can be quite considerable even on a fast machine.

Your requirement for speed depends upon what kind of design work you intend using the Mac for; this determines the type of application you will be using (the speeds of different applications vary, even if they are performing similar tasks). If all you require is a paste-up substitute for creating small-format, short documents such as ads, the greater cost of a fast machine may be difficult to justify – it would be like using a Ferrari to make deliveries around town. If you intend doing anything more than the most basic kind of design work, however, you will find increased speed not just useful, but a necessity. Working on long documents which are heavy with graphic devices and tints, working with images and creating complex illustrations are all activities that demand the fastest computing speeds if you don't want your creativity to atrophy during the process.

If you think you may require even greater speed than the fastest Mac can provide, you will need an accelerator card (see p.48).

MEMORY Vying with speed as the most important criterion when choosing a computer is the amount of random access memory (RAM) the computer has (don't make the common mistake of confusing *memory* with *storage* – see p.23).

RAM is less important than it used to be, not only because additional RAM chips are now both inexpensive and easy to install, but also because System 7 and its developments brought with it the facility of virtual memory (see p.25). However, because virtual memory is significantly slower than installed, or *real* RAM, it makes sense to have as much real RAM installed as you think you'll need – and the answer to that is, as much as will fit into your machine. You will also become interested in the rising price of new memory following a chip factory mishap, and in its fall once the market settles down again.

There are currently three types of RAM chip on offer to expand your Mac's memory – two are different configurations of SIMMs ("single in-line memory modules") that relate to earlier Macs – the other is the DIMM type ("dual in-line memory module") that is used in recent machines. There are other types specially designed to fit portable Macs. As usual, there is more to this than meets the eye. Every Mac has an absolute upper limit to the amount of real RAM it can accept. These limits are always increasing, as are the chances that a new sort of RAM chip may come along. This is no problem until you try to transfer your hoard of RAM from an old machine to a new one.

It is not necessary to commit yourself to buying huge quantities of extra RAM at the moment of purchasing your Mac – when you need more, you can just buy it and install it yourself. Having a lot of RAM is good, and having a very

Inside a Macintosh All the components of a typical Macintosh computer are connected to one another via a single circuit board called the motherboard (**1**). This houses the many microchips which process data and switch it from one component to another. At the core of these microchips is the central processing unit (CPU) (**2**). In some models the processor itself can be removed and a new one fitted. Random access memory (RAM) is held in banks of chips called double in-line memory modules (DIMMs) (**3**), which are plugged into sockets on the motherboard – extra RAM chips can easily be fitted. Existing Video RAM (VRAM) chips (**4**) can also be augmented. Specialist "cards" are designed to slots into the motherboard. A PCI (Peripheral Component Interconnect) card (**5**) like this is typically used to enhance performance on large monitors. The floppy disk drive (**6**) and CD-ROM drive (**7**) are accessed via openings on the front of the computer. There is an additional bay (**8**) on this Macintosh to take another externally-accessed drive. The main internal hard disk (**9**) for data storage is a sealed unit and there is a bay with space and a power supply for another. The Mac's power supply (**10**) adjusts itself to any voltage and is cooled by a built-in fan. Power-on is indicated by a green light on the front of the computer (**11**).

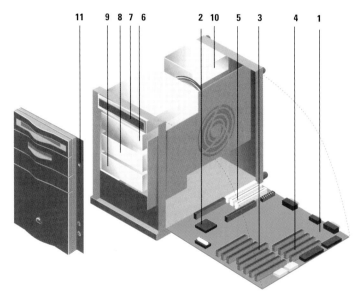

large amount of RAM is very good indeed. You will only need hundreds of megabytes of RAM if you deal with image-intensive documents such as those used at the pre-press stages of reproduction, or for memory-intensive operations such as those undertaken by some CAD (computer-aided design) and multimedia applications.

Although RAM is used by any applications you have open – the more you have open at one time, the more RAM you occupy (see p.25) – it is also required in certain "invisible," or background, areas. System files, and most particularly fonts, in use eat up RAM, as do large color monitors. And if you're interested in making and editing movies, your need for RAM will become intense.

STORAGE All Macs come fitted with an internal floppy disk drive, an internal hard disk (drive) and, almost certainly, a built-in CD drive. The floppy drive will be able to read a variety of 3½in disks, including those formatted in PC style (see p.117), though earlier machines may need extra software to achieve this. The more powerful machines have empty internal drive bays already fitted with a suitable power supply and connections to the CPU. You can insert additional hard disk drives (or almost any other sort of storage device) by removing a panel and making the appropriate connections.

It may seem obvious that the greater the hard disk's capacity the easier it is to work, but since Parkinson's Law always prevails (in this context, the fact that your work, in the form of data, will always occupy the space available for it), I am convinced that, contrary to the advertising which generates increasing pressure for greater storage, a *smaller* disk capacity is sometimes preferable, simply because it encourages neater housekeeping. However, if you intend working extensively with images (scanned or drawn), large documents or multimedia applications, you really will need the largest capacity disk you can afford; a single image, for example – even scanned at a low resolution – can easily occupy several Mb of disk space. The question of response time offered by the hard disk can also influence your choice; for multimedia use, for example, you'll need a drive with the quickest response time and the highest continuous data transfer rate. Helpfully, such drives are labeled "AV."

CONNECTIVITY The gaggle of connector sockets (ports) at the back of the Mac, and slots inside, will be the hardest part for you to deal with when you start out. Mercifully most of them are common to all Macs and, with the exception of specialist audio and video requirements, they shouldn't influence your purchasing decision. The following list shows typical ports found on various models. Not all ports exist on all Macs.

Apple Desktop Bus (ADB) port The mouse connects to the keyboard which then connects to the Mac via the ADB port. If you have an additional input device such as a graphics tablet, you'll need a Y-shaped adaptor to provide an extra connection. Since the cable carries a current (albeit a small one), do observe the precautions advised in the manual, especially when adding peripheral devices. When in doubt, shut everything down and then do the changeover – you'll be protecting the Mac as well as yourself.

SCSI or SCSI2 (small computer system interface) port Pronounced "skuzzy," this port is used to connect peripheral devices such as external drives and scanners. Although you will find only a single SCSI port on all Macs, several devices (up to seven, including the internal hard drive) can be "daisy-chained" together, using the one port (see p.106).

Serial ports These two ports are used by LocalTalk and GeoPort, Apple's own cabling systems, to connect the Mac to printers, modems (and therefore to the Internet), or to a network of Macs or other computers.

Ethernet ports These can be used in the same way as serial ports but offer much higher rates of transfer.

Sound-in and sound-out ports Where the Mac is not fitted with a built-in microphone, an external microphone is plugged into the sound-in port. The sound-out port is a low-power source suitable for headphones or re-amplification by powered external speakers.

Monitor port If the Mac has no built-in screen, this port provides the signal for a monitor. It is also possible to fit an additional video card inside the Mac. In this case the card has its own monitor port, offering the possibility of running two screens side-by-side from one machine. This output is complemented in "audio-visual" Macs by further, separate audio and video links (see below).

AV ports A collection of ports allows VCRs and camcorders to feed directly into and out of a Mac. Composite video signals (just like a home TV set) are accompanied by high-quality stereo audio feeds. Using these connections, the Mac can be used to control video editing equipment.

Internal slots These sockets are accessed inside the Mac, and are designed for plug-in cards which are semi-permanently installed. All kinds of features and enhancements, such as video cards for connecting a monitor, accelerator cards for improving performance, modem and fax cards for connecting to telecommunications lines can be added via these slots.

Before you buy a Mac, give serious consideration to what enhancements you may eventually add. This is the "expandability" question. If you think you may at some stage add cards for, say, a large color monitor, an accelerator, full-motion video, or even PC software compatibility, you will eventually need four or more slots. This will seriously reduce your options in the Mac range. Note that the expansion slots in earlier Macs were designed to take "NuBus" cards – they are not compatible with modern PCI cards.

Microphone input port For voice recording (better done through dedicated sound ports – see above). If, however, you like the idea of controlling your Mac with voice commands, this slot will provide hours of amusement.

VRAM slot The demands of high- and variable-resolution color monitors mean you may have to add more video RAM to that already provided.

MONITORS Monitors work in much the same way as ordinary television sets, where the screen inside a cathode ray tube (CRT), coated with light-sensitive phosphor, is bombarded by a stream of electrons. When impacted the phosphor glows briefly, creating an image. Compact Macs have screens already built in to their cases, so it is not necessary to choose one. However, since it is likely that you will be buying a modular Mac, there are several things about working with monitors that you should know.

Resolution As far as design work is concerned, the most important consideration – even before size and color – is the resolution of the screen. Effectively, this refers to the crispness of the image on the screen – particularly important when you are working with small type sizes. The screen image is represented on screen by tiny square dots, or "pixels," which create a picture by being either on or off. The more pixels there are per inch, the smaller they are and the better the resolution of the screen, thus the sharper the image. Most high-resolution monitors have 72 dots per inch (dpi) or more. If a salesperson tries to seduce you by raving on about the total pixel count of a monitor (and they do), don't listen – 1,920,000 pixels may sound impressive, but you'd expect that kind of number on a 21in screen. It's still only 72dpi, though.

Size Monitor sizes are always described in inches, measured diagonally from corner to corner. This is a tradition perpetuated by cathode tube manufacturers, but is misleading when it comes to establishing the actual dimensions of the total image area of a computer monitor. A 19in screen may *look* huge when it's switched off, showing a potential image area of an adequate 11½ x 15¼in but, when it is switched on may display only 10¾ x 13⅜in – not quite enough height for a letter-size page. To establish the usable image area of a monitor, all you need to know is the number of pixels both horizontally and vertically, plus the resolution (in dpi) of the monitor. You then simply divide each of the horizontal and vertical pixel counts by the resolution – thus a screen described as 19in, with a horizontal pixel count of 1024, a vertical pixel count of 808 and a resolution of 75dpi will produce an image area of 10¾ x 13⅜in. Incidentally, don't be confused by the *appearance* of a monitor – a monitor marketed by one supplier may look identical from the outside to a different product marketed by another. This is because the tube and casing will have been manufactured by a third company, but is used by the two suppliers as a vehicle for displaying their wares – the video card circuitry design and software.

For most design work, a 15in monitor is quite adequate, but if you work extensively with page layouts where you need to see a two-page spread, you really need a larger screen.

Color Monitors are either monochrome, "grayscale," or color. Monochrome monitors, as the name suggests, display pixels as either black or white, with no intermediate grays (a semblance of grays is achieved by alternating black pixels with white ones). Grayscale monitors, on the other hand, are able to display pixels in a range of grays, the exact number depending on the "pixel depth" of the monitor, but usually providing 256 grays.

Color monitors operate on much the same principle as

grayscale monitors, but instead of the pixels being different shades of gray, they are different colors.

Pixel depth becomes important on color monitors since, if you opt for a color monitor, you will be faced with a choice of its being either 8 bits or 24 bits per pixel – perhaps more. The difference is startling – 8 bits produces a mere 256 colors whereas 24 bits produces more than 16 million! This doesn't mean that you can only display 256 colors or tints because, as with four-color halftone printing (which, after all, produces a pretty good range with only *four* colors), a group of different colors in close proximity optically merges to form a variety of colors that is adequate for most purposes.

The question of color fidelity is a vital one for the designer. It would be great to choose a color on screen and see it perfectly reproduced when the job comes back from the printer. This joyful match is hard to achieve – and almost as hard to maintain. We know that different press systems have different color characteristics, and that's before considering paper color and finish. For a start, the vibrant color screen is much more intense than the printed page; it can show much greater apparent contrast and color saturation. Top-of-the-range color monitors for reproduction are equipped with sophisticated calibration systems (you'll need a top-of-the-range pocketbook to afford one). The way ahead for the rest of us is more labor-intensive, but affordable and efficient once you have set some standards of your own.

Load your Mac with a color image – ideally one you have had printed before – maybe adding the scanned test transparency you'll find in your image-editing software package. Make up a page and fill it with items you often print, such as clients' logos, favorite tint backgrounds, colored type on colored panels and so on. Take your disk to your most favored print shop, and with great good humor, suggest that a *very* economical print estimate for a few copies would bring happiness to all concerned. If this approach fails, invest instead in a high quality colour print from a bureau and find another printer. Compare your new print with the screen display, making a note of all the settings which you used when making the artwork. You will see variations from the image you expected, but at least you have a basis on which to make better judgments in the future. Don't forget either that you have all the traditional techniques at your disposal – specifying tints and spot colors from reference charts, quoting either percentages of process colors or reference numbers, or including printed color samples with the disk. With monochrome or grayscale monitors, the same is possible – you can still specify colors (assuming, of course, that your application allows you to) even if you can't see them – and you can still produce them as separated film.

All Macs have video circuitry already built in so that you can plug a simple (256-color) monitor straight in. If you do decide to buy a non-Apple monitor, you will need to add a video or graphics card to one of your Mac's expansion slots – you cannot simply plug the monitor into the back of your Mac. Be warned, though – opening your Mac's case voids the warranty unless done by an Apple-approved engineer. (This is something of an anomaly, since to maximize use of your Mac's expandability, you've *got* to open up your Mac sometime – perhaps Apple figures that by the time you've gathered enough confidence to open up your Mac, the warranty will have run out anyway.)

Refresh rate This is a background, but still important, consideration when choosing a monitor (it's to do with comfort and, since you will be staring at a screen all day, should not

Resolution Computer monitors, although similar to television screens in that they utilize cathode ray tubes, display images at much higher levels of definition or "resolution" than televisions. Typical monitors have a resolution of between 72 and 87 dots, or pixels, per inch. Despite this high resolution, small sizes of type can be difficult to read on screen (**right**), thus most applications incorporate a "zoom" feature so that you can work with type at any size by enlarging it on screen.

Lorem ipsum dolor sit amet, consectetuer adipiscing elit, sed diam nonummy nibh

7pt Univers

Lorem ipsum dolor sit amet, consectetuer adipiscing elit, sed diam nonummy nibh euismod tincidunt ut

7pt Garamond

Lorem ipsum dolor sit amet,

12pt Univers

Lorem ipsum dolor sit amet,

12pt Garamond

Lor

36pt Univers

Lore

36pt Garamond

Below In color monitors, each pixel is made of three phosphors: red, green, and blue (RGB) – the additive primaries which, when mixed in pairs, form the subtractive pigment primaries of cyan, magenta, and yellow. When all three colors are combined they form white light – as distinct from the subtractive primaries which form black when combined.

Above It is possible to drive two monitors from one Mac. The relative positions of the screens are configured via the Monitors Control Panel so that the pointer moves smoothly from screen to screen. Typically, you could view the main application on one screen and use the other as "parking space" for the toolboxes and floating menus featured in most applications. Don't be surprised to lose sight of the pointer now and again.

be dismissed lightly). Put simply, it relates to whether or not the screen may flicker – the slower the refresh rate, the more likely it is to do so. Refresh rate is measured in hertz (Hz), referring to the number of times that the electron beam "rakes" the screen from top to bottom. For example, a refresh rate of 67Hz means that the screen is "refreshed" 67 times each second. Do not confuse refresh rate with screen "redraw," since the latter refers to the time it takes for the screen image to redraw itself after you make a change.

The most important thing to do when you buy a monitor is to view the screen image for yourself. While other people's opinions are useful, particularly if they are graphic designers, there is no substitute for making a decision based upon your own criteria. For example, if you do a lot of fine, intricate work, you'll want a monitor with the crispest

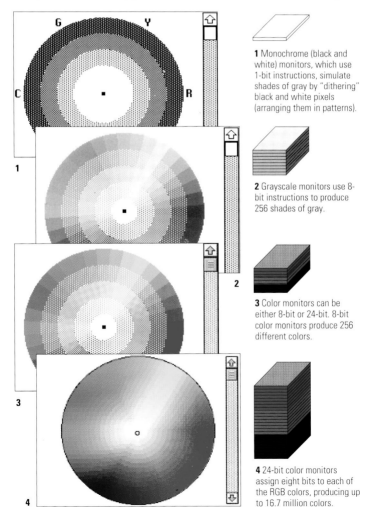

1 Monochrome (black and white) monitors, which use 1-bit instructions, simulate shades of gray by "dithering" black and white pixels (arranging them in patterns).

2 Grayscale monitors use 8-bit instructions to produce 256 shades of gray.

3 Color monitors can be either 8-bit or 24-bit. 8-bit color monitors produce 256 different colors.

4 24-bit color monitors assign eight bits to each of the RGB colors, producing up to 16.7 million colors.

image you can find, whereas if you work a great deal with color, you'll be looking for color fidelity.

STORAGE MEDIA Computer memory (RAM) is erased when the computer is switched off. "Storage" is the computer facility for preserving your data by allowing you to copy data from RAM to one of a variety of storage media so that it is permanently saved.

MAGNETIC MEDIA There are four basic types of media for magnetically storing data; all are made up of a metal or plastic substrate coated with iron oxide particles. When data is "written" to (recorded on) the media, these particles are magnetized and aligned in one of two directions ("north" or "south") by the disk drive's "read/write heads," this polarity corresponding to either a 1 or a 0 according to the data being written (see "bits and bytes," p.14). Because of their sensitivity to magnetic fields, you must always keep disks away from magnets such as those found in telephones and audio speakers (and be careful about putting disks on top of disk drives as well).

Floppy disks These are the most basic of all forms of storage, magnetic or otherwise. Floppy disks for the Mac comprise a single, circular platter of magnetically coated flexible plastic (thus the term "floppy"), which is housed in a rigid plastic case. You use a floppy by inserting it into the slot on the front of the Mac, this slot being the entrance to the drive mechanism. The drive spins the disk and contains the read/write heads for reading data from, and writing it to, the disk as it spins beneath the heads. All Macs contain at least one floppy disk drive.

Floppy disks for the Mac are 3½in in diameter and are double-sided high-density (1.44Mb). "Double-sided" means that the disk is magnetically coated on both sides, each side being read and written to by its own head – you don't need to turn it over. These disks are called "FDHD" (floppy disk, high density). The disk drive is also able to read from and write to the old-style 400k single- and 800k double-sided disks. The main uses of floppies are for software install-ation, transferring documents between non-networked computers, limited backups, and for sending files to service bureaus.

Hard disks In principle, these are similar to floppy disks. The significant differences are that the disk substrate is rigid; the disk itself may actually consist of several disks (each one called a "platter") stacked one on top of another with a space in between for access by the read/write heads; the disk is housed permanently within a sealed, dustproof unit. Hard disks provide the primary means of storage and can be fitted internally in your computer or connected to your Mac as an external device.

Removable hard disks Because of the limited capacity of floppy disks and the inconvenience of transporting hard

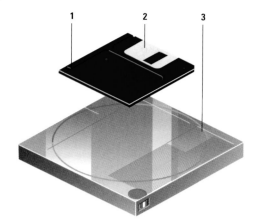

Left The most basic medium for storing computer data is a magnetized disk, which can be either "floppy" or "hard." Floppy disks (**1**) are typically 3½in diameter, consist of a flexible disk contained within a rigid plastic case, and are transportable. The disk is inserted into the computer's floppy disk drive, which gains access to the disk via a protective sliding shield (**2**). Another transportable medium is the "removable" hard disk (**3**), which is considerably more capacious than a floppy disk.

drives, external drives with removable hard disks are becoming increasingly popular. There are several makes of removable hard disk drive which, although none are interchangeable, are broadly similar in that a rigid hard disk, usually measuring 5¼in, is housed within a plastic cartridge. There are only a few manufacturers (known as "original equipment manufacturers," or OEMs) of the basic drive equipment, but there are many companies who combine their own components with drives made by these manufacturers, and who use their own name on the outside of the box.

Storage capacities of removable hard disks are smaller than than those of the fixed type, but still considerable, which makes them ideal for transporting large files such as scanned images. Response times, equally, are not as fast as fixed disks, but often quite sufficient for occasional use as the primary working disk with the Mac. Although it might seem that this type of storage would be vulnerable to all kinds of hazard, particularly dust, they have generally been found to be extremely reliable. Your choice of the many types available should be influenced by the kind in use by your print house and/or your clients.

Tape drives Much the same as audio and video tapes, these consist of a reel of magnetic tape housed in a removable cartridge. Unlike disks, on which data can be accessed from any point with equal facility, tape data can only be accessed as the tape runs from one end to the other. This makes them very slow in comparison to every kind of disk format. Use them for long-term backup.

OPTICAL MEDIA These drives also offer a range of formats and capacities.

CD-ROM The large capacity available on CD-ROM has made it useful both as a back-up device and as a method of transferring large image files. The disc (platter) is light,

Below A typical hard disk drive consists of several disks, called "platters" (**1**), which are sealed within a dust-free box (**2**). This unit may be housed within the computer (internal), or mounted inside a free-standing box which incorporates a separate power supply and suitable ports for connection to the computer (external). The platters consist of a rigid substrate which is coated with magnetized iron oxide particles. These particles are aligned in one of two directions (corresponding to 0 or 1) by a read-write head which changes their polarity by transmitting a magnetic field as the platter spins beneath it (**3**). The magnetic field is generated by the varying voltage of a servo coil (**4**). Each side of a platter (**5**) is served by its own read-write head. Data is written to and read from different parts of the platter by the head as it oscillates rapidly back and forth on its spindle (**6**). For data storage, each platter is divided into concentric rings, called "tracks"(**7**), and each track is divided into segments, called "sectors"(**8**). A single data file may occupy several non-contiguous sectors on different parts of a volume, in which case it is said to be "fragmented."

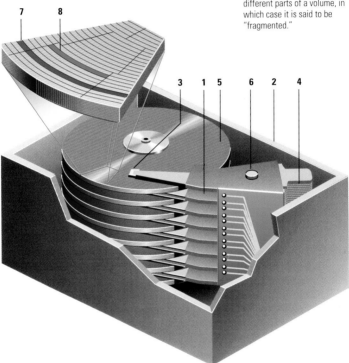

inexpensive, tough and therefore easy to mail. It's basically the same as an audio compact disc (CD) in that data is stored by means of tiny pits burned into the disc's surface, the size of which determines a 1 or a 0. The physical nature of writing data in this way means that the disk can only be written to once, unless it is specially partitioned to accept more than one session of recording.

Industrially, CD-ROMs tend to be used for mass refer-ence data such as encyclopedias, but some type foundries also supply their complete font library on CD-ROMs (not that you necessarily need to buy a whole font library – in some cases, you are supplied with a disk containing an entire library, but are only supplied with access codes to unlock individual fonts as you pay for them.

Because of the ability to store digitized audio data, optical media are particularly important in multimedia and music activities, with most drives providing standard hi-fi output jacks. Various machines offer further sophistication borrowed from audio CDs, including "jukebox" arrangements for multiple disks.

With a CD writer and a supply of discs, you can consider making your own productions for commercial sale. Your disc will need to be tested on a range of machines to ensure successful playbacks under different circumstances.

Magneto-optical Sometimes termed "MO" or "MOD," this kind of drive uses tiny magnetic particles imbedded into the surface of the disc; the polarity of these particles is determined by a combined laser (acting as a heat source) and electromagnet. This dual approach means that data cannot be corrupted by stray magnetic fields. One format externally resembles the classic floppy disk, though it's twice as thick and rejoices in the description "floptical." Another kind – the "phase-change" drive – turns the surface of the disc opaque (on) or transparent (off), using either two laser beams or one beam with variable intensity.

LASER PRINTERS As an intermediate stage to producing high-quality output in a form acceptable for commercial printing, such as bromide or film, you will need to see what your work looks like on paper. To achieve this you will need a printer – which almost certainly means a "laser" printer. Screen quality, although supposedly "WYSIWYG" (pronounced "wizzywig" – "what you see is what you get"), does not render an image with anything like the accuracy that you need to assess the finer subtleties of a design. You should never rely on laser printer output to make typographic judgments – always have a sample run out on an imagesetter. This is not to undervalue the role of laser printers in electronic design – their ability to produce excellent results contributed at the outset to the widespread acceptance of the computer as a professional design tool.

There are other kinds of printer, such as dot matrix, bubble-jets and ink-jets, but, as far as professional graphic design is concerned, laser printers head the list of those producing better quality output at an affordable price. And, more importantly, PostScript (see below) is available only on laser printers.

Laser printers work by means of a pulsating laser light beam exposing a bitmap pattern (the image) onto the light-sensitive surface of a cylindrical drum. The printing (or, sometimes, non-printing) areas of the drum are electrically charged to attract particles of toner, a fine, black, magnetic powder, to its surface. The image is then transferred to paper by means of an electrically charged wire which,

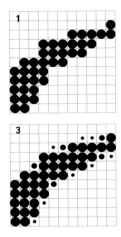

Laser printers transfer an image to paper by means of a laser light which exposes the image onto a light-sensitive surface to which toner ink is attracted or repelled by an electrical charge. The toner is then fused onto plain paper by heat. The fineness of print, or "resolution," is determined by the number of dots per inch, typically 300 or 600. Usually, these dots are all of equal size (**1**), but because of their relatively low resolution (imagesetters use 2540 dpi), stepping is often visible,

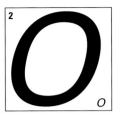

particularly on type (**2**). To compensate for this coarseness, some laser printers smooth out the edges of black areas by interspersing smaller dots in appropriate places to give an optically smoother result (**3**).

again, attracts the toner. Finally, the toner is fused to the paper by heat. These mechanical components of a printer are called its "engine."

PostScript or non-PostScript? When you "send" a page design to a laser printer, it is intercepted by a kind of mini-computer called a "controller." The controller uses a program to "interpret" the computer code comprising your design, which it then "describes" to the printer engine in a language that the engine can use to re-create your design on paper. This language is known as a "page description language" (PDL). PostScript is one such language and is licensed by Adobe Systems Inc. to various manufacturers who use it with their printers' own, built-in controllers.

With the Macintosh, the alternative to printers using PostScript interpreters are printers that use Apple's "Quick-Draw" routines. This means that instead of having a controller built into the printer, some QuickDraw printers are able to use the Mac itself as the controller, gaining a cost advantage.

TrueType fonts (see p.94) can be printed by any printer that uses QuickDraw as well as by PostScript printers, whereas PostScript fonts can only work properly on PostScript printers unless you use a utility program called Adobe Type Manager (ATM). However, the advantages of PostScript printers outweigh those of any other type, not least because so many graphic design-related applications utilize PostScript as a file format. There are, however, software packages (PostScript emulation programs) that enable PostScript files to be printed at an acceptable standard on QuickDraw printers, although because they have difficulty handling complex images, emulators are not as satisfactory as the real thing.

Printer resolution Like monitor screens, printers use bitmaps (see p.60) for creating images, thus outline fonts and object-oriented images must be converted to bitmaps by the interpreter before they can be printed. And, again like screens, because bitmaps are made up of dots, the more dots per inch (dpi) that a printer can handle, the better the resolution, or quality, of the printed image. However, resolution of laser printers is less of a consideration since the majority of them output images at only 300–600dpi, compared with the 1270–2540dpi output of imagesetters. 1000dpi laser printers are also available, but at more than twice the price of most 300dpi printers.

Paper size Most laser printers will only print pages up to a maximum of size 8½ x 14in, although the actual usable image area may be smaller than that. If you need larger printed pages, many applications support "tiled" printing whereby the image is printed onto several sheets of paper – the number depending on the size of the image – which you then join together with the help of small register marks in the corners of the sheets. Laser printers that will print on B-size (11 x 17in) paper are also available – but at more than three times the cost of most smaller printers. In most circumstances, you will find it acceptable to simply reduce the printing size of your page so that it will fit onto the smaller paper size.

Color printers If a large proportion of your work involves color presentations, you may consider buying a color printer – if not, don't bother, since the cost will probably be disproportionate to your needs. Better to take your work to a service bureau which has invested in the best equipment. However, if you do opt for the convenience of in-house color, there is a bewildering and constantly changing range from which to choose. You can select a color laser printer which uses the familiar technology of toner (or rather toners, since all four process colors have to be dealt with) or the dye-sublimation type for a more "photographic" style of output. Be aware of the so-called "consumables" costs associated with color printers: over time they can add up to very large sums indeed.

SCANNERS The rapid technological advances made in desktop scanning equipment may create something of a dilemma for you as a graphic designer. Up until now, you have probably been sending your color transparencies to a color origination house for separation on sophisticated scanning equipment, operated by highly skilled and experienced technicians. But now you've been told that, with a scanner attached to your Mac, you can actually do it yourself. Well, you can – or, at least, you can try. Yes, the equipment exists that enables you, in theory, to achieve good results, and, yes, your favorite color separation house is now using Macs (probably not entirely, but somewhere along the line), but the reality is that if you start spending your time getting embroiled in the intricacies of quality color separation (and by that I mean the high quality you have been used to), you

Right Pixels are used to display images on screen, for low-resolution laser printing, scanning input, and high-resolution imagesetting, all with varying degrees of resolution. Conventional halftone screens are also measured in dots (expressed as lines per inch). "Pixel depth" refers to the number of bits used to define each pixel – 8 bits enables 256 values to be assigned to each pixel (**below**).

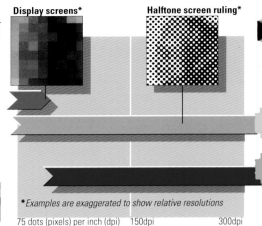

Display screens*

Halftone screen ruling*

Pixel

*Examples are exaggerated to show relative resolutions

75 dots (pixels) per inch (dpi)   150dpi   300dpi

will find that your chosen profession is rapidly displaced by another. However, a scanner can be a substantial aid to your work, more especially if you're in multimedia where the demands of high resolution are not such a big deal.

There are four main uses that print designers have for scanners: scanning in line artwork – this is routinely successful; scanning in images to be used as positional guides (particularly useful for cutout images); inputting text copy by means of optical character recognition (OCR) software; and scanning images for subsequent manipulation with special effects. In time, and with an appropriate scanner, you will probably find that you are able to scan in black-and-white continuous tone originals to produce halftones to an acceptable reproduction standard.

Not only is there a wide variety of makes of scanner, but of types of scanner, too: a scanner may be monochrome, grayscale or color, it may be flatbed, sheetfed, handheld, overhead, a video digitizer, or a transparency scanner. Each type is designed for a specific purpose and, frustratingly, none combines all of these capabilities.

Scanners work by employing a light-sensitive scanning head, called a "charge-coupled device" (CCD), which responds to the various intensities of light being reflected from an original by generating an electric charge – black reflects little light, thus producing a low charge, whereas white is very reflective and generates higher voltages. This electric charge is then converted into a series of 1s and 0s, each one representing a single pixel (in 1-bit mode) which corresponds to the original image. A 1-bit scan will respond to the tones on either side of a mid-tone threshold, reducing the image to pixels which are either on or off – black or white, thus producing a line image. An 8-bit scan offers 256 combinations of 1s and 0s per pixel, thus being capable of 256 grays or colors. Mid-range desktop color scanners offer 24-bit color depth.

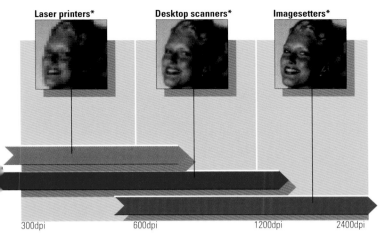

| Laser printers* | Desktop scanners* | Imagesetters* |

300dpi 600dpi 1200dpi 2400dpi

Resolution Just as with monitor screens and printers, the quality of a scanned image depends upon the resolution of the scanner – the more dots per inch, the sharper the result. However, the final appearance of an image depends entirely upon how it is to be output – there is no point in scanning a continuous tone original at a high resolution if you only need it as a positional guide and thus will be printing it on a 300dpi laser printer. (The default halftone screen applied to the image will probably be around only 60 lines per inch, so it's much more sensible to scan images at lower resolution if you are only using them for reference). Conversely, images for halftone reproduction will always stand a better chance of fidelity if scanned at higher resolutions than the halftone screen ruling.

High resolution scanning is, surprisingly, important when scanning line artwork, since an image scanned at the typical resolution of 300dpi may display noticeable lack of smoothness when printed at a higher resolution on an imagesetter. When you look at machine specifications, remember that high resolution is not always what it seems. When you select the highest possible resolution you may well be getting a software-enhanced illusion of more defini-tion. You'll need to work hard at the controls of your scan-ner to get the best results, given the array of adjustments and the wide variety of images you'll be scanning.

File sizes Before even considering buying a scanner, you should be aware of the voracious appetite of scanned image files in terms of both RAM space and disk storage space. An 8 x 10in image scanned with 256 gray levels at a low, but typical, resolution of 300dpi will demand around 7Mb of both disk and RAM space. This rises to more than 20Mb if you scan with 24-bit color. These are demands you will have to accept if you hope to process images for print. Things are easier with multimedia – the basic 640 x 480 pixel screen image is about 900k on the disk.

Hand-held scanners You may still find one of these, the most basic type of scanner. The scan head "sucks" up the image as it goes, almost like a vacuum cleaner, as you drag it across an original by hand. It is difficult to scan images without distortion and most can only scan images up to 4in or 5in wide. However, if you think you will only very occasionally have need for a scanner, consider one of these – it is cheap, small and portable, but you won't be able to use it for anything more serious than rough reference scans and the odd bit of OCR text scanning.

Flatbed scanners These work much like photocopiers – you place your original face down on a glass screen and a scan head then passes under the original. They are all RGB devices – recording the red, green, and blue components of the image. A quick preview scan is normally made to check the image position and to allow for some adjustment of color, brightness and contrast. The high-resolution scan takes longer – in some machines the scan head makes three passes, one for each color. Flatbed scanners are probably the most useful for design purposes, being easy to use, capable of reasonably faithful line artwork scans and grayscale scanning, and very good for OCR work. You can get a transparency attachment, or hood, which contains similar machinery to the base unit. If your need is to scan 35mm transparencies, however, you will be far better off with a dedicated slide scanner (see below).

Sheetfed, or edge-feed, scanners These are similar to flatbed scanners, but, instead of the scan head moving across the original, the original is passed under a fixed scan head. Sheetfed scanners don't really offer the designer any advantages over other types of scanner, being aimed primarily at high-volume work. Furthermore, because the original artwork is fed beneath a stationary scan head, there are limitations on the thickness of material you can pass through it. One development in this area is a small device which sits in front of your machine to scan in text and images presented as single sheets. It will do quick OCR scanning and is intended to act as a subsidiary keyboard.

Overhead scanners These usually consist of a scanning camera mounted above a copy board on which the original is placed. The advantage of these scanners is that you can deal with three-dimensional and large originals, although they can occasionally be difficult to focus.

Slide scanners These are effectively scanning cameras housed inside a box, the slide original being placed between the scan head and a light source. At the lower end of the quality-for-price scale, slide scanners offer little for designers. The higher end can provide quality approaching that of conventional professional color separation, but to get the best results, you will need to acquire the skills of a highly experienced repro house operator.

Bits per pixel (pixel depth)	1	4	6	8	24
Colors or gray shades	1 (b/w line)	16 grays	64 grays	256 grays or colors	16.7 million colors
File size of 4 x 5in image	300K	900K	1.3Mb	1.7Mb	5.2Mb
File size of 8 x 10in image	900K	3.5Mb	5.2Mb	6.9Mb	21Mb

Images scanned by desktop scanners demand large amounts of disk storage space, the amount occupied increasing with image size, pixel depth (the number of bits assigned to each pixel), and scan resolution. The chart (**above**) is based on images scanned at 300dpi, and the file sizes are approximate.

The problem of file size can be partially alleviated by using file compression software or, if you intend working extensively with scanned images, a special file compression card which is installed inside the computer.

Line art, 72dpi, 1-bit

Line art, 300dpi, 1-bit

Line art, 800dpi, 1-bit

Halftone, 72dpi, 8-bit

Halftone, 300dpi, 8-bit

Halftone, conventional repro

File size notwithstanding, desktop scanning of halftone and color images is only acceptable for reproduction when scanned at a high pixel depth. Many designers prefer to use images scanned at low resolutions for positional guides; final reproduction is carried out conventionally. Line artwork, however, when scanned at 600dpi or more, generally achieves adequate quality.

Color, 300dpi, 24-bit

Color, conventional repro

Digital cameras Many types of digital camera are available. The underlying technology is related to that used in flat-bed scanners. The resolution offered depends on the density of packing of the tiny light-detecting devices located where the film plane would be in a conventional camera. Beginning at the rough-and-ready end, you can go out, shoot about 100 low-resolution images on a miniature camera, return to your Mac and download the ones you like the look of for reference purposes, or, if you are skillful, for immediate use in multimedia applications. The controls on this type of camera are reminiscent of the early days of photography – you may have brighter/darker as an exposure option – so don't expect sparkling results in less than ideal conditions. Higher up in the marketplace are conventional high-quality cameras adapted to work electronically. You can enjoy all the advantages, for example, of a sophisticated 35mm single-lens reflex camera system in terms of lenses, filters and so on. These systems are intended to produce repro-duction quality work and so have their own dedicated stor-age attachments to accommodate the resulting large file sizes. Even the classic large format systems have their digi-tal equivalent. This equipment, like its ancestors, is bulky, difficult to set up and mind-numbingly expensive. Probably best left to the more financially adventurous photographic studios.

TRANSMITTING FILES If you design for print, you will in-evitably need to send out large files. While it's nice work for the courier companies to drive or fly around the country loaded down with your disks and cartridges, there comes a point when electronics must intervene. It's not just the fact that the disks rarely seem to come home again. Connecting your Mac to a modem, and the modem to the telephone line is as easy as networking one Mac to another. In other words, you have to work at it. For a start, not all modems are identical in ease-of-use on the Mac. Some of the control-ling software betrays its native PC origins, and you are like-ly to find yourself spending valuable time fiddling with settings before you make any contact. If you have only one telephone line, for example, you'll need an adaptor and an "intelligent" switch to distinguish between voice and modem transmission.

A modem (from *mo*dulate/*dem*odulate) is an electronic device which enables you to use telephone lines (by con-verting outgoing data from digital to analog signals and vice versa for incoming data) to connect your Mac to remote computers. As a bonus, you will be able to send E-mail, con-nect to the Internet (see page 76) and send faxes to ordinary fax machines. The true enthusiast on the move can even link up a portable Mac via a mobile phone. Although the efficacy of telecommunications depends as much upon the software as on the hardware, there are two main points to bear in mind when you set out to purchase a modem: speed and compatibility.

Speed You will find the speed of modems described in either "bauds" or "bits per second" (bps). Essentially, these descriptions equate to the same thing although, because the meaning of a "baud" (one unit per second) can be somewhat imprecise in this context (two or more bits can be contained in a single event), "bits per second" has become more widely favored. Inside your Mac, the 8 bits of data comprising a character (8 bits = 1 character, or byte) travel together side-by-side along parallel paths. A modem, on the other hand, uses what is called a "serial" communications path – that is, the bits travel along a single wire one after the other: since 8 bits are needed to make up a single character, two additional bits – the "start bit" and the "stop bit" – are required to indicate the beginning and end of each byte, expanding each character to 10 bits. (The use of start and stop bits when transmitting data is known as "asynchronous" communication).

Thus modem speed is important since transmitting 10 bits one after the other takes a lot longer than sending 8 bits all at once. As in most areas of hardware purchase, you need the fastest speed you can afford. The longer you are on the line, the bigger your phone bill and the more chance of errors creeping into the transmission. If you use the Internet, a slow modem will be a real liability.

Compatibility In the early absence of an organized standard for modem design, it fell by default to Hayes, one of the earliest manufacturers of modems, to define it. The V34 standard and its successors ensure that the modem you buy will work with every service you are likely to come across. Your own modem will try to work at its highest rated speed. If the information is coming down the line at a faster rate than it can handle – no problem, it just keeps plugging away at the speed it was born with. Equally, if it pitches up against a slower modem, it will be forced to operate at the slower speed.

Transmitted data is only as good as the line it is being sent along and, just as you encounter line interference in a telephone conversation, so your data can also be confused by the same kind of line noise. Some garbage data may be acceptable when transmitting, say, text for editing, but if you are considering sending page layouts to a service bureau for imagesetter output, don't – the effect of such noise on your design will be catastrophic. This is a job for ISDN (see below). In order to reduce the effects of line interference, many modems are equipped with noise filters. Although these are by no means totally effective, they may clean up transmission well enough for you to use a modem to send material for, say, urgent approval or proofreading. The more sophisticated modems can regain contact and resume where they left off when a connection is temporarily interrupted.

ISDN (Integrated Services Digital Network) High-quality services like ISDN offer much faster and more reliable file transfer than conventional telephone lines. Unlike modem-based transmission, there is no need for data to be converted from digital to analogue and back again – the whole procedure is digital. For organisations with constant heavy loads of files to transfer it makes sense to have dedicated ISDN lines open continuously. The installation and running costs of ISDN connection are overall greater than those of modem systems, but this is an area in which intense competition will inevitably drive prices downwards.

ACCELERATOR CARDS When you start out looking for the right Mac to buy, the last thing you'd think about is ways of speeding it up – why not just buy a fast Mac at the outset? At first, while you find your way around your Mac and the applications you have chosen, you won't even notice its speed, or lack of it. It could also be the case that your Mac will operate at a pace that you will always feel comfortable with – probably meaning that you made the right decision in the first place.

However, it is also quite likely that you will become increasingly frustrated by even the briefest pause while your Mac computes some complex task or other – especially if you use one of the slower machines to carry out memory-intensive tasks such as those generated when you create color illustrations with a drawing application, or when your own ambitions outstrip the pace of even the fastest off-the-shelf Mac.

You can turn to a range of accelerators which fall into two broad groups. One group acts upon the Mac's existing microprocessor, increasing the clock speed, or in some versions, providing a "cache" so that the Mac can respond rapidly with recently accessed material. The second group is more software-specific, typically taking over some of the processing load of large image files, for example. All these types are installed in very much the same way as extra RAM chips – and, in the long term, may suffer from the same lack of portability when you change machines.

Or what about a higher specification Mac? Or upgrading a recent Mac with the aid of a complete CPU upgrade? The possibilities are endless.

INPUT DEVICES When you buy a Mac, you may just get the basic machine, so it's up to you to select an input device.

Keyboards You will probably find that the standard Apple Keyboard is perfectly adequate for most purposes. If you decide to go beyond the routine Apple product, you should look at non-Apple keyboards, most of which provide at least the same features as the Apple Extended Keyboard for less money. Many of them sport more features – for instance, modular key clusters which enable you to configure each group of keys in whatever way you want. Consider also the ergonomic aspect. Even the least literate designer has to type quantities of text from time to time, and there are curving keyboards and padded wrist-rests which may help relieve problems with fingers and wrists.

Mice Apart from the Apple standard-issue mouse which, like the Apple Keyboard, you will probably find perfectly adequate, there are several alternative non-Apple pointing devices. These include mice with additional buttons which allow you to assign frequently used commands to each button. There are mice which dispense with the familiar ball and rely instead on a mouse mat with a tiny checker pattern. Movement across the mat is detected by electronic sensors in the underside of the mouse.

Another device, a "trackball," takes the form of a stationary upturned mouse, with which you move the pointer by rotating the ball rather than by moving the mouse. It's equipped with separate buttons for making selections on the screen. There is also a cordless mouse, which does away with connecting wires by using an infrared light connection to the Mac. You might also be interested in the "trackpad" – you move your finger over a small panel to direct the screen cursor and double-click by double-tapping your fingertip. This pad is also available integrated into a standard keyboard.

Tablets The standard mouse is a very blunt instrument when it comes to drawing on screen. If you expect to draw in any kind of freehand style, you'll need a "graphic tablet." This device enables you to draw on screen almost as you would on paper – if your application offers the appropriate drawing tools and will respond to the features offered by the tablet. In its most basic form, a tablet consists of a rectangular pad on which you draw with a pencil-like stylus. The tip of the stylus is pressure-sensitive, enabling you to simulate the marks that a pen or brush would make if you pressed it harder onto paper. Like an ordinary lead pencil, some are fitted with an "eraser" at the blunt end – just flip the stylus over and it rubs out your work.

You may see other, larger tablets that come with full-size mice. These are intended for digitizing engineering, architectural, and cartographic originals – you creep over the surface entering co-ordinate points as you go. For regular design purposes, you would be better off using a flatbed scanner to input this kind of work.

Most input devices connect to the Mac's Apple Desktop Bus (ADB) port, and can either be daisy-chained together or plugged into adaptors. All such devices should be thought of as complementary to, and not a replacement for, the conventional keyboard. Even if you mean to draw all day, you'll eventually want to type out an invoice.

3
SOFTWARE

When you start exploring the options for application software, you will understand why I suggested earlier that choosing a Mac will seem relatively easy.

Your choice of application depends on which main area of design you work in and on how you envisage a Mac helping you in that discipline. Avoid the temptation to go too far, too fast. The Mac is an easy machine to learn how to use, but many applications are very powerful and complex, particularly at the professional end, and take considerable time and practice to master. It takes a while before your new tool becomes productive (i.e. revenue-earning) and it will pay you to ease your new knowledge gently into your traditional way of working.

One of the first things to understand is that a Macintosh will not take over the job of *design*, nor will it make you a better designer, no matter how powerful your software or technically sophisticated your output. Don't be too eager to throw away your markers, pencils and pads – designing directly on-screen is not necessarily better or quicker.

So how will a Mac change things? It's first worth reviewing the traditional shape of the design process. Starting with thumbnail sketches of ideas on paper, one or more concepts begin to dominate the surrounding landscape. Although the designer tries hard to keep all options open, these favored ideas beg to be translated into more finished form. To make a comp, colored markers and photographs cut from magazines are employed to simulate the printed job. Greeked type fills up (some of) the spaces in between. Headings might be set, carefully traced or even made from rubdowns. The result probably looks great, but the designer's suppressed desire for an absolute facsimile of the real thing brings a touch of disappointment at the sight of obvious hand-work and compromise. No longer.

The Mac offers to stand the problem of the rough visual and comp on its head. It's very hard to make a rough on the Mac. A keyboard shortcut would be a useful keystroke, but there's little prospect of it. With a very fast Mac, every font available (to give you the freedom of choice you have hitherto had), tons of RAM, a high-capacity hard disk, a color monitor, a color scanner and a dye-sublimation printer – all the output looks very much like the finished job. More seriously, the finished job looks very much like the first visual. Keep a pencil at least.

All the comments above apply to design for print, where the Mac represents the industry standard. Its empire now embraces multimedia and the Internet, and in these areas the development of ideas is conducted inevitably on the screen. The finished product will generally be viewed on the same kind of screen as the one on which it was created (i.e. 72 dots to the inch). The demand for print-style high resolution is therefore absent. No cause to rejoice, however, because the number and size of multimedia files is enormous. The incoming raw material will be film, video, QuickTime movies, sound files and scripts. Trade in your pencil for a conductor's baton.

CHOOSING SOFTWARE You will spend hours appraising the advantages of rival applications. If you research each software package in some depth and ask a lot of questions, you will become aware that an application currently leading the herd in a particular area may soon be left behind by an "upgrade" to one of its rivals (see p.53).

You can try "test driving" potential applications; most software developers offer demonstration programs which work normally apart from file-saving and printing functions. These are commonly found on magazine cover-mounted CD-ROMs. Select a likely candidate and copy it to your hard disk. An "installer" utility may be provided to ensure you get all the right files into the right place on your Mac – keep an eye on where they go so you can trash them at the end of the trial. (If the installation process crashes or hangs up your Mac, restart and consider some different software.) Even when you get a successful installation, you may be asked to restart to use the software. Remembering that none of your trial efforts can be saved or printed, try to give the package a realistic test on your own kind of work. There's usually a help application to get you started.

Since the Mac's introduction (with a word processor and a black-and-white painting application), a great mountain of knowledge and opinion on the relative merits of hundreds of different software packages has grown. You'll find my own, design-oriented, list on page 82. Look at as many magazine reviews as you can (although these are sometimes over-technical for the Mac novice) and talk to as many Mac users as possible, even if they are not designers. There is bound to be a "Macintosh User Group" ("Mug" for short) in your area, and there is often a sub-group which specializes in design matters.

Be very wary of advice on software from people who are trying to sell you hardware – it's not that they necessarily lack knowledge, but as their prime concern is the machinery, you may not receive the most objective and practical advice from this quarter. They may, however, know a lot about accounting packages and databases.

If you are thinking in terms of equipping several designers with Macs, you should consider employing a consultant to study the kind of work that you do, your methods of producing it, and to discover the attitudes of your personnel toward the introduction of new technology. The same advice holds good if you are already in the Mac domain but considering expansion, networking and external communications. The consultant will then advise on the level at which you can integrate the technology into your practice and suggest the most appropriate hardware and software for your kind of work. Ask the consultant about the provision of on-site training, which should be geared to achieving an acceptable standard of competence and productivity with minimum disruption to schedules.

Having made your selection of software, make sure that you are buying the latest versions of the various applications, and that they are specific to your country of operation. Check the paragraph on upgrading software, below.

TRAINING There are three levels of Mac expertise. First, as a novice, you must learn how to use the Mac itself or, more specifically, the Finder and certain items of system software. This involves learning the basic functions of the Finder – how to move things around the desktop, how to use menus, create and open folders, organize files, install vital system enhancements (such as fonts), and so on. A useful explanation of the most elementary of these is provided, in the form of a guided tour program called Macintosh Basics which is supplied with your Mac. More help is contained in other accompanying manuals, one of which will be related to your particular machine. With this library of clear and concise instructions, you will quickly teach yourself how to use a Mac, thus confirming its reputation as an "easy to learn" computer.

The second stage of the learning process involves the applications that you are going to use. This is a more complex proposition since, in order to produce work at a professional level, you need some of the most powerful and sophisticated applications available. Don't be embarrassed to follow conscientiously the tutorial tasks provided – however grotesque the restaurant menu and greetings card examples may seem. It's unfortunate that you can't get to see the manual before buying the software, since it is very often a reflection of the quality of the actual package.

In many cases it should be possible to teach yourself the application, but at first you may want to consider buying some professional instruction from a training service. Make absolutely certain that the person doing the training is expert with the Mac and is familiar with the particular version (update) of the software that you want to learn – try to find someone who is recommended. If you do decide to go it alone, help is nearly always offered by developers of the software or by their distributors; many have dedicated "helpline" telephone numbers which may be toll-free, at least for the initial months after purchase.

The third level of expertise is optional. The Mac is set up to offer the optimum straightforward working environment to the greatest number of users. Install your selected major software packages, add a few fonts, select a tasteful desktop pattern and you will be flying. But doubts will set in. A glance through the Mac's system folder is enough to show that there is another world beneath the desktop. The small choice of standard alarm sounds, for example, is not sufficient for the true enthusiast. On any shareware disk you'll find add-on collections of curious and often disgusting noises to accompany every one of your actions. More useful are the small utilities which Apple forgot to design, and which are the preserve of an energetic army of Mac developers. Some are commercial products and are listed in this chapter, some are free- or share-ware. Some are FMTTTW (far more trouble than they're worth) but you won't know that until your Mac trips and crashes over one. If you enjoy this sort of crusade for enhancement, the Mac underworld will keep you occupied indefinitely. Suitable computer games for designers are listed on page 233.

UPGRADING SOFTWARE If you are thinking of "borrowing" an application or two from a colleague, think twice. Apart from committing an illegal act (see the paragraph on copyright, below) you will be missing out on one of the most important aspects of buying an application – that of keeping up with the developer's constant "tweaking" of the product.

Upgrades are made for two reasons: the addition of new features (most software can be improved one way or another, not least to gain the edge over the competition), and to "debug" the application (the fixing of problems which have been identified after its release). The addition of new features may simply involve minor enhancements, or it may involve a complete rewrite of the application. The first versions of major rewrites are usually identified by the use of a whole number (e.g. 3.0), as distinct from minor upgrades which employ a decimal figure (e.g. 3.1). You may come across software with the suffix "b" for "beta" – on a magazine cover-mounted disk, for example. This means that it has probably been distributed for testing purposes to a select panel, and has escaped into the public domain. You'd be absolutely right to be wary of getting into a "beta" version aircraft. Use the same caution here.

When you buy an application, the package includes a

registration card, the return of which will entitle you to various benefits such as free minor upgrades, reduced prices for major upgrades, use of a toll-free helpline for technical support and newsletters. If you don't want your details passed onto other mailing lists, you are entitled to say so or check the relevant box.

COPYRIGHT The copyright in software is an extremely sensitive issue among developers, which is quite understandable considering how easy it is to copy software. In the past, most software was "copy protected," meaning that an application would require some kind of "key" to enable it to be run – usually in the form of an encoded, non-copyable disk to be inserted every time the application was opened. Although the practice of copy protecting products has largely died out, due mainly to consumer resistance and impracticality, some software (usually expensive and of a specialist nature) is still copy protected.

The package of a brand new application is usually fastened by a seal, with the warning that by breaking the seal you are accepting the terms and conditions of the license agreement printed on the outside of the pack. Effectively, this means that the price you pay for an item of software is a license fee, and if you fail to comply with any of the conditions specified, you are in breach of the license agreement. When you read the small print of a license agreement, you will find the restrictions quite extensive – you cannot, for example, copy the program (except for backup purposes), or lend it to anyone. Although you have paid money for it, the developers insist that it's not your property in the usual sense. Once the seal is broken, you may not re-sell it. It's easy to dismiss the legalese as just being saber-rattling by the software developers, but when software is pirated or misused, it is the end-users who will ultimately suffer – dwindling revenues are bound to erode a software developer's commitment to a product. This issue becomes very much clearer if and when you yourself develop a saleable item of Mac software.

PAGE MAKEUP APPLICATIONS Also called "page layout" or "desktop publishing" applications, these are the real workhorses of virtually all graphic design work done on the Mac.

All page makeup applications at the professional end of the scale, of which there are few – there are many more at the so-called "entry-level" – use only slightly varying means to achieve the same end. They allow you to enter text either directly (word-processing features tend to be fairly divergent between applications, and some are quite limited) or by importing it from another application. They enable you to make fine typographic adjustments (some to within .001 pt) to kerning, tracking, and scaling. They all provide a limited selection of drawing tools, enabling you to create boxes, circles and ellipses, rules and, in some cases, polygons and freeform shapes. Most of them provide a facility to lay percentage tints either as spot or process colors which can then be output into color-separated film.

All applications come with preset default values (selected settings), many of which (particularly kerning) may not be acceptable to you. However, most defaults can be overridden relatively easily by the user, and then saved to be applied to further jobs. Typically, you might set your preferences so that each newly created picture box repels the text that's already on the page. This preference will dominate succeeding jobs until you reset it.

As with much other specialist software, selecting a suitable page makeup application is not easy – there is little to choose between the most popular applications: PageMaker and QuarkXPress. Since most offer more or less the same features at more or less the same price, your criteria for choosing one revolve around fewer and fewer differences. Nonetheless, you should consider the following features: the degree of accuracy with which you can specify certain attributes such as the positions of pictures and blocks of text; typographic flexibilities such as kerning, editing, and rotatable text; document length – the maximum number of pages you can create in a document varies considerably between applications and, depending on their complexity, can slow down the application quite dramatically; file-importing features, both of text and pictures – although applications are becoming increasingly universal in this respect; color separation features – all professional applications will provide separations of colors and tints created within the application, and separate imported picture files without additional software; and finally, the extent to which additional facilities are available, either from the developer or from third parties.

QuarkXPress (Quark, Inc.), commonly known as "Quark" or "XPress." The world welcomed the end of the so-called "Cold War." The reporting of successes and failures on both sides had filled the news for years. In the Mac environment, QuarkXPress v. PageMaker rumbles on. QuarkXPress dominates the professional end of makeup applications because it addressed that market's needs before its rival did. It was first to enable precise positioning of items and sophisticated type control. It has been widely adopted by the design industry as a whole – a significant consideration when choosing *any* software. There are now hundreds of add-on products (XTensions) produced by third party manufacturers which can be used to enhance the main application. A few of these XTensions are items which should have been built-in anyway; others are virtually applications in their own right. The universality of QuarkXPress extends into the prepress areas of the production process where it is able to interface directly with high-end scanning software. QuarkX-

Anatomy of a page makeup application A typical professional page makeup application allows you to combine all the functions of layout, type-setting, and camera-ready art so that your work can be output as color-separated film. The two principal applications competing in the field are QuarkXPress and PageMaker. Both offer very precise positional control of text and images. QuarkXPress works exclusively on a box, or "frame" basis, while PageMaker can switch between that system and its traditional free-form method

using a text-insertion tool.

The illustrations (**below**) are from QuarkXPress and show a few of its features, many of which can also be found in other applications. A feature which XPress shares with PageMaker is a pasteboard (**1**) where you can play around with ideas, outside the page area. This text box (**2**), can be re-sized using the surrounding "handles" or repositioned by dragging with the pointer. Text boxes can be linked together using the linking tool (represented by a chain link in the toolbox) so that text flows automatically from one to the other.

The File menu (**3**), similar in almost all applications, allows you to create, open, save and print documents. The Edit menu (**4**) includes a "preferences" section which lets you control, for example, the unit of measurement; the quality (and therefore speed) of screen display, and the behavior of the tools in the toolbox. In the same menu you can edit colors, style sheets (consistently used styles for fonts, leading, indents, etc, which can be applied by a single keystroke), and hyphenation and justification parameters. The Edit Color feature enables you to define

process colors for tints (**5**) or to specify PANTONE and spot colors, or to select a PANTONE color (**6**) which can be automatically output in the correct percentages of process color tints. The Style menu (**7**) lets you select typeface, type size, leading, scaling, kerning, etc. The Item menu (**8**) allows you to apply specific measurements to such items as text and picture boxes, rules, run-arounds, etc. The Page menu (**9**) enables you to add, move, re-order or delete pages within a document and to set automatic page numbering. The View menu (**10**) is where you choose the size at which

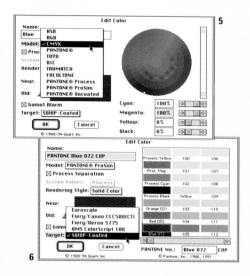

your document appears on your monitor and also enables you to control the appearance of guides and floating palettes.

The Utilities menu (**11**) includes facilities for checking spelling, making hyphenation exceptions, identifying fonts and pictures used within a document, and editing tracking and kerning values – you can customize any kerning pair Kerning Table Edit (**12**). Extra features, called Quark XTensions, also appear here (**13**). As well as those supplied with the main application, you can choose from a range of several hundred third-party XTensions. QX Effects, for example, will produce soft drop-shadows on type and graphics without the need to launch a separate image-editing application.

There are a variety of "floating palettes" which you can choose to display and position anywhere on

the screen: the Toolbox (**14**) is where you select various tools which enable you to undertake tasks such as creating, modifying, and moving boxes, drawing rules and shapes, and linking text; Measurements (**15**) duplicates some of the commands in the Style and Item menus and displays the attributes of the currently selected item; Document Layout (**16**) allows you to rearrange the pages in your document and design master pages; Library (**17**) enables you to store frequently used items, such as a logo, and retrieve it in any document; Value Converter (**18**) makes instant conversions of measurements; Colors (**19**) applies colors to frames, type and backgrounds; Style Sheets (**20**) assigns pre-determined styles to text; Trap Information (**21**) allows you to edit the way different colors will print with respect to their neighbors.

Press is also the springboard to Quark's own multimedia authoring package, QuarkImmedia (see page 73).

PageMaker (Adobe Systems, Inc.) Effectively the first serious page makeup application for the Mac, PageMaker is well established as the leading application among desktop publishers and has for some years provided the benchmark which its competitors have striven to surpass. However, despite – or, perhaps, because of – the easy-to-use nature of the product, it concentrated its sights more upon DTP users than on professional designers, presumably because the former constitute a much larger market. It seemed to be leaving the higher end to its competitor. For example, its features for positioning items and rotating text were not originally as powerful as those of QuarkXPress; only one master page style was allowed per document whereas a QuarkXPress could have 127; and the color separation department was notably ho-hum. All this has changed. Now re-cast as a companion product with Illustrator and Photoshop, and benefiting from seamless transfer between them, it rivals QuarkXPress on all fronts. Additionally, Web pages can be created either from scratch or by employing existing PageMaker files. To doubly reinforce the extent of its improvement, it can even import "old" QuarkXPress documents for transformation.

Ventura Publisher (Ventura Software, Inc.) This application, like PageMaker, was originally written for the PC world where, along with PageMaker, it is dominant. Unlike PageMaker, it has made a rather uncomfortable transition to the Mac. Ventura is best suited to longer, more complicated documents than those discussed previously and, as such, is not really suitable as a multipurpose design tool. It is also quite difficult to learn.

FrameMaker (Adobe Systems, Inc.) The strength of this application has always been its ability to handle lengthy and complicated documents. FrameMaker possesses extensive word-processing features and drawing tools, as well as the most sophisticated table creation system. With features such as an equation editor, it is specially appropriate for preparing scientific and technical documents.

UniQorn (SoftPress) is a relative latecomer to the field. It uses Apple GX technology to facilitate type manipulation, but its main feature is the ability to transform its pages into a form which can be opened and read by any Java-capable internet browser – that is, a separate "viewer" application is not needed by the recipient.

Interleaf (Interleaf, Inc.) is a specialized integrated word-processing, drawing, and page makeup application. It can handle documents with hundreds of pages and multiple footnotes. It is mainly used for producing technical manuals.

DRAWING APPLICATIONS Just as you sometimes need to create illustration artwork when preparing conventional pasteup, so you will need a facility for doing the same on your Mac. The "office" type application suites provide some drawing and painting tools along with word-processing, page layout, and communications facilities. These integrated packages might provide you with a grounding, but their limitations, especially in fine typographic control, will be ultimately frustrating. Neither will your files be very welcome at the output bureau. The answer inevitably is a standalone application.

Drawing applications are "object-oriented" programs (the shape and characteristics of a drawn line are stored as data in a single point, or "vector"), as distinct from painting and image-manipulation applications (see p.64) that produce "bitmapped" images. This distinction is becoming less clear with every upgrade of the two leading applications in the field (Illustrator and Freehand).

The object-oriented nature of drawing applications has two other distinct advantages over bitmap applications. First, because they store the instructions for drawing a line, rather than the line itself, an object-oriented illustration can be output at any resolution. Quality is determined wholly by the resolution of the output device – the higher the resolution, the finer the end result. In bitmapped images, the input resolution determines the output quality. Second, object-oriented files are smaller (regardless of the physical dimensions of the drawing) than bitmap equivalents and thus occupy less storage space. This economy has another welcome side effect; you can set the application to allow a variable number of "undo" commands. You can therefore try out many different ideas and safely retrace your steps if things begin to go wrong.

The best drawing applications offer one or more built-in library or color-system based on printing ink models. The familiar range of PANTONE colors, for example, can be output as spot color film or fully separated film for four-color process printing. This is not to say that the color on the screen will necessarily closely resemble the patch in your sample book, but it has every chance of printing out correctly on the page. Whichever application you choose, accurate screen rendering of specified colors is very difficult to achieve and maintain – even with 24-bit color and a color calibration device.

Other features offered by drawing applications include "auto tracing" (an outline of, say, a bitmapped image can automatically be traced – useful if you want to create an editable version of a scanned design); "graduated fills" for creating smooth, graduated tints; and "blending," which allows you to create graduated tones – for example, around the side of a curved object. Drawing applications also allow you to import most types of picture file format, although you may not be able to edit them.

Because of their facility to allow the alteration of previously drawn shapes, drawing programs are extremely versatile and can be used for a wide variety of purposes, such as technical illustration, diagrams and charts, maps and all manner of graphic decoration, as well as for general purpose illustration of a more mechanical nature. Being object-oriented, drawing applications also offer the valuable feature of being able to alter and manipulate outline fonts, thus providing an invaluable aid to logo design and also the means for extensive typographic variations. Some drawing applications also provide powerful typographic features, giving them the ability to be used, within limits, for page makeup.

There is little practical difference between the two leading drawing applications, **Illustrator** (Adobe Systems, Inc.)

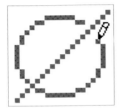

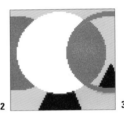

Bitmapped graphics
When you use a paint application to create an image, marks are made by switching pixels on and off (**1**) – a line comprises a series of linked pixels and a solid shape consists of a block of pixels. The color of each pixel depends on how many bits are assigned to each pixel – a one-bit

program only renders black (when the pixel is on) or white (when the pixel is off), whereas an 8-bit program can render 256 grays or colors. This is called a bitmapped graphic. Although the use of pixels permits a wide variety of effects, it can also make editing shapes difficult – when a shape is created (**2**),

the pixels used to render the shape replace any existing pixels such as those forming part of a background. Thus, if a shape is moved, a white space is left (**3**). Likewise, because the shape consists of a solid block of pixels, it can only be modified by adding and/or removing pixels.

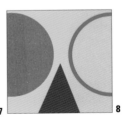

Object-oriented graphics
A drawing application stores information about a drawn line at each end of the line (**6**) or at points along its length. This means that only the data for a section of line between two points need be stored, as distinct from the need of a bitmapped graphic to store

data relating to each individual pixel. Consequently, the file size of an object-oriented illustration depends on its complexity rather than the area it occupies, unlike a bitmapped graphic, the file size of which increases proportionally to the area – thus the number of pixels –

it uses. A line can be edited by selecting it and making alterations as necessary – changes which affect only the data relating to that line (**7**, **8**), and not any other element of the illustration. Some paint applications incorporate object-oriented drawing features.

and **FreeHand** (Macromedia, Inc.) I use FreeHand because I prefer to make adjustments to an illustration in "preview" mode – the view that allows you to preview tints, colors, etc., as distinct from the monochrome keyline view. Long ago, when I made my software choice, this facility didn't exist in Illustrator, although it does now. Probably the most objective advice is, if you can't decide which to get, toss a coin or, if your budget permits, get both.

As an alternative comes **Canvas** (Deneba Software, Inc.) which, as well as offering powerful drawing and text features, allows you to import and export files in just about every format available. Unusually, it allows vector-based drawing to coexist with bitmap painting.

Relatively new to Mac users, **CorelDraw** (Corel, Inc.) has long been the dominant package in PC graphics. It is

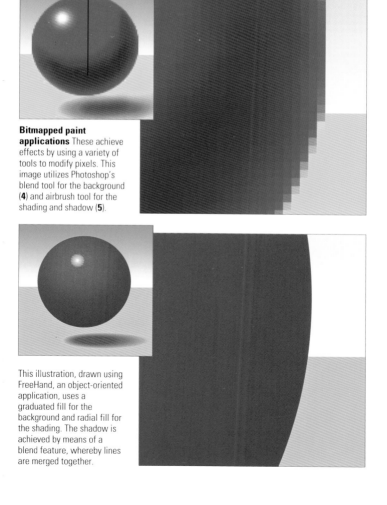

Bitmapped paint applications These achieve effects by using a variety of tools to modify pixels. This image utilizes Photoshop's blend tool for the background (**4**) and airbrush tool for the shading and shadow (**5**).

This illustration, drawn using FreeHand, an object-oriented application, uses a graduated fill for the background and radial fill for the shading. The shadow is achieved by means of a blend feature, whereby lines are merged together.

Anatomy of a drawing application Graphic designers may need to complement their page-makeup application with one that provides extensive features for creating drawn artwork. Although page-makeup applications offer drawing tools, none achieves the power of a dedicated drawing application. Likewise, no drawing application provides the power of a dedicated page-makeup application. Designers of information graphics can use "graphing" in Illustrator and "charting" in FreeHand, to enter statistical data into a spreadsheet that automatic-

ally configures the graph, which you can customize to your design.

Typically, a drawing application (**below**, from FreeHand) provides the standard File and Edit menus (**1**, **2**) for opening, closing, saving, copying, pasting, etc. In the View menu (**3**) you can control various display options such as floating panels, the Toolbar of miniature icons at the top of the screen, magnification of the page view, rulers, grid, and guides. "Snapping," which enables accurate drawing by attracting an element to the nearest point, guide, or grid, is also

controlled from this menu.

The Modify menu (**4**) is one route by which you can change the attributes of all the elements in your drawing. Detailed inform-ation is entered through the Inspector panels (**5**), which are linked to the other floating panels such as Color and Color Mixer, here shown grouped together (**6**) for ease of use. The Color panel gives access to built-in PANTONE and rival color libraries, as well as the conventional RGB and CMYK palettes. The Color Mixer offers a set of sliders to modify ready-made colors by one per cent increments. Layers (**7**)

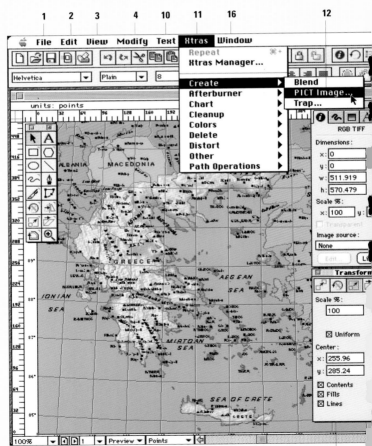

9

controls the hierarchy of drawing layers in the document, enabling you to assign objects to different layers. You can "hide" other objects, lock them to guard against unwanted changes, or send them to the background where, though visible, they will not print.

Styles (**8**) enables frequently-used attributes, both of text and objects, to be saved and re-applied. Transform (**9**) offers scaling and skewing. Most of these floating panels can be accessed via the Toolbar icons. The Text menu (**10**) allows you to attribute typographic styles and also

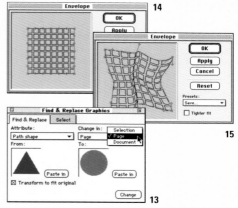

to convert letterforms to "paths" (see below). The multi-function Extras menu (**11**) includes filtering and path manipulations. In this example, the entire page is being re-created (**12**) as a PICT image for subsequent export. On the same menu, objects can be searched for by attribute (**13**) and then modified or replaced. The "Envelope" function (**14, 15**) offers Bézier curve-based distortions.

Window (**16**) gives another way of controlling floating panels. More

usefully, it can open another view of the same document. In this way you can, for example, view changes simultaneously at large magnification and page size.

Object-oriented applications employ mathematically defined lines, or paths, which allow accurate manipulation of a shape by utilizing handles which project from a point on a curve. This means that fonts, which use the same method of describing a line, can be manipulated within a drawing application.

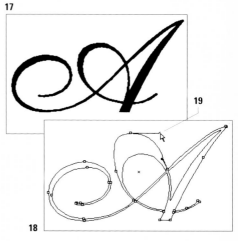

Several object-oriented applications enable you to customize any PostScript font you have installed on your Mac by converting a word or character into paths

(above, **17,** from Illustrator). This generates points along the path (**18**) which can be moved or from which curves can be modified via a "direction point" (**19**).

capable of many of the manipulations offered by its rivals, but lacks their ease of use.

PAINTING AND IMAGE-EDITING For many people, their first glimpse of a Mac will have been at an entrancing demonstration of a painting, or "paint," application – it's impressive to see a computer achieve myriad paint effects so cleanly. But it is disappointing that the media has bombarded us with a stream of ill-conceived computer "painted" images, most of which look more like an attempt to exploit every trick an application has to offer, rather than to devise a suitably considered graphic solution to a given problem. Yet a paint application is an innovatory graphic tool that, in the right hands, can provide the means of producing appropriate, original, and stimulating work. If you produce a lot of illustration work, the computer offers great potential as an alternative illustration medium. But the main reason for using a paint application will probably be for image processing – whether for preparation for color printing or for multimedia.

All image-editing software of this type needs to be allied with large amounts of RAM and considerable hard disk space for file storage. It is no coincidence that most magazine reviewers set a filter manipulation in Photoshop as their benchmark "hard thing to do" when testing new machines. You might easily get involved in the purchase of an additional hard disk, and/or some form of dedicated accelerator card. To take advantage of the application's sophisticated color capabilities, you should really be thinking in terms of a 24-bit color card and monitor. Image-editing on screen with a mouse is hard work. With a graphics tablet that has a pressure-sensitive stylus, you can simulate the way you would normally work with a pencil or paintbrush, enabling you to vary the thickness of your line just as you would with a brush (see below).

The different software packages offer similar painting features, but with varying degrees of sophistication in their additional features. They all have adjustable airbrush tools, most allow you to control the opacity of paint, most possess image-editing tools, allowing you at least to blur or sharpen a scanned image, and some allow you to draw Bézier curves. Although all paint applications produce images as bitmaps, some also feature object-oriented drawing tools or at least object-oriented text capabilities, both of which you will probably find useful, whatever type of work you do. Other criteria relate to whether or not the application permits you to make direct process color separations and, if so, whether it allows you to adjust halftone screen resolution (although this is not too much of a problem since you can always save the file in a format that can be separated by another application); and whether the application supports the color library of your choice.

The dominant force in this field is, bizarrely, an application whose original, rather humble, task was to transfer graphics files from one format to another. **Photoshop** (Adobe Systems, Inc.) has evolved into the standard by which the others are judged. Like QuarkXPress, it has an accompanying flock of third-party add-ons in the form of filters and special effect "plug-ins." Chief amongst these are items from **MetaTools**, all distinguished by their extraordinarily off-beat interfaces.

Competition comes from applications which try to address the lack of speed inherent in Photoshop. While Photoshop goes right ahead and applies your commands to the actual image as you work (and this can slow things down quite considerably), **Live Picture** and **xRes** operate on a "proxy" system. It appears on screen that your actions have been executed, but they have in fact only been recorded temporarily. When you save the document, the actions you have input are then applied all together. This last stage is relatively slow, but the overall process can save a lot of time.

Other important paint applications, so-called "natural media" software, including **Painter** (Fractal Design) attempt to simulate artists' tools such as pencil, charcoal, pastel, watercolor and oil paint. These are allied to simulated textured paper surfaces. With a graphics tablet connected, you can also control, via the pressure-sensitive pen, the "wetness" of the "paint" loaded onto a "brush" and the rate at which it "dries." Equally, the brush can be made to paint with two different colors. The results can be exported in a variety of image formats or even exchanged in near real-time over the Internet.

If you have no need for the multiple features of the software described so far, try **Color-It!** (MicroFrontier, Inc.) or one of the many simpler shareware offerings.

SPECIAL EFFECTS The drawing and painting applications described up to now can between them produce an extraordinary variety of images. From time to time, the results appear to leap off the screen, but *really* convincing three-dimensionality is the preserve of two inter-related groups of applications. Three-dimensional modelling (3D) begins the process and "rendering" finishes it off.

3D applications used to be synonymous with "computer-aided design" (CAD), a term which seems outmoded now, but it was originally the preserve of architects, industrial designers and product engineers. The applications were consequently highly sophisticated, complex, and ran on mainframe computers. However, there is now a wide selection of practical, and cheaper, alternatives. Many 3D applications also provide animation capabilities and most have built-in rendering features. Popular 3D applications among designers are **Dimensions** (Adobe Systems, Inc.), **Strata**

Anatomy of a "natural media" paint application

Many paint applications now support graphics tablets with pressure-sensitive styli, making them increasingly attractive to illustrators. Paint applications achieve a wide variety of effects (**right**), by modifying the characteristics of groups of pixels and the way in which they behave in relation to their neighbors.

The illustration below shows a document open in Painter, which, typical of many paint applications, allows you to add a wide variety of paint effects to scanned images (**1**) as well

as create paintings from scratch. Painter was the forerunner of the so-called "natural media" applications, so named for their use of simulated watercolor paper backgrounds and arrays of "brush" effects. The File and Edit menus (**2, 3**) are standard Macintosh. The Effects menu (**4**) in this example shows "3D Brush Strokes" (**5**) selected to modify this image which has already been treated with the alternative selection, "Paper Grain." Other effects available include "marbling" and "auto van Gogh-ing" of an existing image. Canvas (**6**) offers options for paper size

and base color, as well as for "wet" and "dry" brushes. The Tools palette (**7**) resembles that found in most painting applications, but it is in the Tools menu (**8**) that the most powerful items in the Painter armory are found. New brush effects and "paper textures" can be created here. Also controlled by the Tools menu, the extraordinary Image Hose can spray patterns such as the plants (**9**) from a built-in collection of "nozzles" which, once again, can be added to by creating and copying new images. The last option in this section is a facility to record a "session" of brush strokes so that successful maneuvers can be repeated whenever required. The Objects Sessions palette (**10**) controls the playback of

these recordings. Brush effects created in the Tools menu are added to the default styles, then all are organized and selected in the Brushes palette (**11**). In this case, the Chalk group is displayed. Colors and patterns are similarly controlled in the Art Materials palette (**12**). As well as the usual range of colors and textures, Painter offers a number of unusual patterns including a range of fabrics like the Buchanan plaid (**13**).

The Movie menu (**14**) controls the playback and modification of QuickTime movies imported into Painter. You can literally "paint" upon the surface of

each frame to produce an animation of your own.

Window (**15**), the last section in the main menu, turns individual palettes on and off.

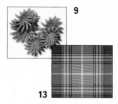

Continuing the underlying "paint and paper" metaphor, the Advanced Controls palette (**16**) gives fine control of brush behavior and the water as well.

7 12   11

Plug-in filters All the principal image-editing and painting applications can use plug-in filter modules from third party developers. The filters can usually be re-configured by the user. Using filters from various manufacturers, the

top row shows, from left to right, the original transparency, and the effect of Canvas and Dabble. Second row: Impressionist, Oil Painting, and Sketch. Third row: Threads, Water, and Charcoal.

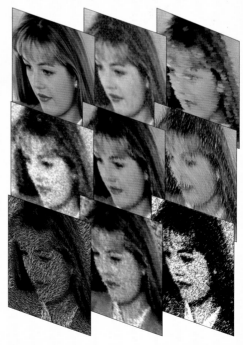

16

Anatomy of an image-editing application It is now routine for the Mac designer to attempt complex image manipulation as part of the day-to-day working process. This "desktop repro" has an irresistible side-effect; designers can be illustrators (or, at least, montagers) too. Confronted by the facilities offered by Photoshop, Live Picture and xRes, it would be a dull Mac designer indeed who was not tempted to interfere with the image on screen.

The Photoshop example (**1**) demonstrates the use of layers. The three people are separate images from BodyShots, a business clip-art resource.

The File menu (**2**) includes a module for direct acquisition of images via a scanner. Edit (**3**) contains the normal cut and paste tools; Image (**4**) controls, amongst other things, the color mode – RGB in the example shown.

The Layer menu (**5**) is associated with the Layers floating palette (**6**) which is the center for most Photo-shop manipulations. The 5 layers of this document are all visible, controlled by the eye device. The active layer (**7**) is colored yellow and marked by the brush symbol. It is being used to finesse the edge of the model's hair on the layer below. Adjustment layers

can also be created to experiment with the effect of changing image values. As with regular layers, they can be turned off and re-ordered in the layer stack.

The Select menu (**8**) includes controls associated with the Channels palette (**9**). The constituent red, green, and blue channels of the composite image are displayed, along with masks for use in separating out backgrounds and applying selective effects. Such masks are produced by painting or, more usually, by drawing paths with the Pen tool, shown in its extended form in the Toolbox (**10**). The Paths palette (**11**) displays the results.

All in-built filters are accessed through the Filter menu (**12**) as are any additional third-party plug-ins. Application of these filters, and many other user-defined routines, can be automated with the Actions palette (**13**).

Magnification of the screen image is controlled both by the View menu (**14**) and the Navigator palette (**15**).

Colors are selected in the Colors palette (**16**) or by double-clicking on the color patches at the foot of the Toolbox (**10**). The latter gives access to the Custom Colors dialog box where various color libraries can be selected.

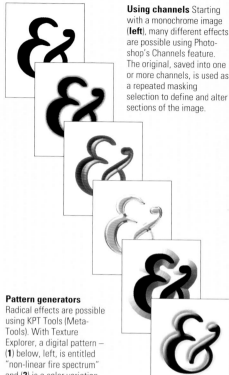

Using channels Starting with a monochrome image (**left**), many different effects are possible using Photoshop's Channels feature. The original, saved into one or more channels, is used as a repeated masking selection to define and alter sections of the image.

Pattern generators
Radical effects are possible using KPT Tools (Meta-Tools). With Texture Explorer, a digital pattern – (**1**) below, left, is entitled "non-linear fire spectrum" and (**2**) is a color variation of "utterly shattered shutters." KPT's Spheroid Designer is further applied to make random spheres (**3**) and the Glass Lens filter produces the result shown at (**4**). Similar kaleidoscopic and geometrical effects can be obtained with Terrazzo (**5**) (Xaos Tools Inc.) .

6   7

11   9

1   2

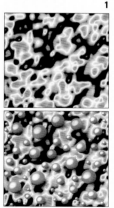

3

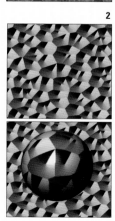

4

Studio Pro (Strata, Inc.), **Infini-D** (Specular), and **Extreme 3D** (Macromedia, Inc.). Modelling the human figure in 3D is notoriously difficult, but **Poser** (Fractal Design Corp.) offers ready-made figures which you can manipulate and modify.

Rendering applications enable you to apply the surface effects of materials such as wood, metal, or marble to an object which has been created in a different 3D application. If the surface choices supplied don't do the job, you can make your own by working in a painting application. Manipulation of the intensity, color, and direction of the light sources illuminating the object is routine; some applications also offer mist, fog, and differential focusing. Depending on your need, you can create powerful still scenes, or complex animation sequences for inclusion in multimedia produc-

Applications for special effects 3-dimensional (3D) and rendering applications now combine high power with ease of use, although some, such as StrataVision 3d, are so powerful that they require a considerable learning effort – but perseverance will be hugely rewarding. Generally speaking, 3D applications follow the same basic principles in the way that they create images, and the illustrations (**right**) show how an image is rendered using Swivel 3D Professional: an object is constructed by first drawing a cross section, plan and/or elevation of your image. The object may be either "extruded," in which case the cross section can be thought of as a sort of die through which material is forced, or "lathed," whereby a profile of your image is rotated along an axis just as if you were carving it on a lathe. The program then creates a 3-dimensional "wireframe" or "mesh" of the object (**1**), the facets of which are filled in to render the object with shading

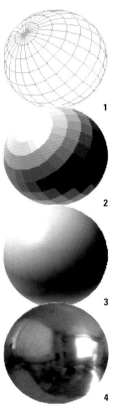

according to a pre-determined light source (**2**). The shading is then smoothed (**3**), and an effect or texture can be applied, or mapped, to the object's surface (**4**). A constructed object can be freely rotated around various axes (**5**), and can be combined with other objects (**6**).

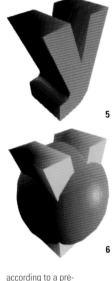

tions. Because of the sheer processing power required, there are serious hardware implications to consider. The trial renderings you make to check your progress are relatively speedy, but when you finally press the button marked "high quality render" be prepared to have your Mac tied up for *very* long periods. Two leading applications in this field are **Ray Dream Designer** (Ray Dream), which is also a 3D modelling application, and **Mac RenderMan** (Pixar).

ADVERTISING The leading dedicated application is **Multi-Ad Creator** (Multi-Ad Services, Inc.), which offers a quick result using templates, borders, and graphic devices. Advertising studios in the print field commonly use conventional page makeup applications such as QuarkXPress, adding images through Photoshop and the major drawing packages. The increasing importance of electronic media calls

The degree to which 3D effects can be controlled are extensive; for example, Ray Dream Designer (**right**), can configure various qualities of light and Swivel 3D Pro allows you to add up to eight light sources from any direction (**far right**). Although many 3D applications offer rendering features, others – such as StrataVision 3d, Ray Dream Designer, and Mac RenderMan – allow virtually unlimited possibilities.

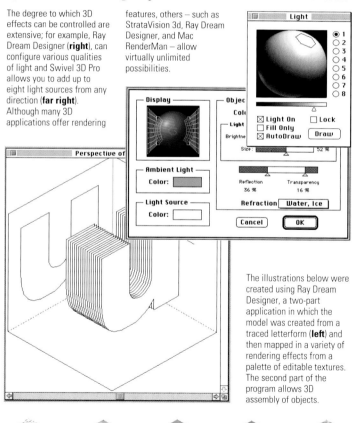

The illustrations below were created using Ray Dream Designer, a two-part application in which the model was created from a traced letterform (**left**) and then mapped in a variety of rendering effects from a palette of editable textures. The second part of the program allows 3D assembly of objects.

for applications which can deal with a wide variety of inputs, and re-define them for use on screen (see pp.82– 3).

MULTIMEDIA This area of activity presents the professional Mac designer with a wide range of enormous challenges – creative, intellectual and, not least, financial. For the novice Mac designer it's a mountain which rises on top of the much smaller hill labeled "learning to use the Mac." The development of multimedia as an idea, and the introduction of the machines and software to make it work has not been a smooth progress. There was an initial explosion of excitement at the early efforts – apparently the result of taking virtually everything it was possible to do on a Mac and throwing it haphazardly into a single pot. The password of the moment was "interactive." Of course, such a scenario presented both the hardware and software marketing teams with a dream, but euphoria soon gave way to embarrassment when it was realized that end-users of this new medium were as much bewildered as they were excited by it. The efforts of software producers and hardware manufacturers needed to be rationalized and channeled to a commercially productive end. Several potential uses became apparent – educational materials, disk-based reference, museum guides, sophisticated business presentations, and so on.

For the designer there is a neat parallel between multimedia and Hollywood. Stay on for the closing credits next time you're at the movies. Which job would you like out of the hundreds listed? Producer, director, editor, or maybe all of them. In multimedia terms, you could provide the graphics, but who, for instance, will write the words, compose the music, record the sound, take the photographs, and direct the video sequences? And if you decide to simplify matters by using existing material, who owns the copyright of each individual element? And, when you've eventually hunted the owners down, will they let you use it – and if so, for how much? An important factor to bear in mind before embarking on the multimedia odyssey is the level of hardware you will require – the list would include most of the following: color scanner, digital camera, video-capable inputs, CD-ROM recorder and associated fast and vast storage, sound recording and editing equipment, and so on and so on.

Software for programming multimedia productions comes in two flavors. First come high-powered "authoring" programs like **SuperCard** (Allegiant Technologies, Inc.), **MacroMind Director** (Macromedia, Inc.) and the hugely expensive **Authorware Professional** (Macromedia, Inc.). These all allow you to write or modify program "scripts" (a simplified form of program language). Ready-made scripts are selected from a comprehensive collection, modified if necessary, and assembled in order. There is a learning curve to be negotiated – each package has its own script language which looks like English but has a very specific grammar.

This is the closest that the average Mac designer is likely to come to true programming. Second, and a bit easier to use, are packages such as **QuarkImmedia** (Quark, Inc.), which operates in tandem with the QuarkXPress page makeup application. Events are managed by selecting buttons with particular properties, then making links by pasting them to objects and animations. With this kind of software and some sound capabilities, you will be able, in theory at least, to produce really complex shows. If your ambitions are less grand, try a much stripped-down application like **ProView** (E-magine). With this you can make, for example, a rolling portfolio presentation, complete with sound.

WEB AUTHORING All the major multimedia applications can be used equally for Web page production – even the classic drawing applications can transform their output into Web-ready form. The overall disciplines for successful page production are entirely different from those of the printed page. They are not dictated by the characteristics of the particular software package nor even by your abilities as a designer. They are determined simply by the efficiency (or lack of it) of the delivery system, although developers will almost certainly improve this in the foreseeable future. You'll find limitations, for example, on the available color palette, range of usable typefaces, and speed of animation playback. Simplicity is the keynote. Pages with slowly-unrolling graphics are likely to be cut off in their prime by impatient users. Typical authoring software include **Home Page** (Claris Corp.) and **Page Mill** (Adobe Sysytems Inc.). Browsers such as **Netscape Navigator** (Netscape Communications Corp.) and **Internet Explorer** (Microsoft Corp.) offer page creation as an additional feature. The only constant here is change.

TYPE DESIGN AND MANIPULATION Font technology for the Macintosh is a complex subject and is discussed in greater detail in Chapter 4 (p.84). But the computer is a godsend to the typographic designer when it comes to typeface design – even if it is also frequently a scourge as far as some other typographic activities are concerned. Using a suitable application, it is a relatively straightforward matter to create an entire typeface from scratch and then use it as you would any other font. It is also easy to modify every character of any existing font installed on your Mac and then use it as a new typeface. **Fontographer** (Macromedia Inc.) is capable of either generating new faces or modifying existing ones. Use it for drawing up logo designs, particularly if you intend to incorporate the logo into typeset copy.

If you still can't get the font you like, you can go digging in the pre-history of the Mac for old "type 3" fonts and use Fontographer to bring them up to date. However, fonts converted from one format to another may be degraded by conversion at a lower resolution than that of the original font format.

WORD PROCESSING Applications such as QuarkXPress and PageMaker can read many "foreign" text formats directly into your document's text box, but a word processor may be of use if this process goes wrong or the format proves too exotic. This can work also in reverse – after you have fitted text you may have to re-export it to your client in word processed format for further editorial changes. Sounds crazy, but it happens. You will also one day be faced with a corrupt or damaged file, from which text, but not much else, can be rescued via a file recovery utility and read by a word processor. For all these reasons, and to write an occasional invoice, choose from the most widely used applications. Among these are **MacWrite Pro** (Claris Corp.), **Nisus Writer** (Paragon Concepts, Inc.), **WordPerfect** (Novell), and the most widely used of all, **Microsoft Word** (Microsoft Corp.). All "office" packages, such as **ClarisWorks** (Claris Corp.), include word processors.

OTHER APPLICATIONS So far, I have described applications which relate directly to the work of the graphic designer. There are thousands of others that don't appear relevant, but in the crowd there are some useful subsidiary packages.

Presentation When you need to make slide shows, try **Persuasion** (Adobe Systems Inc.) and **PowerPoint** (Microsoft Corp.). They have been available on the Mac for a very long time, and their ability to make quick and colorful sequences could get you out of a jam.

Spreadsheets and accounting You'll find spreadsheet facilities in the "office" packages. These can be useful for budgeting complex jobs such as juggling levels of print specification and run lengths to achieve a final price. The useful features will soon become apparent, enabling you to ignore all the heavy mathematical stuff. If you want to do your own accounting on the Mac, beware of the large, powerful applications that are really designed for the corporate sector. You may spend more time inputting financial data than designing. **Quicken** (Intuit) is perhaps more suitable for the freelance designer. You may find a personal database such as **Day-to-Day Contacts** (Portfolio Software, Inc.) useful.

Text scanning Optical character recognition allows you to use a scanner to input typewritten or typeset text into your Mac. **OmniPage** (Caere, Inc.) handles a wide variety of inputs, including multi-column and tabular material. The interpretation or "recognition" of the actual words is now very sophisticated, with selectable dictionaries to allow scanning of texts in foreign languages.

UTILITIES AND SYSTEM ENHANCERS There are thousands of little applications, or "utilities," available as commercial items, "shareware" or "freeware." Useful ones include:

Adobe Type Manager Deluxe (ATM) (Adobe Systems, Inc.) renders PostScript Type 1 fonts smoothly on screen, and anti-aliases others to achieve a better result.

Adobe Type Reunion (Adobe Systems, Inc.) organizes your font menus by family, with style and weight submenus alongside, cutting font lists to a more manageable size.

Suitcase (Symantec Corp.) is a useful font-management utility that enables you easily to add fonts to or remove them from your system without the need for dragging them in and out of your System file.

QuicKeys (CE Software Inc.) enables you to assign keyboard shortcuts to menu items or to repetitive actions.

Virus protection A virus (see glossary) wreaks havoc by causing repeated crashes or files to vanish. Many utilities are available for detection and elimination, such as **Disinfectant** (Northwestern University) and **SAM** (Symantec Corp.).

Screen savers are now in the entertainment category. Modern screens are not so susceptible to burn-in as their predecessors. **After Dark** (Berkeley Systems, Inc.) continues the tradition.

Disk recovery and optimization One day your hard disk will get damaged – files may disappear, or the disk may not appear on the desktop. You may be able to save the day with a recovery utility such as **Norton Utilities** (Symantec Corp.). These utilities will also "optimize" your disk. The more a disk is used, the more it becomes "fragmented": as the disk gets full, the files get broken up and distributed over different parts of the disk, slowing access time. A disk-optimizing utility will find all the parts of a file, join them together to make them contiguous, and rearrange them on the disk, restoring quick access.

File compression One way of economizing on disk space is to use a file-compression utility. In addition to creating space on your hard disk, such a utility is useful for archiving files (for instance, storing old jobs that you need to keep but are unlikely to require regular access to) and for transporting large files to a service bureau. If you are mailing disks to an unfamiliar destination, you would be advised to use a compression utility that is used universally, such as **DiskDoubler** (Salient Software) or **StuffIt Deluxe (**Aladdin Systems). There are other compression utilities which may be more useful for compressing certain types of image file.

Backup utilities The golden rule in computing is: back up your files. Regularly, and without question. A computer is a complex machine, but even simple machines break down. To make the chore of backing up as painless as possible, there are several specially designed backup utilities, the appropriate one depending upon what media you are backing up to (hard disk, removable disks, tape streamers, or floppy disks, etc.). You can back up your hard disk simply by copying the files to another disk, but this means that every time you back up, you must laboriously copy the *entire* disk. A backup utility, on the other hand, will only back up changes made to files since the last time you backed up.

Anatomy of a multimedia application Multimedia presentations must open and run smoothly on all types of machine, respond instantly to an untutored user's commands, play sounds on cue, and finally,

quit when instructed. These are heavy demands and are reflected in the complexity of the authoring software.

In the example below, SuperCard is being used to orchestrate a CD-ROM production on gem stones.

The viewer will be able to navigate back and forth through a series of screens, many of which contain animations. Incoming still images are saved as PICT files at 72 pixels per inch. The other raw materials —

QuickTime movies and PICS files, for example, and audio files are first processed in applications like Première and Sound Edit 16 (**opposite page**). The aim is to make as small a file as possible, for smooth playback, without losing quality.

In the SuperCard menu (**above**), the normal File and Edit menus are augmented by Go (**1**) with commands to test the "project" (Super Card term for the job in

hand). Objects (**2**) and the Property Inspector palette (**3**) control the position and properties of all components, of which the most important is the "Card." Cards are the containers for all other objects and are linked by "scripts." Tools (**4**) controls the conventional Toolbox (**5**), Colors palette (**6**), Text palette (**7**), and Toolbar (**8**), but also opens the crucial ClickScript window (**9**). Text (**10**)

controls on-screen type (not all faces are suitable for multimedia display). Internet (**11**) offers possibilities of embedding the project, within limitations, into a Web site. Windows (**12**) and Utilities (**13**) are simple lists of options. The animated rotating button (**14**) is under the control of the Animation palette (**15**). After testing on a variety of computers, the project will be saved as a standalone application.

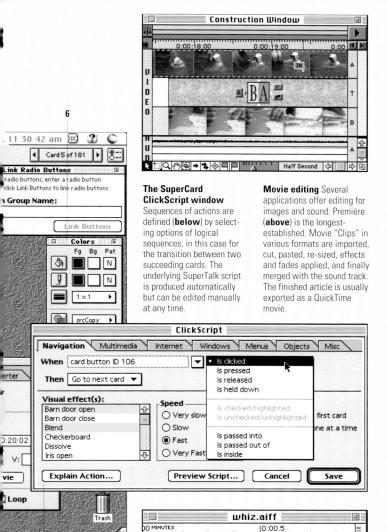

6

The SuperCard ClickScript window
Sequences of actions are defined (**below**) by selecting options of logical sequences, in this case for the transition between two succeeding cards. The underlying SuperTalk script is produced automatically but can be edited manually at any time.

Movie editing Several applications offer editing for images and sound. Première (**above**) is the longest-established. Movie "Clips" in various formats are imported, cut, pasted, re-sized, effects and fades applied, and finally merged with the sound track. The finished article is usually exported as a QuickTime movie.

9

Sound editing The Mac is increasingly able to take in and process high-quality stereo sound. In Sound Edit 16 (**right**), sound tracks are edited graphically. The sound shown here (a kind of extra-galactic pulsating whoosh) was entirely created on the Mac desktop from one existing tone, distorted, split into three tracks, flipped backwards, pitch-shifted, and finally re-merged.

Anatomy of a Web authoring application

Beneath all Web applications is a seething morass of HTML (Hypertext Markup Language). Fortunately Page Mill (Adobe Systems Inc.), Home Page (Claris Corp.) and others hide it away. There is an increasing trend for this type of authoring to be bolted on as an addition to page makeup and drawing applications. In either case the ambition is the same – to make a Web site that downloads quickly and contains links that work correctly. The page as delivered to the viewer should retain the qualities you designed into it. Because of the nature of Internet transmission, this is not always the case.

The basic output of an application like PageMill, below, is not a "page" in print terms, but a single continuous column of text with graphics inserted as if they were also pieces of text. For now, the eventual viewer sets the page width and depth, and your words, however you styled them, only appear in the typefaces and colors active on the viewer's computer.

Although it is possible to insert complex graphics and animations into a site, limitations of bandwidth and modem speed mean that potential visitors will likely become impatient of long download times, and simply abandon the attempt.

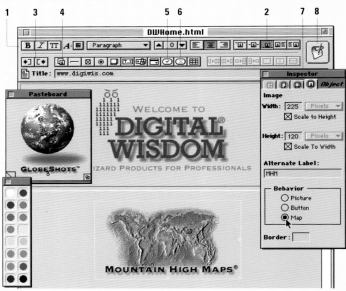

In the PageMill window the menu bar is replaced by miniature icon buttons. The upper rank of icons (**1**) deals primarily with the text – the right hand group (**2**) controls its relationship with images. In the lower toolbar, icon (**3**) set column indents. The next group, starting with "insert image" (**4**), create page elements. Some are simple objects – but most contribute to the interactive qualities of the page. Submit (**5**) and Reset (**6**), for example, will be active links within the finished site. All items can be accessed through the Inspector palette (**7**). A preview button (**8**) shows the behavior of the finished page.

Using the Web There are many on-line resources which designers can access. Macromedia, for example, offer electronic software support (**1**), and Adobe operate a type-vending service (**2**).

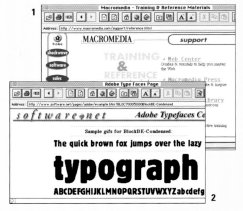

Resources The items on this page are not strictly software – they continue the long-established graphic arts tradition of "clip art" and "stock shots." The intention in both cases is to save you, the designer, the trouble and expense of commissioning illustration and photography from scratch.

Textures High resolution scans of natural textures such as elm burl (**left**) and marble (**below**) make useful backgrounds. The images (from Artbeats) are also provided as tileable fills for making repeating patterns and borders.

Photo libraries The major photo libraries offer their stock on CD-ROM. A browser (**right**) allows a search of the stock by scanning thumbnails or typing in subject keywords. You can download a low-resolution image (**far right**) for use in a presentation, then order and pay for the real thing by phone or E-mail. You must still credit the photographer and agency in the usual way in this case Deborah Gilbert/ Image Bank. You can imitate this process with your own photographs using the Kodak PhotoDisc system. Through your photo dealer, 35mm slides can be scanned on to CD-ROM (they appear as icons, right) and browsed with a slide-show viewer application.

Illustration libraries In order to be usable at a wide range of sizes, images are often saved as Illustrator documents for subsequent rasterizing into Photoshop. The jaguar (**below**) comes from a Clipables (C.A.R. Inc.) collection.

Specialist resources Several manufacturers offer libraries of specialist clip art. The globe view (**right**) is from one of the Mountain High Maps collections of world and regional maps, as is the background to the montage (**above**). Conventional "atlas" style mapping complete with editable layers is also available. The harassed executive is from Body Shots, a series of photographs reflecting the business environment.

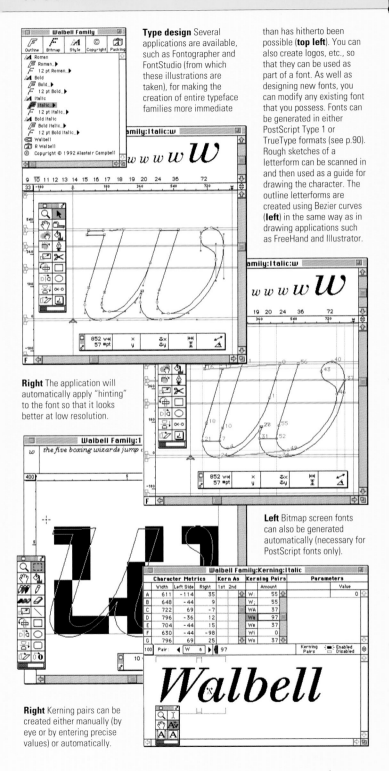

Type design Several applications are available, such as Fontographer and FontStudio (from which these illustrations are taken), for making the creation of entire typeface families more immediate than has hitherto been possible (**top left**). You can also create logos, etc., so that they can be used as part of a font. As well as designing new fonts, you can modify any existing font that you possess. Fonts can be generated in either PostScript Type 1 or TrueType formats (see p.90). Rough sketches of a letterform can be scanned in and then used as a guide for drawing the character. The outline letterforms are created using Bezier curves (**left**) in the same way as in drawing applications such as FreeHand and Illustrator.

Right The application will automatically apply "hinting" to the font so that it looks better at low resolution.

Left Bitmap screen fonts can also be generated automatically (necessary for PostScript fonts only).

Right Kerning pairs can be created either manually (by eye or by entering precise values) or automatically.

Font effects Applications such as Illustrator and FreeHand provide features for manipulating fonts, but there are several dedicated to rendering a wide variety of effects – ideal for logos and display lettering. In addition to providing a palette of predetermined distortions for Type 1 fonts (**below**), effects can be freely achieved by manipulating Bezier curves (**right**).

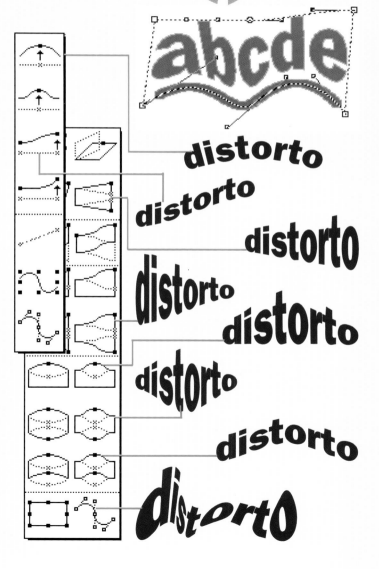

This chart summarizes a variety of applications of particular relevance to professional graphic designers. Utilities, system enhancements and clip-art resources are also listed.

Category	Animation	Clip/Art Resource	Image manipulation	Color retouching	Drawing	Effect rendering & 3D	Font manipulation	Multimedia	Page layout/makeup	Painting	Plug-in	Utilities & communications	Web page design	Word processing/general
Acrobat Adobe Systems Inc.												①		
Andromeda Filters Andromeda Inc.											②			
Artbeats Artbeats		③												
ATM Deluxe Adobe Systems Inc.												④		
Authorware Macromedia Inc.	●							⑤						
Canvas Deneba Software			●		⑥					●				
ClickWorks Scitex Corp. Ltd.	●							⑦						
CorelDraw Corel Corp.			●		⑧									
DeBabelizer Equilibrium								●				⑨		
Dimensions Adobe Systems Inc.						⑩								
Director Macromedia, Inc.	●							⑤						
Disinfectant Shareware												⑪		
DiskDoubler Connectix												⑫		
Eudora Qualcomm Inc.												⑬		
Excel Microsoft Corp.														⑭
Extreme 3D Macromedia Inc.	●					⑩		●						
FileMaker Pro Claris Corp.														⑮
Fontographer Macromedia Inc.							⑯							
FrameMaker Frame Technology									⑰					
FreeHand Macromedia Inc.					⑧									
Home Page Claris Corp.													⑱	
Illustrator Adobe Systems Inc.					⑧									
Infini-D Specular International	●					⑩								
Internet Explorer Microsoft Corp.												⑲		
Kai's Power Tools MetaTools			●								②			
KPT Bryce MetaTools										⑳				
KPT Vector Effects MetaTools			●								②			
Live Picture Live Picture Inc.				●						㉑				
MacDraw Claris Corp.					⑧									
MacWrite Claris Corp.														㉒
Morph Gryphon Software Corp.	●				㉓			●						
Mountain High Maps Digital Wisdom Inc.		㉔												
Multi-Ad Creator Multi-Ad Services									㉕					
Navigator Netscape Comms. Corp.												⑲		
Nisus Paragon Concepts														㉒
Norton Utilities Symantec Corp.												㉖		
Now Up-to-Date Now Software Inc.														㉗
OmniPage Caere Corp.														㉘
PageMaker Adobe Systems Inc.									⑰					
PageMill Adobe Systems Inc.													⑱	
Paint Alchemy Xaos Tools Inc.											②			
Painter Fractal Design			●							㉙				

Legend:
- **1** Primary features (numbered circle)
- **●** Secondary features (solid dot)

Product	Animation	Clip/Art Resource	Image manipulation	Color retouching	Drawing	Effect rendering & 3D	Font manipulation	Multimedia	Page layout/makeup	Painting	Plug-in	Utilities & communications	Web page design	Word processing/general
PhotoDisc Photodisc Inc.		30												
PhotoShop Adobe Systems Inc.			●	●	●					21				
Poser Fractal Design Corp.										31				
Premiere Adobe Systems Inc.	●							32						
QuarkImmedia Quark, Inc.								5					●	
QuarkXPress Quark, Inc.									17					
Quicken Intuit														33
Ray Dream Designer Ray Dream Inc.	●					10				●				
Retrospect Dantz Dev. Corp.												34		
SAM Symantec Corp.												11		
Sound Edit Macromedia Inc.								35						
StrataVision 3d Strata Inc.	●					10		●						
Streamline Adobe Systems Inc.												36		
StuffIt Deluxe Aladdin Systems												12		
Suitcase Symantec												37		
SuperCard Allegiant Technologies Inc.								5						
Type Reunion Adobe Systems Inc.												38		
VideoShop Avid Technology								32						
Word Microsoft Corp.														22
xRes Macromedia Inc.			21											

Key

1. Creation of portable documents which can be distributed for reading without the original software or fonts.
2. Plug-in effects filters for Photoshop and similar applications.
3. Natural textures and backgrounds.
4. Improvement through anti-aliasing of screen rendering of bitmapped fonts. Font management and display.
5. Creation and organization of multimedia presentations.
6. Combination vector and bitmap drawing.
7. Flowchart-based multimedia authoring.
8. Vector-based drawing.
9. Automated image-processing and conversion.
10. Creation and rendering of 3D objects.
11. Virus protection.
12. File compression utility.
13. E-mail handler.
14. Spreadsheet application.
15. Database creation and management.
16. Font creation and modification.
17. Design and layout of text and images for print.
18. Web page design.
19. Web browser and E-mail application.
20. Digital landscape generator.
21. Image creation and editing. Color correction and retouching.
22. Word processing.
23. Image distortion, still-frame, and movie creation.
24. Range of detailed terrain maps with atlas overlays.
25. Template-based design for press advertisements.
26. Disk diagnosis, optimization, and recovery utility.
27. Calendar and time management utility.
28. Document scanning for optical character recognition.
29. "Natural media" painting application.
30. Stock photography library.
31. 3D human figure templates for manipulation.
32. Movie and video editing and effects.
33. Accounting and financial planning package.
34. Archiving and back-up utility.
35. Sound editing and effects.
36. Auto-tracing of bitmapped images.
37. Font management utility.
38. Font menu re-organization.

4
TYPOGRAPHY
TYPE MEASUREMENT/TYPE CHARACTERISTICS/
POSTSCRIPT/TRUETYPE/FONT CONFLICTS/
FONT ORGANIZATION/DIGITIZING FONTS/
BUYING FONTS

In the old days – you remember (or maybe you don't) – when you selected a typeface for a job, you probably spent a little time flicking through type sample books from a few of your preferred typesetting houses. If you didn't see what you wanted in one book, you reached for another, and then another until you found what you were looking for. You then marked up your text with type specifications and sent it to the typesetter, who got to work implementing your instructions. Meanwhile, you got on with something else, never giving a moment's thought to the technicalities involved in turning your marked-up copy into high quality typesetting.

A few hours, days or even weeks later you would receive galleys back from your typesetter.

Now that you are the owner of a Macintosh computer system, a whole new world has opened up in front of you – and one that may force you to question the wisdom of your decision to get a Mac at all. The printer that you have bought, along with the Mac, comes with a few (*very* few) built-in fonts, most of which are not particularly appropriate for professional graphic design. Hence your first realization – that you need more typefaces. So, you do as you used to; you reach for a type sample book. But now you find that you are faced with a choice based not just on esthetic criteria but on a whole new set of considerations, many of them technical, and none of which would ever have concerned you in the past.

Just as you once had to choose between typesetting houses, you now have to choose between font vendors – some of whom appear to be offering some fonts which are exactly the same as those offered by another. And having made your choice of typeface, you find that you are also offered a choice of font format – TrueType or PostScript (two kinds, 1 and 3 if you're looking in a very old catalog, now just Type 1). Then comes the crunch – a typeface in a set of about eight styles (light, roman, semi-bold and bold, with their respective italic variations, for example) is *very* costly

– it may even cost more than your fee for the job. And, to cap it all, you discover that to get the full mix of styles and weights, you must purchase not one, but two font sets (or more – an entire typeface, Helvetica 25 through to Helvetica 95 for example, may be split into *three* sets).

Once you've made your decision and ordered the font, you face your next problem: how do you get all those 20,000 words of typewritten manuscript into your machine? (see p.116 for the answer). Having input the text into your Mac, formatted it to your desired specifications and printed out a proof, you discover that there is something not quite right about the kerning, or about the character or word spacing of justified text; but now you can't go back to your typesetter to get it fixed – you've actually got to do it yourself. By now you may be forgiven for wondering whether you are still a designer or have become a typesetter.

However, typography on the Mac is far from a negative experience. If you discipline yourself to stay within certain parameters – always using the same font format, for instance, or always buying fonts from the same foundry, or always using the same application to output text to your printer or to an imagesetter – you will encounter few problems and will come to rejoice at the typographic control you now have over your work, and the amount of waiting time you'll save.

TYPE MEASUREMENT The earliest type consisted of solid blocks ("body") upon which the area to be printed ("face") was "punched". All measurements of type relate to these three-dimensional objects – even the digitized type commonly used today.

In the past, printing was an inexact science, and no two printers could agree on a standard system of type measurement, which meant that units of type cast in different foundries were incompatible. Eventually, in the mid-18th century, the French typographer Pierre Simon Fournier proposed a standard unit which he called a "point." This was further developed by Firmin Didot into a European standard which, although their systems were based upon it, was not adopted by Britain or the U.S.

The Anglo-American system is based on the division of one inch into 72 parts called points and, mathematically, one point should equal 0.013889in – but, in fact, it equals 0.013837in, meaning that 72 points only make 0.996264in. The European point equals 0.0148in and 12 of these form a unit measuring 0.1776in. This 12-point unit is called a *cicero* in France and Germany, a *riga tipografica* (*riga*) in Italy, and an *augustijn* (*aug*) in the Netherlands. There is no relationship between the Anglo-American point and the Didot point, and neither of them relates to metric measurement.

While it was thought that there would be a gradual move toward the metrication of typographic measurements, the

Much of the nomenclature and measuring systems of traditional typography remain standard language on the Macintosh. Traditional type measurement on the Mac derives from the body size of a non-printing piece of metal, and even though computer type has no physical basis, this idea has been extended for measuring computer-generated letterforms – instead of being based on the physical body size of metal type, computer type is based on an imaginary em square. The unit of measurement used to describe type is still the point. However, PostScript defines one point as being 0.013889in. (exactly ½in.) as distinct from the traditional Anglo-American point size measuring 0.013837in. (72 of which make slightly less than an inch). The terminology relating to different parts of typeset characters is extensive, but the terms most commonly retained by Macintosh parlance are listed here.

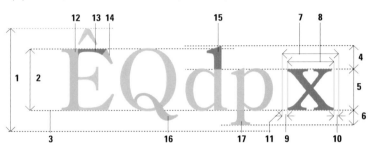

advent of the Mac as a design tool has probably established a new international standard of measurement (or, at least, it may have delayed metrication in some countries) based on the Anglo-American system. On the Mac however, one point measures 0.013889in, and 72 points really do equal one inch. It is no coincidence that the basic Mac screen resolution is 72dpi.

TYPE CHARACTERISTICS Among the many basic considerations of typographic design, perhaps the most important are the varying widths of type characters and the spaces between them. An understanding of these elements is essential in order to achieve the twin aim of esthetic appeal and legibility.

The width of characters, or the space allotted to them, depends largely on the equipment used to produce them. For instance, a manual typewriter, in order to maintain consistent letter spacing, uses exaggeratedly wide serifs on thin letters such as "i" and "l" (*viz* i and l). This gives a string of characters an even appearance by reducing the amount of white around them. On the Mac, however, the width of each character is able to be defined closely to accommodate that particular character and is adjusted to suit the design of the typeface. This provides the potential for perfect optical spacing between characters.

The spacing of words in a line of text owes as much to a convention employed by scribes in medieval times as it does to the evolution of typographic design – because they wanted to make facing pages in books symmetrical, scribes insisted that both the left- and right-hand edges of text should be vertically aligned. This ideal could only be

1 Body height, or em height
2 Cap height
3 Base line
4 Ascender height
5 x height
6 Descender depth
7 Character width
8 Body width
9 Left sidebearing
10 Right side-bearing
11 Character origin
12 Stem
13 Arm
14 Beak
15 Ascender
16 Tail
17 Descender
18 Apex
19 Spine
20 Stroke
21 Serif
22 Bowl
23 Link
24 Ear
25 Counter
26 Cross-stroke
27 Horizontal stem or crossbar
28 Spur
29 Bracket
30 Loop
31 Finial

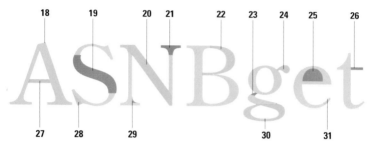

achieved by abbreviating words, which led to the introduction of additional symbols, called contractions, being used to fill short lines or the spaces remaining after words had been abbreviated.

This convention was continued by Johann Gutenberg (c.1397–1468), who came up with the idea of printing from movable (and thus re-usable) type as long ago as 1436, although its continuation reflected mechanical requirements more than esthetic considerations. In order to make an impression from a group of pieces of type, all the pieces had to be locked together under tension in a metal frame called a chase. This meant that all the lines of type, including spaces, had to be of the same length, otherwise all but the tightest line would fall out of the chase as soon as it was lifted. In other words, the whole area between each edge of the chase had to be filled with wood or metal – either type or spaces. The convention of vertically aligning edges of blocks of text was made possible by distributing approximately equal spaces between each of the words along a line of text. This is what we know today as "justified" text, and the technique of achieving it remained more or less unchanged until the advent of alternative methods of setting type in the latter half of the 20th century.

After the introduction of movable type, the next significant change came with the invention, patented in 1884, of the Linotype machine by a German-born American engineer Ottmar Mergenthaler. This was the first keyboard-operated composing machine to employ the principle of a "matrix" from which molten metal was used to cast type. Each line of type was composed from a row of matrices,

SCREEN AND PRINTER FONTS

To use fonts successfully, you will find it necessary to familiarize yourself with the distinction between font files that are used to display the font on your monitor and font files that are used by a printing device for output. For monitor display, letterforms are made up of pixels and are called "bitmapped" or "screen" fonts. The printer, on the other hand, uses an object-oriented version of the font, an outline capable of output at any size and at any resolution. These fonts are called "printer" or "outline" fonts.

Font formats There are two formats from which to choose: PostScript and True-Type. If you opt for Post-Script, you will find files on the disk for both screen fonts and printer fonts. True Type fonts are supplied with only one file – an outline font file which is used both for printing and for creating bitmapped screen fonts.

Screen fonts To render a PostScript font on screen with a semblance of what it will look like when printed ("WYSIWYG" – what you see is what you get), a screen font must be installed in several sizes. If not, the font is drawn from the nearest available size and results in "aliasing," a jagged appearance ("jaggies"), making it impossible to fine-tune typographic design.

ATM The introduction of Adobe's Type Manager (ATM) resolved this problem

by using the "hinting" information stored in the PostScript printer outline font to render more accurate bitmapped letterforms on screen. With ATM installed, only one size of bitmapped screen font is required (so that the font name appears in menus). The more recent ATM Deluxe will also anti-alias (or smooth) the appearance of bitmapped fonts even in the absence of the relevant outline font.

Hinting Hints modify character shapes to look better at low resolutions (both monitor and printer). Normally, a screen font will instruct a pixel to turn on if more than half the area of the pixel is covered by the font, resulting in anomalies (**1**). A hinted character, on the other hand, knows how the character should *look* – that the two stems of an "n" should be the same width, for example (**2**).

Font organization Type 1 screen font files are con-

tained within "suitcases" (**3**). These, and their related PostScript printer font files (**4**, **5**, for example) are placed within the Fonts folder (**6**, see opposite). The screen fonts will then be available within all applications, and the printer fonts will auto-matically download to the printer when required. TrueType font files (**7**) should also be placed inside the Fonts folder. Double-clicking a PostScript screen font icon will produce a list (**8**) of the individual weights and sizes it contains. Double click on an item in the list to see a sample (**9**) of its screen appearance. The TrueType font icon responds in the same way. The ATM control panel (**10**) allows a variable size font cache to be allocated. More cache space is needed to render very large point sizes.

Alternative installation As a designer, you will use a lot of fonts; thus font menus may become very lengthy, and fonts can absorb a great deal of RAM. A utility such as *Suitcase* will allow you to open and close suitcase files of screen fonts easily. First, make a new folder and name it "Font Suitcases" (**11**). Drag your screen fonts and printer fonts into the new folder.

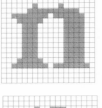

1

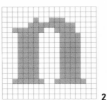

2

Garamond 24

Sample
How
razorback-jumping
frogs can level six
piqued gymnasts!

To use this font, drag it onto your System Folder

9

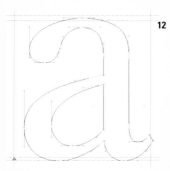

12

13

Suitcase will generally let you turn screen font suitcases on and off, without quitting the application in which you are working. It will warn you if the font you are trying to close is in use. Equally, there will be an alert if a newly introduced font shares a font ID number with one already active. There is an option to temporarily change the ID number of the offending font. The best plan, however, is to de-select the active font.

Making your own suitcases To group together a selection of useful fonts for a new job, do the following: make copies in the Finder ("Duplicate," in the File menu) of all the screen font

suitcases you intend to use. Rename one of them "New Job Suitcase," for example, then drag the remaining suitcase copies into the

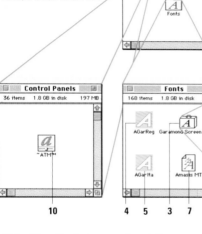

renamed suitcase icon. Double-click on the renamed icon and you will find it contains all the styles and weights of all the selected fonts. If you don't need every style and weight of every font for that particular job, just drag the surplus ones to the Trash. Close the modified suitcase. It can then be used in exactly the same way as all your other screen fonts, either in the Fonts folder under the contol of the System, or in your own Font Suitcases folder, using *Suitcase* or a similar utility.

10   **4 5 3 7**   **8**

Below The outline font construction (**12**) is shown next to its 60pt imageset character. The hinted bit-mapped screen character (**13**) is generated from the outline font by ATM; also

shown is the appearance of the 60pt character on screen. Without ATM, the 60pt character is constructed (**14**) from the installed bit-mapped font of the closest size, in this case 24pt. In

paint applications like PhotoShop, anti-aliasing (smoothing of the edges by inserting grayscale pixels) will improve the screen image (**15**).

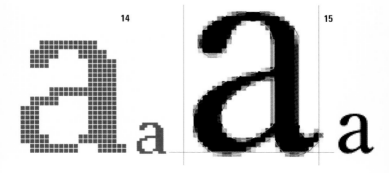

then cast as a single, solid piece (hence the name Linotype), called a "slug."

One year after the patenting of the Linotype machine came the Monotype process, invented in 1885 by Tolbert Lanston of Ohio. His keyboard-operated composing machine cast type as individual letters, using large numbers of matrices (which was feasible because of the invention of a mechanical punch cutter by L.B. Benton).

In the 1950s, photomechanical typesetting machines were introduced, and they employed matrices stored as negatives on glass disks or strips. Output was produced photographically onto bromide paper for subsequent lithographic reproduction.

The first digital typesetting machines appeared in the early 1970s. Letterforms made up of digitized data were generated on the screen of a cathode ray tube (CRT), from which an image was projected onto photographic film or paper. This method of generating digitized type has gradually been replaced by the laser imagesetter, which was first introduced in the mid-1970s.

The Macintosh computer arrived in 1984, but it wasn't until 1988 that it began to be taken seriously by the various graphic arts industries. Their resistance was understandable. The first fonts were bitmaps (made up of square pixels) which were designed to be both displayed on screen and printed. The Mac could only output its very limited range of fonts on a low-resolution dot-matrix printer. While some of the type looked great on the screen, it could not be got out of the machine in a usable form. The new dawn finally arrived with PostScript (see below) and the Laser-Writer. Nowadays, the amount of control the Mac user has over word and letter spacing is almost limitless. Freed from the constraints of the old three-dimensional piece of type, you can experiment with negative leading, in which successive lines collide (please don't), horizontal and vertical scaling (worth it in moderation – see p.104) and kerning adjustment (makes all the difference). Applications such as QuarkXPress offer numerous alternative hyphenation and justification permutations; just as the medieval scribe determined his own criteria for spacing out lines of text, so the graphic designer must now be in total control of word and character spacing.

POSTSCRIPT PostScript is the proprietary page description language (PDL) of Adobe Systems Inc. A page description language is the program that the printer uses to interpret data from the computer into a form that the printer can use to print from. The PostScript PDL is also used to describe graphic images, such as tone images, tints, rules, etc., as well as fonts, to a printer, so a PostScript printer is still a necessary part of your equipment even if you use non-PostScript fonts (TrueType, for example).

When you buy a PostScript font, you get three items in the package – a "suitcase" file containing screen fonts, individual printer font files (one for each style – italic, bold, etc.), and a folder containing Adobe "font metrics" files (AFMs).

The screen fonts are the bitmapped fonts that are designed to display the font on-screen at a variety of fixed sizes (as well as being called bitmapped fonts, PostScript screen fonts are also occasionally referred to as "fixed-size" fonts, especially by Apple). Screen fonts generally reside in the Fonts folder in the System folder on your hard disk. The problem with bitmapped screen fonts is that they give an ugly, stepped appearance (known as "jaggies") on screen, which is exacerbated when you specify a size that is not one of the fixed sizes that you installed in the System file.

Printer font files, generally recognized on-screen by an icon incorporating their manufacturer's logo, are the "outline" fonts containing data that describes the outline shapes of type characters, from which any size can be drawn and filled in by the output device (printer fonts may also be called "scalable" fonts). The advantage of outline fonts is that, as well as providing a single set of data for any size, they can be output at any resolution, whether it be the 300dpi of a laser printer or the 2540dpi of an imagesetter.

The third part of the package, the AFM files, is required by very few applications such as Scitex Visionary and Interset's Quoin.

Type 1 and Type 3 fonts Originally Adobe protected their PostScript font technology by reserving a font format for their own type designs. This format, called PostScript Type 1, was encrypted (locked), and the fonts were thus unalterable. Type 1 fonts employed a technique called "hinting," which was designed to enhance the display of fonts at small sizes – it also improved the appearance of small sizes of type when printed on low-resolution printers.

Type 3, on the other hand (there was no Type 2), was the PostScript format that other (non-Adobe) foundries used for their fonts – unless they were prepared to pay a license fee to Adobe for their Type 1 format, which very few did. Although Type 3 fonts did not contain hinting, they were alterable, which meant that by using applications such as Fontographer you could change the design of any character, or even of an entire font. But the real drawback of Type 3 fonts was that Adobe Type Manager (see below) worked only with Type 1 fonts.

Adobe Type Manager When Apple announced that they were to offer an alternative font format to PostScript, Adobe responded by releasing a font utility called "Adobe Type Manager" (ATM). This little utility made a huge impact on the Mac world generally, and particularly on designers, as a typographic tool. So far as the user is concerned, all ATM

KEYBOARD CHARACTERS

Keyboard layout is generally standard, but some fonts may use different keys, such as "expert sets," with additional characters. To view the character set of any of your installed fonts, use the Apple-supplied Key Caps (**below**) utility in the Menu which displays all available characters for the various modifier keys.

Shift + character keys	Option + Shift + character keys
Character key only	Option + character keys

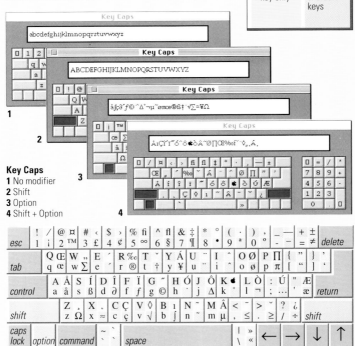

Key Caps
1 No modifier
2 Shift
3 Option
4 Shift + Option

Above All the characters accessible by using combinations of the Shift and Option modifier keys.
Below The commonly available characters and the modifier key combinations for generating that character (where appropriate). There may be slight variations depending on the version of the system software that you use. For example, the # and £ characters are transposed on the US and UK systems. The following abbreviations are used for the modifier keys, followed by the character to be pressed.
S = Shift key
O = Option key
SO = Shift + Option keys
/ = two keystrokes

Sym.	Character	Key
´	Acute	**O**e
Á	Acute cap A	**SO**y
Í	Acute cap I	**SO**s
Ó	Acute cap O	**SO**h
Ú	Acute cap U	**SO**;
&	Ampersand	&
	Apple	**SO**k
≈	Approximately equal to	**O**x
*	Asterisk	*
{	Brace, open	{
}	Brace, close	}
˘	Breve	**SO**.
•	Bullet	**O**8

Sym.	Character	Key
ˇ	Carib diacritic	**SO**t
Ç	Cedilla, cap	**SO**c
ç	Cedilla, l/c	**O**c
¢	Cent	**O**4
^	Circumflex	**SO**n
^	Circumflex, ASCII	^
Â	Circumflex, cap A	**SO**m
Î	Circumflex, cap I	**SO**d
Ô	Circumflex, cap O	**SO**j
:	Colon	:
,	Comma	,
@	Commercial at	@
©	Copyright	**O**g

Sym.	Character	Key
†	Dagger	**O**t
Ø	Danish cap O	**SO**o
‡	Double dagger	**SO**7
.	Decimal	**SO**9
°	Degree	**SO**8
Δ	Delta	**O**j
¨	Diaeresis/umlaut	**O**u
	Diaeresis, cap I	**SO**f
Œ	Diphthong, cap OE	**SO**q
œ	Diphthong, l/c oe	**O**q
Æ	Diphthong, cap AE	**SO**'
æ	Diphthong, l/c ae	**O**'
÷	Divide	**O**/
$	Dollar	$
.	Dot accent	**O**h
ı	Dotless i	**SO**b
…	Ellipsis	**O**;
—	Em rule	**SO**-
–	En rule	**O**-
=	Equals	=
ß	Eszett	**O**s
!	Exclamation	!
ƒ	Florin	**O**f
⁄	Fraction bar	**SO**1
`	Grave, ASCII	`
Ò	Grave, cap O	**SO**l
>	Greater than	>
≥	Greater than or equal	**O**.
«	Guillemet, open double	**O**\
»	Guillemet, close double	**SO**\
‹	Guillemet, open single	**SO**3
›	Guillemet, close single	**SO**4
#	Hash	**O**3
˝	Hungarian umlaut	**SO**g
-	Hyphen	-
∞	Infinity	**O**5
∫	Integral	**O**b
¤	International currency	**SO**2
<	Less than	<
≤	Less than or equal	**O**,
fi	Ligature, fi	**SO**5
fl	Ligature, fl	**SO**6
¬	Logical not	**O**l
◊	Lozenge	**SO**v
¯	Macron	**SO**,
µ	Mu	**O**m

Sym.	Character	Key
≠	Not equal to	**O**=
˛	Ogonek diacritic	**SO**x
Ω	Omega	**O**z
ª	Ordfeminine	**O**9
º	Ordmasculine	**O**0
¶	Paragraph	**O**7
(	Parentheses, open	(
)	Parentheses, close	)
∂	Partial differential	**O**d
‰	Per thousand	**SO**e
%	Percent	%
.	Period	.
π	Pi	**O**p
+	Plus	+
±	Plus or minus	**SO**=
"	Prime, double	"
'	Prime, single	'
∏	Product	**SO**p
?	Query	?
"	Quote, open double	**O**[
"	Quote, close double	**SO**[
'	Quote, open single	**O**]
'	Quote, close single	**SO**]
„	Quote, double baseline	**SO**w
‚	Quote, single baseline	**SO**0
√	Radical	**O**v
®	Registered	**O**r
°	Ring	**O**k
§	Section	**O**6
;	Semicolon	;
/	Solidus	/
¡	Spanish exclamation	**O**1
¿	Spanish query	**SO**/
[	Square bracket, open	[
]	Square bracket, close	]
£	Sterling	**O**3
Σ	Summation	**O**w
Å	Swedish cap A	**SO**a
å	Swedish l/c a	**O**a
˜	Tilde	**SO**m
~	Tilde, ASCII	~
™	Trademark	**O**2
_	Underscore	_
I	Vertical bar	I
¥	Yen	**O**y

Right Some accented characters are only accessible by two keyboard operations (an o acute is generated by first pressing Option + e together, then o). Some accented caps also have their own key(s).

Accent	Characters	Key
Acute	Á É Í Ó Ú á é í ó ú	**O**e/character
Grave	À È Ì Ò Ù à è ì ò ù	**O**`/character
Diaeresis	Ä Ë Ï Ö Ü Ÿ ä ë ï ö ü ÿ	**O**u/character
Tilde	Ã Ñ Õ ã ñ õ	**O**n/character
Circumflex	Â Ê Î Ô Û â ê î ô û	**O**i/character

does is to draw a font on-screen by using the data contained in the printer outline font file, the result being a smooth screen rendering of the type design. This did away with the need for bitmap screen fonts (although one bitmapped font is still required to be in the System file so that the font name can be accessed and therefore appear in font menus).

The differences between Type 1 and Type 3 fonts were to all but disappear when Adobe, in response to the imminent release of Apple's new font format, unlocked their Type 1 format and made it available to all developers. This means that, by using a suitable font conversion program, any Type 3 font can now be converted to a Type 1 font. It also means that you can create your own Type 1 typeface, with the advantage of rendering it on-screen with ATM. Individual Type 1 outline fonts, and therefore whole alphabets, can be edited using applications such as FreeHand and Illustrator.

TRUETYPE For a variety of reasons, not least to avoid paying licensing fees to Adobe for the use of PostScript, Apple deemed it necessary to develop their own outline font tech-

Rules Page makeup and object-oriented drawing applications offer a wide variety of rule styles at virtually any size. While useful, rule styles supplied with applications do not normally allow a great deal of flexibility, particularly in controlling the relative thickness and spacing of different lines which make up the same rule. It is important, when attributing a size to a rule, not to rely on laser proofs for esthetic decision-making. In most circumstances, a laser printer will print a hairline rule (0.25pt) at 0.5pt, and thus you would be advised to run out an imageset sample before committing to a size.

300dpi	2400dpi	300dpi	2400dpi		
				0.25pt	0.0882mm
				0.3pt	0.1058mm
				0.4pt	0.1411mm
				0.5pt	0.1764mm
				0.6pt	0.2117mm
				0.7pt	0.2469mm
				0.8pt	0.2822mm
				0.9pt	0.3175mm
				1.0pt	0.3528mm
				1.25pt	0.4410mm
				1.5pt	0.5292mm
				1.75pt	0.6174mm
				2.0pt	0.7055mm
				2.25pt	0.7937mm
				2.5pt	0.8819mm
				2.75pt	0.9701mm
				3.0pt	1.0583mm
				3.25pt	1.1465mm
				3.5pt	1.2347mm
				3.75pt	1.3229mm
				4.0pt	1.4111mm

nology, which they named TrueType. There are two main distinctions between TrueType and PostScript. The first is that TrueType fonts are rendered both on screen and by the printer from a single set of outline data, thus using up less space on your hard disk than an equivalent PostScript version of a font. There is no need for a separate bitmapped screen version, not even for font menu purposes – unlike ATM, which requires a screen font in order to display the name of the font. The second is that TrueType fonts can be printed on any printer, whether PostScript or not – although TrueType is not a PDL, so you still need a PostScript printer to output graphics.

The use of a single file for screen and printer rendering, whether in TrueType or PostScript formats, reduces the possibilities of error – for example, the number of characters in a line of text displayed on-screen using a bit-mapped version may not be the same as that output by a printer using the outline version.

Traditionally, each size of metal type was cast from its own matrix, and because of this, changes could be made to the design of a face at different sizes in order to adjust optical aberrations that may occur when a face is enlarged or reduced. The problem with outline fonts on the Mac, whether they are TrueType or PostScript, is that each size of a font is scaled from a single set of data, ignoring the fact that, to achieve optimum results, it may be necessary to

2400dpi	2400dpi	2400dpi	2400dpi
0.25pt	2.0pt		2.5pt
0.3pt	2.25pt		3.0pt
0.4pt	2.5pt		3.5pt
0.5pt	2.75pt		4.0pt
0.6pt	3.0pt		4.5pt
0.7pt	3.25pt		5.0pt
0.8pt	3.5pt		5.5pt
0.9pt	3.75pt		6.0pt
1.0pt	4.0pt		6.5pt
1.25pt	4.25pt		7.0pt
1.5pt	4.5pt		
1.75pt	4.75pt		2.5pt
2.0pt	5.0pt		3.0pt
2.25pt	5.25pt		3.5pt
2.5pt	5.5pt		4.0pt
2.75pt	5.75pt		4.5pt
3.0pt	6.0pt		5.0pt
3.25pt	6.25pt		5.5pt
3.5pt	6.5pt		6.0pt
3.75pt	6.75pt		6.5pt
4.0pt	7.0pt		7.0pt

Fractions Few fonts provide fractions as part of their standard character set. However, variations on fonts called "expert sets" provide, among other things, a range of "true" fractions (a single keystroke composite) plus a facility for setting "piece" fractions (**below**) from numerators (**1**), separators (**2**) and denominators (**3**). The selection of fonts for which expert sets are available is limited.

$1/8$ $1/4$ $1/3$ $3/8$ $1/2$ $5/8$ $2/3$ $3/4$ $7/8$
Expert set true fraction

$1/8$ $1/4$ $1/3$ $3/8$ $1/2$ $5/8$ $2/3$ $3/4$ $7/8$
QuarkXPress fraction with virgule (fraction bar) separator

$1/8$ $1/4$ $1/3$ $3/8$ $1/2$ $5/8$ $2/3$ $3/4$ $7/8$
QuarkXPress fraction with solidus separator

$1/32$ $3/32$ $5/32$ $3/16$ $5/16$ $7/16$
Expert set piece fraction

$1/32$ $3/32$ $5/32$ $3/16$ $5/16$ $7/16$
QuarkXPress fraction with virgule (fraction bar) separator

$1/32$ $3/32$ $5/32$ $3/16$ $5/16$ $7/16$
QuarkXPress fraction with solidus separator

1
2
3

QuarkXPress provides an editable "make fraction" feature, but if you require extensive fraction setting, this can be laborious. Alternatively, create your own fraction font using an application like Fontographer in which you can copy any of your fonts, create fractions any way you like, and assign each one a little-used keystroke (**right**).

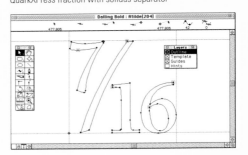

Numerals Traditionally, fonts were often cast with options for numerals both as aligning and non-aligning choices. Standard fonts offer only one choice, but expert character sets provide another.

1 2 3 4 5 6 7 8 9 0
Expert set non-aligning numerals

1 2 3 4 5 6 7 8 9 0
Aligning numerals

Ligatures Standard character sets provide two ligatures – fi and fl. Expert character sets, however, provide more choices. A Quark XTension is available for converting appropriate characters. Ligatures should not be used on small sizes where tracking is tight.

fi ffi fl ffl ff
Expert set roman ligatures

fi ffi fl ffl ff
Expert set italic ligatures

Small caps Expert sets provide specially designed small caps which give a more even weight relative to the capitals of that font, as distinct from the reduced caps of standard fonts.

Aa Bb Cc Dd
Expert set small capitals

Aa Bb Cc Dd
Small capitals generated via Small Caps command

make changes to the design of a font at different sizes. However, this inadequacy of the current font formats may be redressed by the introduction of TrueType Optical Scaling, which offers a choice of design for different sizes of the same font. Adobe's Multiple Master font format, which generates several weights from a single set of font data, does not offer a choice of design for different sizes.

As for deciding between TrueType and PostScript – it doesn't really matter, since neither format is better than the other. You can mix both formats within the same document, but check with your output house first. If you are just starting out, you will have received some TrueType fonts with your Mac, so you may want to stick with TrueType as your preferred format – at least you can then take advantage of any special display designs of a typeface. However, for some time yet, you will find that foundries offer a wider choice of PostScript fonts, although the selection of PostScript as against TrueType will eventually balance out. Whichever you decide upon – TrueType or PostScript – if you can't find the font that you need in one format, don't hesitate to get it in the other (if you adopt a TrueType-only policy, but need a PostScript font, just make sure you have ATM installed on your Mac).

FONT CONFLICTS Every font is given an identity number (ID) so that it can be identified by your Mac. Originally, the Mac only made provision for 255, half of which were reserved for use by Apple, the remainder by other foundries. When they were used up the range of ID numbers was increased, but not by enough to meet the rapidly growing number of fonts being made available. This led to an anomaly where different fonts (occasionally, even from the same foundry) might bear the same ID number. A font selected from a menu could produce a screen rendering of a different font, or the font printed might differ from the one displayed on screen. Fortunately, a number of font utility programs are available that will check the IDs of your fonts and reassign any that clash.

FONT ORGANIZATION With time, you will probably accumulate a large number of fonts, many of which you would like permanently on call. In the scrolling alphabetical font menu, if you use PostScript fonts you will see names such as "Sbl 1 Stone Serif SemibdItal"; worse than that, all the semibold italic weights, for example, of all your active fonts will be grouped together. Type Reunion (Adobe Systems, Inc.), is a small utility which renames fonts in menus with more helpful names – Stone Serif Semibold Italic, in this case – saving space by listing all their weight and style variations in sub-menus.

Even by rationalizing your font collection using a utility such as Type Reunion, you could still end up with an impractically long list in your font menu. It is, however, a simple matter to install and de-install fonts – you simply drag them in and out of the System file as necessary. Be aware, though, that PostScript outline printer fonts must reside in the Fonts folder of the System folder for ATM to work. It is sometimes more practical to create a separate font suitcase for each job that you are working on and use a font utility to open and close the suitcase as and when you need the fonts. You could even have a separate suitcase to hold the fonts you use regularly, regardless of the job you may be working on.

DIGITIZING FONTS With a suitable application it is possible to scan in (or draw) any font – for instance, one from an extinct foundry or an old woodcut face – fine-tune it, assign kerning values and so on, then produce it either as a PostScript Type 1 font with hinting or as a TrueType font. Even existing fonts can be regenerated in this way and without infringing copyright (curiously and, to my mind, outrageously, copyright only exists in the *name* of a font and not in its *design*, enabling you to copy a typeface and reissue it under another name – something that you may notice is prevalent among some foundries). Page 99 lists a selection of font name synonyms. If you need to use a special symbol frequently, you can replace a seldom-used character with it. Make a note of the keystroke you've modified and make sure your output house knows what your intentions are – you'll have to supply the revised font in bitmap and outline form to be sure that your new symbols print correctly.

BUYING FONTS Fonts are generally supplied on CD-ROM. You can view, or browse a vast range of fonts on screen, some suppliers allowing you to copy all the bitmapped screen fonts to your hard disk. Some CD-ROMs are free, and most offer a small selection of fonts (or rather weights of font) as a gift to celebrate your first unlocking. You pay a supplier (probably not the actual typeface manufacturer), usually by charge card, to gain a code to unlock your selected font. This number is only good for this font on your particular CD. Most foundries also offer their entire font libraries unlocked on a single CD-ROM which, although hugely expensive, is probably more economical than buying fonts individually if you need the ultimate in choice.

You may be lucky enough to find a usable shareware font designed by a fellow typographic enthusiast. Remember to do the honorable thing and pay your dues as requested. Bear in mind also that this new font might not have the secondary characters, or even a lower case, provided with commercial products. You will only discover this as you do the last revisions before going to output. Of course, you will still need to buy fonts on floppies if you select a newly released font that wasn't included on your CD-ROM from a font library.

Font names The relative ease with which typefaces can be copied, modified, or created from scratch on a computer has brought about a proliferation of fonts from various suppliers. Curiously, copyright in a font exists not in the *design* of the font, as you might expect, but in its *name*. This has resulted in many foundries producing, as well as their own new designs, the same fonts as other foundries, but with different names. Listed here are some common typefaces and their alternative names.

Numbering fonts If you create your own typeface using a font design application such as FontStudio, it is important that you assign to it a "font family number," since many applications identify fonts by their number rather than by their name. Certain ranges of font family numbers have been reserved by Apple for specific purposes, such as foreign language scripts. If you intend to distribute the font commercially, you must register it with Apple:
Font Registration Program
Developer Technical Support
Apple Computer Inc.
20525 Mariana Avenue
M/S 75-3A
Cupertino, CA 95014

If you intend using the font only on your own system, its font family number must fall between 1024 and 3071, which Apple has reserved for non-commercial fonts. These do not need to be registered.

Antique Olive
Alphavanti
Berry Roman
Incised 901
Oliva
Olive
Olive Antique
Oliver
Olivette
Olivette Antique
Olivia
Provence
Avant Garde
AG
ITC Avant Garde
Avanti
Suave
Baskerville
Basque
Baskerline
Beaumont
BK
Fry's Baskerville
Baskerville Display
Baskerville Old Face
Bembo
Aldine 401
Aldine Roman
Ambo
Bem
Griffo
Latinesque
Bodoni
BO
Bodoni No. 2
Brunswick
Bauer Bodoni
Bodoni B
Euro Bodoni
Headline Bodoni
Caslon Bold
Caslon No. 3
Caslon 74 Bold
Caslon Bold 482, 483
New Caslon
Caslon
Caslon Old Face
Caslon Old Style
Caslon 76
Caslon 128

Caslon 471
Caslon 540
Caslon 2
Caslon 74
Caslon 484, 485
Century Expanded
Cambridge
Expanded
CE
Century
Century Light/II
Century X
Century Oldstyle
Cambridge Oldstyle
Century Schoolbook
Cambridge
Schoolbook
Century Medium
Century Modern
Century Text
Century Textbook
CS
Schoolbook
Cheltenham
Cheltenham Old
Style
Cheltonian
Chesterfield
Gloucester
Kenilworth
Nordhoff
Sorbonne
Winchester
Franklin Gothic
Gothic No. 16
Pittsburgh
Futura
Alphatura
Atlantis
FU
Future
Photura
Sirius
Utica
Garamond
American Garamond
Garamond No. 2
Garamond No. 3
Garamond No. 49
Garamont

GD
Grenada
ITC Garamond
Garamet
Stempel Garamond
Garamond
Garamond Antiqua
Garamond Royale
Euro Garamond
Original Garamond
Gill Sans
Eric
Gillies
Glib
Graphic Gothic
Hammersmith
Humanist 521
Sans Serif 2
Goudy
Goudy Old Style
Grecian
Number 11
Helvetica
Aristocrat
Claro
Corvus
Europa Grotesk
Geneva/2
Hamilton
HE
Helios
Helv
Helvette
Holsatia
Megaron
Newton
Spectra
Swiss 721
CG Triumvirate
Vega
Video Spectra
Palatino
Andover
Compano
Elegante
Malibu
CG Palacio
Paladium
Palatine
Palermo

Parliament
Patina
Pontiac
Zapf Calligraphic
Perpetua
Felicity
Lapidary 333
Percepta
Perpetual
Rockwell
Geometric Slabserif
712
Rockland
Slate
Times Roman
Claritas
Dutch 801
English
English Times
Euro Times
London Roman
Pegasus
Press Roman
Sonoran Serif
Tempora
Tiempo
Timeless
Times New Roman
TmsRmn
TR
Varitimes
Trump Mediaeval
Activa
Ascot
Continental
Knight
Kuenstler 480
Olympus
Renaissance
Saul
Univers
Alphavers
Aries
Boston
Eterna
Galaxy
Kosmos
UN
Versatile
Zurich

JUSTIFICATION SETTINGS

Most page makeup applications offer features for controlling the way space is apportioned between words and characters in justified and unjustified text. In justified text the program will attempt to insert spaces according to an optimum value, but failing that will space out a line according to defined minimum and maximum values. In unjustified text, only the optimum value is used. Usually, the optimum word space represents the normal space width of a font. Using default values in justified text with a short column measure may result in dramatically inconsistent spacing from line to line (see **7**), and the values should be modified (**8, 9**). Among these examples are the default values of QuarkXPress (**1, 5**), and Pagemaker (**4**).

---

1 Unjustified, ranged left
Auto hyphenation off
Word spacing
Minimum: 100%
Optimum: 100%
Maximum: 150%
Character spacing
Minimum:　0%
Optimum:　0%
Maximum:　15%

Lorem ipsum dolor sit amet, consectetuer adipiscing elit, sed diam nonummy nibh euismod tincidunt ut laoreet dolore magna aliquam erat volutpat.

Lorem ipsum dolor sit amet, consectetuer adipiscing elit, sed diam nonummy nibh euismod tincidunt ut laoreet dolore magna aliquam erat

---

2 Unjustified, ranged left
Auto hyphenation off
Word spacing
Minimum: 100%
Optimum: 85%
Maximum: 100%
Character spacing
Minimum:　0%
Optimum: −5%
Maximum:　0%

Lorem ipsum dolor sit amet, consectetuer adipiscing elit, sed diam nonummy nibh euismod tincidunt ut laoreet dolore magna aliquam erat volutpat.

Lorem ipsum dolor sit amet, consectetuer adipiscing elit, sed diam nonummy nibh euismod tincidunt ut laoreet dolore magna aliquam erat volutpat.

---

3 Unjustified, ranged left
Auto hyphenation on
Word spacing
Minimum: 100%
Optimum: 110%
Maximum: 150%
Character spacing
Minimum:　0%
Optimum:　5%
Maximum:　15%

Lorem ipsum dolor sit amet, consectetuer adipiscing elit, sed diam nonummy nibh euismod tincidunt ut laoreet dolore magna aliquam erat volutpat.

Lorem ipsum dolor sit amet, consectetuer adipiscing elit, sed diam nonummy nibh euismod tincidunt ut laoreet dolore magna aliquam erat

---

4 Justified
Auto hyphenation on
Word spacing
Minimum:　50%
Optimum: 100%
Maximum: 200%
Character spacing
Minimum: −5%
Optimum:　0%
Maximum:　25%

Lorem ipsum dolor sit amet, consectetuer adipiscing elit, sed diam nonummy nibh euismod tincidunt ut laoreet dolore magna aliquam erat volutpat.

Lorem ipsum dolor sit amet, consectetuer adipiscing elit, sed diam nonummy nibh euismod tincidunt ut laoreet dolore magna aliquam erat volutpat.

Lorem ipsum dolor sit amet, consectetuer adipiscing elit, sed diam nonummy nibh euismod tincidunt ut laoreet dolore magna aliquam erat volutpat.

Lorem ipsum dolor sit amet, consectetuer adipiscing elit, sed diam nonummy nibh euismod tincidunt ut laoreet dolore magna aliquam erat

5 Justified
Auto hyphenation on
Word spacing
Minimum: 100%
Optimum: 100%
Maximum: 150%
Character spacing
Minimum: 0%
Optimum: 0%
Maximum: 15%

Lorem ipsum dolor sit amet, consectetuer adipiscing elit, sed diam nonummy nibh euismod tincidunt ut laoreet dolore magna aliquam erat volutpat.

Lorem ipsum dolor sit amet, consectetuer adipiscing elit, sed diam nonummy nibh euismod tincidunt ut laoreet dolore magna aliquam erat

6 Justified
Auto hyphenation on
Word spacing
Minimum: 75%
Optimum: 100%
Maximum: 125%
Character spacing
Minimum: 0%
Optimum: 0%
Maximum: 0%

Lorem ipsum dolor sit amet, consectetuer adipiscing elit, sed diam nonummy nibh euismod tincidunt ut laoreet dolore magna aliquam erat volutpat.

Lorem ipsum dolor sit amet, consectetuer adipiscing elit, sed diam nonummy nibh euismod tincidunt ut laoreet dolore magna aliquam erat volutpat.

7 Justified
Auto hyphenation on
Word spacing
Minimum: 90%
Optimum: 90%
Maximum: 100%
Character spacing
Minimum: − 5%
Optimum: − 5%
Maximum: 0%

Lorem ipsum dolor sit amet, consectetuer adipiscing elit, sed diam nonummy nibh euismod tincidunt ut laoreet dolore magna aliquam erat volutpat.

Lorem ipsum dolor sit amet, consectetuer adipiscing elit, sed diam nonummy nibh euismod tincidunt ut laoreet dolore magna aliquam erat volutpat.

8 Justified
Auto hyphenation on
Word spacing
Minimum: 80%
Optimum: 90%
Maximum: 100%
Character spacing
Minimum: −10%
Optimum: − 5%
Maximum: 0%

Lorem ipsum dolor sit amet, consectetuer adipiscing elit, sed diam nonummy nibh euismod tincidunt ut laoreet dolore magna aliquam erat volutpat.

Lorem ipsum dolor sit amet, consectetuer adipiscing elit, sed diam nonummy nibh euismod tincidunt ut laoreet dolore magna aliquam erat volutpat.

9 Justified
Auto hyphenation on
Word spacing
Minimum: 100%
Optimum: 100%
Maximum: 110%
Character spacing
Minimum: − 5%
Optimum: 0%
Maximum: − 5%

TRACKING VALUES

When text is output, by laser printer or imagesetter, it is scaled from a single outline printer font, and the character spacing values remain the same, regardless of output size. It may be necessary to adjust the spacing between characters ("tracking," as distinct from "kerning," which involves pairs of characters) on various sizes of text setting, depending on the characteristics of the typeface. Tracking values are normally expressed in fractions of an em, the definition of which depends on the application you are using (QuarkXPress defines an em as the width of two zeros of the current type size). Values can be expressed as finely as 0.00005 em ($\frac{1}{20,000}$ em). In XPress a value of 1 equals 0.005 em ($\frac{1}{200}$ em).

Lorem ipsum dolor sit amet, adipiscing elit, sed diam nonummy nibh euismod tincidunt ut laoreet dolore magna aliquam erat volutpat. Ut wisi enim ad minim veniam, quis nostrud exerci tation ullamcorper suscipit lobortis nisl ut

7pt Gill Sans, 0 tracking

Lorem ipsum dolor sit amet, consectetuer adipiscing elit, sed diam nonummy nibh euismod tincidunt ut laoreet dolore magna aliquam erat volutpat. Ut wisi enim ad minim veniam, quis nostrud exerci tation

7pt Galliard, 0 tracking

Lorem ipsum dolor sit amet, adipiscing elit, sed diam nonummy nibh euismod tincidunt ut laoreet dolore magna aliquam erat volutpat. Ut wisi enim ad minim veniam, quis nostrud exerci tation ullamcorper suscipit lobortis nisl ut

7pt Gill Sans, 0.005 em tracking

Lorem ipsum dolor sit amet, consectetuer adipiscing elit, sed diam nonummy nibh euismod tincidunt ut laoreet dolore magna aliquam erat volutpat. Ut wisi enim ad minim veniam, quis nostrud exerci tation

7pt Galliard, 0.005 em tracking

Lorem ipsum dolor sit amet, adipiscing elit, sed diam nonummy nibh euismod tincidunt ut laoreet dolore magna aliquam erat volutpat. Ut wisi enim ad minim veniam, quis nostrud exerci tation ullamcorper suscipit lobortis nisl ut

7pt Gill Sans, 0.01 em tracking

Lorem ipsum dolor sit amet, consectetuer adipiscing elit, sed diam nonummy nibh euismod tincidunt ut laoreet dolore magna aliquam erat volutpat. Ut wisi enim ad minim veniam, quis nostrud exerci tation

7pt Galliard, 0.01 em tracking

Lorem ipsum dolor sit amet, adipiscing elit, sed diam nonummy nibh euismod tincidunt ut laoreet dolore magna aliquam erat volutpat. Ut wisi enim ad minim veniam, quis nostrud exerci tation ullamcorper suscipit lobortis nisl ut

7pt Gill Sans, 0.015 em tracking

Lorem ipsum dolor sit amet, consectetuer adipiscing elit, sed diam nonummy nibh euismod tincidunt ut laoreet dolore magna aliquam erat volutpat. Ut wisi enim ad minim veniam, quis nostrud exerci tation

7pt Galliard, 0.015 em tracking

Lorem ipsum dolor sit amet, adipiscing elit, sed diam nonummy nibh euismod tincidunt ut laoreet dolore magna aliquam erat volutpat. Ut wisi enim ad minim veniam, quis nostrud exerci tation ullamcorper suscipit lobortis nisl ut

7pt Gill Sans, 0.02 em tracking

Lorem ipsum dolor sit amet, consectetuer adipiscing elit, sed diam nonummy nibh euismod tincidunt ut laoreet dolore magna aliquam erat volutpat. Ut wisi enim ad minim veniam, quis nostrud exerci tation

7pt Galliard, 0.02 em tracking

Lorem ipsum dolor sit amet, adipiscing elit, sed diam nonummy nibh euismod tincidunt ut laoreet dolore magna aliquam erat volutpat. Ut wisi enim ad minim veniam, quis nostrud exerci tation ullamcorper suscipit lobortis nisl ut

7pt Gill Sans, 0.025 em tracking

Lorem ipsum dolor sit amet, consectetuer adipiscing elit, sed diam nonummy nibh euismod tincidunt ut laoreet dolore magna aliquam erat volutpat. Ut wisi enim ad minim veniam, quis nostrud exerci tation

7pt Galliard, 0.025 em tracking

Lorem ipsum dolor sit amet, adipiscing elit, sed diam nonummy nibh euismod tincidunt ut laoreet dolore

10pt Gill Sans, -0.015 em tracking

Lorem ipsum dolor sit amet, consectetuer adipiscing elit, sed diam nonummy nibh euismod

10pt Galliard, -0.015 em tracking

Lorem ipsum dolor sit amet, adipiscing elit, sed diam nonummy nibh euismod tincidunt ut laoreet dolore

10pt Gill Sans, -0.01 em tracking

Lorem ipsum dolor sit amet, consectetuer adipiscing elit, sed diam nonummy nibh euismod

10pt Galliard, -0.01 em tracking

Lorem ipsum dolor sit amet, adipiscing elit, sed diam nonummy nibh euismod tincidunt ut laoreet dolore

10pt Gill Sans, -0.005 em tracking

Lorem ipsum dolor sit amet, consectetuer adipiscing elit, sed diam nonummy nibh euismod

10pt Galliard, -0.005 em tracking

Lorem ipsum dolor sit amet, adipiscing elit, sed diam nonummy nibh euismod tincidunt ut laoreet dolore

10pt Gill Sans, 0 tracking

Lorem ipsum dolor sit amet, consectetuer adipiscing elit, sed diam nonummy nibh euismod

10pt Galliard, 0 tracking

Lorem ipsum dolor sit amet, adipiscing elit, sed diam nonummy nibh euismod tincidunt ut laoreet dolore

10pt Gill Sans, 0.005 em tracking

Lorem ipsum dolor sit amet, consectetuer adipiscing elit, sed diam nonummy nibh euismod

10pt Galliard, 0.005 em tracking

Lorem ipsum dolor sit amet, adipiscing elit, sed diam nonummy nibh euismod tincidunt ut laoreet dolore

10pt Gill Sans, 0.01 em tracking

Lorem ipsum dolor sit amet, consectetuer adipiscing elit, sed diam nonummy nibh euismod

10pt Galliard, 0.01 em tracking

Lorem ipsum dolor sit amet, adipiscing elit, sed diam nonummy nibh euismod tincidunt ut laoreet dolore

10pt Gill Sans, 0.015 em tracking

Lorem ipsum dolor sit amet, consectetuer adipiscing elit, sed diam nonummy nibh euismod

10pt Galliard, 0.015 em tracking

Lorem ipsum dolor sit amet, adipiscing elit, sed diam nonummy nibh euismod tincidunt ut laoreet dolore

10pt Gill Sans, 0.02 em tracking

Lorem ipsum dolor sit amet, consectetuer adipiscing elit, sed diam nonummy nibh euismod

10pt Galliard, 0.02 em tracking

A distinctive feature of computer-generated typography is that of horizontal scaling, whereby fonts are scaled along their horizontal axes only, as distinct from uniform scaling which is employed for varying the size of type. Although the technique is useful in many situations, it should not normally be used as a substitute for fonts which have a specially designed condensed or expanded version – the exaggerated distortions of horizontally scaled letterforms rarely surpass the esthetic properties of the real thing. However, rules are made to be broken …

thie

Univers 67 Bold Condensed, no horizontal scaling

thie

Univers 65 Bold, 83% horizontal scaling

Lorem ipsum dolor sit amet, consectetuer adipiscing elit, sed diam	Lorem ipsum dolor sit amet, consectetuer adipiscing elit, sed
12pt Gill Sans Light, no horizontal scaling	12pt Garamond, no horizontal scaling
Lorem ipsum dolor sit amet, consectetuer adipiscing elit, sed diam nonummy nibh euismod	Lorem ipsum dolor sit amet, consectetuer adipiscing elit, sed diam nonummy nibh
12pt Gill Sans Light, 80% horizontal scaling	12pt Garamond, 80% horizontal scaling
Lorem ipsum dolor sit amet, consectetuer adipiscing elit, sed diam nonummy nibh euismod tincidunt ut laoreet dolore magna	Lorem ipsum dolor sit amet, consectetuer adipiscing elit, sed diam nonummy nibh euismod tincidunt ut
12pt Gill Sans Light, 60% horizontal scaling	12pt Garamond, 60% horizontal scaling
Lorem ipsum dolor sit amet, consectetuer adipiscing elit, sed	Lorem ipsum dolor sit amet, consec-tetuer adipiscing elit,
12pt Franklin Gothic, no horizontal scaling	12pt Walbaum, no horizontal scaling
Lorem ipsum dolor sit amet, consectetuer adipiscing elit, sed diam nonummy nibh	Lorem ipsum dolor sit amet, consectetuer adipiscing elit, sed diam
12pt Franklin Gothic, 80% horizontal scaling	12pt Walbaum, 80% horizontal scaling
Lorem ipsum dolor sit amet, consectetuer adipiscing elit, sed diam nonummy nibh euismod tincidunt ut	Lorem ipsum dolor sit amet, consectetuer adipiscing elit, sed diam nonummy nibh euismod
12pt Franklin Gothic, 60% horizontal scaling	12pt Walbaum, 60% horizontal scaling

5
THE RIGHT SETUP

Choosing a computer system can be a daunting task. Advice, and plain old sales talk, will be offered at every turn. You have to decide the nature of your need, not just right now but for the next two or three years. And it's not just the hardware – the decision to commit to a particular choice of software will lock you firmly in for a number of years. You will train yourself, or be trained, in the efficient operation of a page makeup application, for example. The time you spend getting up to speed (keep a note – you'll be amazed) is the true investment – not just the initial software price. Bear in mind that you will be following an upgrade path as well – some software developers are kind to their registered users, while others would not be out of place as defendants in a hostage trial. You might consider a complete package – the so-called "designer's dream" – which repre-sents a dealer's idea of your wilder fantasies. You'll get a better deal, and gain some valuable insights if you develop your own shopping list.

This chapter offers a number of suggestions for a basic setup, and goes on to explore the experiences of some working designers. In the case of Thumb Design, we can follow a decade and more of change which parallels the development of the Mac itself.

WHO WILL USE IT? and who will pay for it? For the low-budget, first-time Mac designer, the choices are few and simple. There are Macs from the 1980s lying unused in clos-ets all over the world. Some are discarded style accessories – the seductively advertised 128k Macintosh was in 1984 a must-have item. Most are the battered souvenirs of Mac design pioneers who cannot face up to the ultimate trashcan for their baby Macs. Find one if you can – all but the most ancient models will run some form of useful software and get you on to the first rung of the ladder. Maybe you don't need a Mac of your own at all. There are many freelancers who work in-house on an ad hoc basis; and specialize in one or more software packages.

If you *do* have a budget, then start out by devoting the greater part of it to the Mac itself. The peripheral devices are just that – they will arrive when you can't do without them any more. All the services you need, apart from the crucial backing up, can be bought at your local service bureau or print shop. As for software, check the list in the Software for Starters box, below right, for a starting lineup.

The diagram on this spread shows a typical studio setup

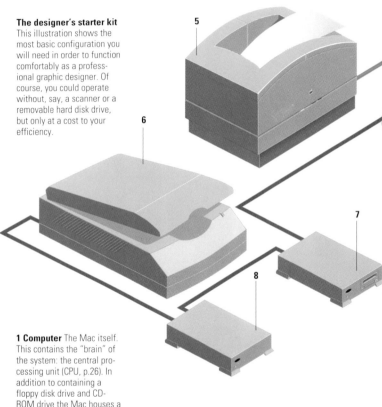

The designer's starter kit
This illustration shows the most basic configuration you will need in order to function comfortably as a profess-ional graphic designer. Of course, you could operate without, say, a scanner or a removable hard disk drive, but only at a cost to your efficiency.

1 Computer The Mac itself. This contains the "brain" of the system: the central pro-cessing unit (CPU, p.26). In addition to containing a floppy disk drive and CD-ROM drive the Mac houses a hard disk for storing your work as data files (p.29). You will need a Mac with plenty of "random access memory" (RAM, p.23). RAM chips (DIMMs) can be added as your need for RAM grows. The speed at which your computer is able to process data is important – complex page layouts may take a long time to "redraw" on screen, which can be very frustrating if you are often switching between pages. In time, you will probably want to add

extra devices, such as a graphics card to drive a more sophisticated monitor, so make sure your Mac has enough slots for future expansion (p.48).
2 Keyboard Much of your interaction with the Mac will be with the mouse, but the keyboard provides an opportunity for shortcuts.
3 Mouse The means by which you "draw" on screen and perform many other

important functions.
4 Monitor The means for displaying your work. There are many permutations of choice, such as screen size, resolution, color, "bit-depth," and more. A 20in screen is desirable for most work. 8-bit color will suffice unless you intend working extensively with scanned images, in which case you may find you need a 24-bit monitor (p.33).

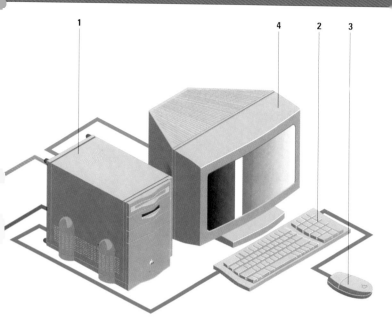

5 Printer Some kind of laser printer is essential for proofing purposes. Most printers have a resolution of 300dpi or 600dpi, compared with up to 2450dpi on a high-resolution imagesetter, so you will still need to sample work on an imagesetter as laser-printed proofs will not display the subtleties you will need to make aesthetic decisions. A PostScript printer is essential even if you only use TrueType fonts (p.94).

6 Scanner You will find a scanner useful even if you intend using conventional methods of origination. You may, for instance, want to scan images for positional guides, or scan rough designs or logos, for recreating on your Mac. Resolution is expressed in dots (actually pixels) per inch, commonly 300dpi across the width of the scan and 600dpi along its length. Software interpolation, which intelligently adds more pixels between those actually scanned optically, can increase this figure to 4800 by 4800dpi, or higher.

7 Backup device Don't think, even for a moment, that nothing will go wrong – it will, so you will need some kind of backup device such as an external hard disk or a DAT drive (p.37).

8 Removable hard disk drive You will find removable media necessary for transporting large files, especially to service bureaus. A removable-media drive is also useful as a backup device and is often used as a primary means of storage.

SOFTWARE FOR STARTERS

Whichever field of graphic design you work in, you will need software which provides you with creative versatility and optimum professional standards. In addition to the system software bundled with the hardware, you will need applications for:

Page makeup for laying out pages (p.54).
Drawing to create artwork which you may wish to incorporate into your layouts (p.59).
Image-editing for creative work with scanned or "painted" images (p.64).
Type manipulation to enable you to design and manipulate fonts and other graphic elements, such as logos, that you may wish to incorporate into a font (p.73).
Fonts – have as many as you need to give you creative freedom (p.84).
System management utilities for enhancing the performance of both your computer and your applications. Among the most important are:
Font management for arranging menus and handling large numbers of fonts (p.97).
ATM (Adobe Type Manager) for making fonts look smooth on screen (p.74).
Backup for protecting your work (p.121).
Disk utilities for managing your disk (p.75).

for one designer. In practice, though, the various items would be closer to hand, and probably be networked to other Macs. This brings several practical as well as economic advantages over "stand alone" Macs. There might be a centralized, high-capacity hard disk which everyone uses – even though each individual Mac has an internal hard disk for day-to-day work. The central disk can store the things everyone needs to use, such as printer fonts, client databases, and job files, so that everyone knows where they are and can examine them when necessary. Similarly, printers and scanners can be shared across the network.

WHICH DESIGN AREA? If your design activities are precisely focused, it may be an easier task for you to define which configuration to go for. For instance, a designer working mainly in information graphics (i.e., the graphic representation of data) will probably be less concerned about a large selection of fonts, document length, text input, and networking, and more about memory and application power. On the other hand, a book designer will be concerned about text input, typographic power, document length, file size, and the practicalities of moving files between several people working on the same job. Illustrators (and designers who aspire to doing their own illustrations) will focus on processing speed, massive storage, and graphics cards for more sophisticated monitors.

DO YOU NEED TRAINING? Mac experience or qualifications are routinely demanded in design job ads. You'll often find ads for computer training companies in the very same newspaper. Prices vary enormously, but the crucial question is how many students are taught at a time? Don't be shy – ask for a trial lesson. With good training you can quickly acquire useful knowledge that the working, untrained Mac designer gains slowly and, quite often, painfully. I speak from long experience. Don't pay money for courses that offer you the absolute Mac basics as a step in your training. If you can point the mouse in the right direction, you can work the Mac system.

HOW FAR DO YOU WANT TO GO? The Mac and its clones, peripherals, software, and communications give you the potential to do the jobs of about two dozen different people. You can do traditional tasks like typesetting as well as jobs that didn't exist before like multimedia authoring and Web page design. The Mac, by its nature, will encourage you along this road and every few weeks the specialist Macintosh magazines will spread out the latest software for your attention. Beware the law of diminishing returns. No-one could possibly be on top of all these skills, even if they could afford the software learning time. If you're exploring the basics of typography, you'll have your hands too full with hyphenation and flush zones to concern yourself with 16-track sound sample manipulation.

CONTROLLING THE COST Buying a complete professional
standard Macintosh setup is a very expensive business, so it
is essential that you shop around. At the start, you'll need
support, preferably readily available at the end of the telephone line. You can often get this type of inclusive deal from
a franchised dealer. Don't sign up for a long-term maintenance contract based on the value of the equipment. In
the unlikely event that your Mac or other hardware turns
out to be a dud, it will show its faults very quickly and you
can get it fixed under the guarantee. The early problems
will more than likely be down to your own inexperience in
connecting everything up. Later on, you can use a call-out
service if hardware repairs become necessary.

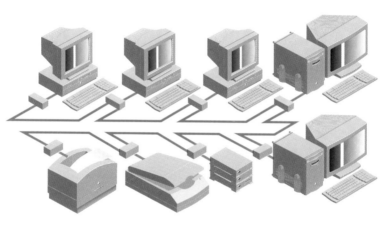

Networking If you work as
part of a group and intend
using several Macs, you will
find many advantages in
linking them together to
create a "network." A
network enables you to
share hardware devices and
programs with other
computers, share your own
files with people using other
computers and *vice versa*,
and automatically update
files on other computers. A
network can be, at its most
basic level, simply two Macs
sharing a single printer or, on
a complex level, hundreds of
computers using different
operating systems and
connected to each other
across continents. As far as
advantages to the average
graphic designer are
concerned, probably the

most relevant is the ability
to minimize capital outlay by
enabling many computers to
share single hardware
devices such as a printer, a
scanner, a fax modem, a
backup device, and a
removable media device.
Automatic updating of files,
using Apple's "publish and
subscribe" feature, can also
be useful to designers on a
network where large jobs
are concerned – for
instance, a corporate
identity where logos and
other graphic devices are
constantly evolving. Central
to a network is the "file
server," a process by which
information is shared
between one device and
another (individual devices
on a network are called
"nodes"). The file server

stores and manages the
information that other users
on the network can access
(at the same time, if
necessary). Apple's own
AppleShare is the entry-
level system. Faster transfer
along similar cables is
achieved with EtherNet.
Networks using LocalTalk
should always be arranged
in a line (a so-called "bus"
network) and not as a
closed circle (although other
networks may be configured
as a "token-ring" whereby a
continuously circulating file
can be accessed by all
nodes). A connector should
be used for each device in a
LocalTalk network.

RIGHT FOR THUMB Thumb Design has an unusual attitude to the use of Macs in design: it lends them to its clients.

The landmark machine in Thumb's history, a 1984 Mac 128k, sits encased in a plexiglass cube in their London office. When Andrew Wakelin, the founding partner, first bought that Mac in 1984, he had already been using an Apple II computer for accounts and spreadsheets. He used the Mac mostly for word processing since he was wary of using computers for design work – although he immediately took to the "friendliness" of the Macintosh. It was not until he started using MacDraw that he realized the potential of the Mac as a design tool. By the end of 1988, Thumb was producing page artwork from an imagesetter via a service bureau. Eventually, they bought their own imagesetter – and found that their typesetting costs fell to 3 percent of the previous year's. Clients were always encouraged to install Macs of their own, and disks with text in progress were couriered around London. Later, with modems and ISDN lines, text files could be exchanged at speed. Although this type of technology saved time, it was error prone because of the vast quantity of documents moving through the system. In two particular areas – company reports and accounts, and holiday brochures – small mistakes of fact or figure could have catastrophic consequences. On the client side many hours were spent collating, issuing and checking material for eventual print. At Thumb's end of the process, valuable design time was spent ensuring that the latest revision they received really was as described.

Above Cover and typical spread from the *Museum of the Moving Image* guide. Pre-dating the introduction of RingMaster, this job would be ideal for the new system as it involves multiple contributors and regular updating. Try to spot the filmic folio numbers. There's even a 21-frame flicker book in the top right corner.

In 1992, Andrew Wakelin first saw an XPress-based newspaper system in action and began to evolve a solution which would relieve his designers of administrative tedium, as well as putting editorial responsibility in the right place – back in the client's office. One hurdle remained. The system had been devised for use in the publishing business in order to integrate a building full of employees. Thumb's own development (which they named RingMaster) extends the system via routing software and ISDN to the client's own Mac. In a typical job, such as the holiday brochure shown here, the basic design is produced and approved. Everyone who has a part to play in the production (i.e., both client and designer) will be assigned a level of privilege to control their contributions. "Checking in" to the system copies the file to the contributor's own hard disk for amendment – "checking out" on completion records the changes and frees the file for the next contributor (or designer). Thumb's designers resented this loss of control in the early days, but

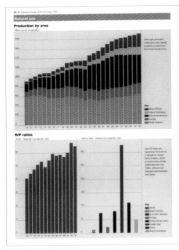

Above A spread from a 40-page report: *BP Statistical Review of World Energy.* Late-breaking information came in from all over the world during its production. The thousands of figures and other data were entered, and subsequently checked, at the client's headquarters on Macs provided to them by Thumb Design.

resistance was short-lived. One big asset was the escape from continual backing up – the server does all that – but more important was the knowledge that the client would do his or her own amendments. The effect of such copy changes is immediately apparent on the client's screen and has a salutary effect on previously wayward contributors. In the first week of RingMaster operation, the designers were charmed to see from the database records that one job had already gone through nine different text revisions without them noticing. Clients print out their own black-and-white proofs, then Thumb supplies a color run-out as a last check. Finally, conventional repro is still used to ensure a high-quality result.

Hardware Some of the IICXs and their like which were the Thumb Design studio workhorses of the early 1990s are now in clients' offices connected by ISDN line to the RingMaster system. The in-house hardware comprises PowerMacs of various specifications and includes powerful servers which handle communications with clients. Failsafe backup is vital, and is achieved with RAID (see Glossary) hard disk systems.

Software RingMaster is based on QuarkXPress; within the system, graphics produced in Illustrator and Photoshop can be amended directly.

Training Thumb has always trained its own designers, but now their Mac evangelism has extended to the client base. Wakelin's stack of testimonials from clients includes the following, ". . . although I had never used an Apple Mac . . . RingMaster was a simple concept and easy to use," and the more lyrical, "thank goodness for your magic machine."

RIGHT FOR STEVE CAPLIN Imagine, if you will, a gothic-style mansion set back from the highway, positioned on a small hill, where things are not what they seem. The occupant, no motel-keeper, is Steve Caplin, electronic manipulator of the human form and part-time saxophonist.

In the 1980s, armed only with a philosophy degree and a Mac Plus, he wrote, designed, edited, and sold a satirical magazine, modestly named *The Truth*. Later, with Photoshop, he produced weekly "black-and-white satirical/political/photo-cartoons" for the British magazine *Punch*. Now his work also appears in newspapers and on billboards, always in color (the brighter the better). Animation for TV is next – and he'd like to bypass the Mac in favor of virtual-reality distorting gloves for that direct, hands-on, approach.

Hardware Image acquisition is a priority. A cheap scanner is used for news shots, combined with Photo CD libraries of the historical and just plain strange. An old, but accelerated, II CX drives the scanner; illustrations are made on a Power Mac. Rough visuals go to clients as JPEG files by e-mail, as do the finished newspaper and magazine jobs; ads and animations are sent by removable cartridge.

Software Photoshop (with a full array of plug-ins and third-party filters) is the mainstay, with AfterEffects for animation. Other packages are always passing through (he's also a reviewer for Mac magazines) but only a few stick.

Training On the job.

Career structure Hard to tell.

Above Distortion of the British Royal family, part of an article on intrusive press coverage.
Below Illustration composed in Photoshop from various elements, including drawing from scratch, a computer catalog shot, and a figure from a commercial Photo CD library. Hands are from the in-house self-portrait collection.

Above Illustration for a magazine article on database software. The wood grain effect was scanned and imported, and everything else was drawn in Photoshop and Dimensions.

6
THE DESIGN PROCESS

PRESENTING ROUGHS/RETAINING CONTROL/STYLE
SHEETS/TEXT INPUT/CORRECTING TEXT/HANDLING
IMAGES/COLOR TRAPPING/ORGANIZING WORK
ON YOUR MAC/BACKING UP/USING SERVICE
BUREAUS

Bringing a Mac into your working life will force you to make some fundamental changes to your way of working. Although it's relatively easy to teach yourself the disciplines of your chosen software package, it's not so simple to develop a pattern of working that will derive the maximum benefit from the Mac. If you've been working "by hand" up to now, producing concepts and comps followed by finished artwork and mechanicals, you'll need to review your methods stage by stage.

PRESENTING ROUGHS The Mac's ability to give a finished look to a design right from the word "go" will bewilder and delight your traditional clients. You can easily take even the most rudimentary design to a finished-looking state by setting headings in an appropriate typeface, indicating text as dummy copy and pictures as dummy scanned images, and then run it out in color. It will look very much like a proof from a printer – that's the fundamental problem. Your enthusiasm for producing more and more alternative designs will be fueled by your client's obvious appreciation at being presented with such a galaxy of choice. This is not

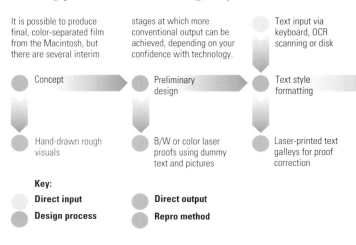

It is possible to produce final, color-separated film from the Macintosh, but there are several interim stages at which more conventional output can be achieved, depending on your confidence with technology.

Text input via keyboard, OCR scanning or disk

Concept

Preliminary design

Text style formatting

Hand-drawn rough visuals

B/W or color laser proofs using dummy text and pictures

Laser-printed text galleys for proof correction

Key:

Direct input

Direct output

Design process

Repro method

necessarily the route by which the best design solution is reached. There is still a strong case for retaining elements of the traditional way. Pencil and marker roughs force the client, (and you, for that matter) into analyzing and discussing fundamental questions of concept and design without the distractions of finish and gloss. Later you can move on to laying the groundwork for a fully resolved Mac-based solution. This progression is vital – ideas take time to evolve and mature on both sides. And there is another issue here. Presented with a shiny color visual complete with logo, apparently working text, and scanned transparencies, your client may suddenly reach across the table and hand it to his printer as finished artwork. It happens, and you'll have plenty of time on the way back to the studio to devise a defense mechanism.

RETAINING CONTROL Software houses would like to sell more software to a wider range of customers. No surprise there. To achieve this aim they need to offer progressively simpler solutions to achieve sophisticated results. You may find "design assistants" and "templates" in your software package; there will certainly be "default" and "auto" settings in abundance. To retain control, send the first two items to the trashcan. Get to know the significance of "auto" in relation to the fine typographic control of your text. The success of a design is often affected by extremely subtle variables, such as the typographic "color" of a piece of text, or the difference between, say, a hairline rule and a half-point rule. The difficulty of assessing these differences on a monitor or a laser proof is amplified when you consider that whereas in an application such as QuarkXPress you can specify a hairline rule, which is 0.25 points wide, it will print on a laser printer only at 0.5 points wide. The ideal answer is to run out your final ideas on an imagesetter (this will show you *exactly* what the end product will look like) before making a final decision.

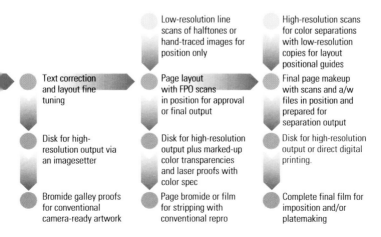

Text correction and layout fine tuning

Disk for high-resolution output via an imagesetter

Bromide galley proofs for conventional camera-ready artwork

Low-resolution line scans of halftones or hand-traced images for position only

Page layout with FPO scans in position for approval or final output

Disk for high-resolution output plus marked-up color transparencies and laser proofs with color spec

Page bromide or film for stripping with conventional repro

High-resolution scans for color separations with low-resolution copies for layout positional guides

Final page makeup with scans and a/w files in position and prepared for separation output

Disk for high-resolution output or direct digital printing.

Complete final film for imposition and/or platemaking

STYLE SHEETS Having decided upon a design solution, you now need to set up a grid and attribute styles to all the elements of your design. This is a particularly acute problem if you are working on a long document full of typographic styles and graphic devices. You can, of course, go through the laborious process of attributing styles to each item individually – by selecting a word, or string of words, and assigning it a typeface, size, weight, leading value, scaling value, tracking value, and so on. Fortunately it is not necessary to go through this time-consuming process. Instead, you can set up a "style sheet" for every possible variation of text style and formatting in a document and assign it a keyboard command of its own. This style will then also be accessible through the regular menu. In this way you can format an entire block of text or an individual word with the desired styles in a single keystroke or menu selection.

Page grids can be set up using the "master page" feature offered by most page-makeup applications. This enables you to set not only page margins, text columns, automatic page numbering, and tints, but also repeating items such as rules and running headings. Some applications allow you to set up a number of master pages – for accommodating design variations such as a different number of text columns – which you can assign to any page.

It is surprising how many designers don't use style sheets and master pages. Setting them up can take a while, but it certainly pays off when a style change becomes desirable or inevitable in a long document. When you create the principal style for running text, for example, ensure that related subsidiary styles are made dependent on the main style. Then, when you change leading or type size parameters, all this type of text will obediently conform to the new style rules without further intervention.

TEXT INPUT Transferring text into the Mac in the first place is not the problem it once was. Some applications are able to preserve the styling choices made in the original writer's word-processing package. You can then reproduce that hierarchy of styles in your page-makeup application. Failing this, you'll see unformatted text appear, either as ASCII or RTF (see page 128 for an explanation).

OCR scanning It is probable that a good deal of the copy you receive will come in the form of typewritten manuscript, or "hard" copy. Sometimes the amount of copy is minimal and it's no big deal just to key it in yourself. Otherwise, hard copy can be input to a Mac and converted to an editable form using one of the many "optical character recognition" (OCR) applications that are available, such as **OmniPage** (Caere Corp.). These applications work in conjunction with most scanners. Even a hand-held scanner (see p.44) can succeed as long as you have only a small amount of text to input. OCR applications don't achieve a

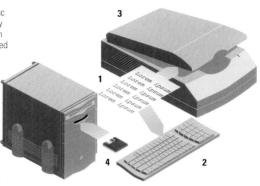

Text may be input to a Mac in several ways. Hard copy which may be type-written or printed (**1**) can be entered by typing it in on the keyboard (**2**) or directly by scanning it (**3**), but you will need OCR software to accomplish this. Alternatively, text may be supplied in disk form (**4**). The Mac can cope with all but the most unusual PC word processing formats. In the last resort, you'll need a conversion utility.

one hundred per cent success rate when scanning in text, but they have reached such a degree of sophistication that, provided the original copy is relatively clean, the error rate is low. Handwriting or underlining on the manuscript are the most likely marks to fool the scanner. OCR applications automatically insert special symbols to flag occurrences where a word may be suspect or where the scanner has not been able to read the copy, making it fairly easy to check scanned text for errors. If you mean to scan Hispanic texts, however, be aware that the default error symbol is often the tilde (~). Change the default to a different exotic character to make life easier.

Text on disk The most efficient way of inputting text to a document is to have it supplied on disk and, if you can persuade your client to co-operate, this is the best way to go. It is quite likely that you will receive copy on a non-Macintosh (probably PC) format disk. All current Macs, and many older models with a small software addition, will accept such a disk without protest. When the job is done, you could even use the disk yourself as it stands, but there is a small glow of satisfaction to be had by erasing it and re-formatting in Mac style. Remarkably, there may even be authors persisting with 5¼in disks – don't despair, you can generally find a bureau to help you out.

Text by modem and e-mail Another fairly efficient means of inputting text is to use a modem, by which you can take in text instantly (called "uploading"). Obviously, this is only possible so long as your client is suitably equipped. This method can also be useful for returning your styled text for editorial correction. If your client does not use a Mac, you will need to go a different route. You can use **Acrobat** (Adobe Systems Inc.) to send sample pages by e-mail (or disk) to your client. The system allows the recipient to check the file even if their machine doesn't have the relevant fonts installed (and even on a PC), but they cannot revise it themselves.

CORRECTING TEXT Taking in corrections to text is more problematical, although if you received text on disk in the first place, you would not expect many corrections to be made. If corrections are light, it is probably best to take them in yourself; if they are heavy, you would be well advised to put the work out to a Mac-based freelancer. If your client is a publisher, text corrections would most likely be supplied on disk. Time and experience with individual clients will let you know whether it's necessary to re-submit corrected text for approval again and again. This additional burden can cause great pain in the designer–client relationship if the latter is in the habit of changing the words every time they see a printout. The Mac, for better or worse, makes it possible to incorporate such changes up to the last minute; some clients will exploit this flexibility to the full, and some beyond that.

HANDLING IMAGES The question is: do you *need* to handle images? Refer to the section on scanners (see p.41) for the pros and cons of being your own repro house. When it comes to "housekeeping" on your hard disk, the largest component to deal with is a great mass of image files. Many print designers do not scan in pictures or output them with reproduction in mind, though the desktop scanner manufacturers would prefer it if they did. Pictures scanned in as a guide for position only (FPO) can be at low resolution, say 72dpi for screen manipulation, and take up little space. If you work with really tight layouts, especially with cutouts and runaround text, you will obviously need to see the images on the page. As for the problem of disk space, a way around this is to keep the picture files on your hard disk only until you are ready to output your job to film – print out sets of laser proofs which include the images, for your reference as well as for the repro house, but delete them from the document prior to final output.

If you intend using scanned images for reproduction, such as line art, halftones or color illustrations, you are obliged to leave them in the document file, and to include

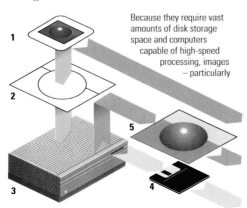

Because they require vast amounts of disk storage space and computers capable of high-speed processing, images – particularly color (**1**) – may be scanned at low resolution (**2**) and used for positional purposes only. Output from the Mac (**3**) is provided in the form of a disk (**4**) for imagesetting to film or bromide, with a laser proof (**5**) showing exact positions and crops. Increasingly, high-resolution scans are made first, a low-resolution copy being returned to the designer for positioning. The low-resolution version is substituted by the high during output (see p.133).

the original picture files in the folder with the document file so that it can be output correctly by the imagesetter. For instance, if you are using a tone picture scanned as a TIFF file and a piece of artwork created in a drawing application and exported as an EPS file, both the TIFF file and the EPS file must accompany your document file to the bureau. Don't forget, by the way, that any font you may have used in making your EPS file must also be included.

COLOR TRAPPING It is important to remember that when you are creating colored artwork, specifying tints or using colored typography, you may need to specify "trapping" values for each color. Trapping a color means that, to allow for imprecisions in printing, you increase the area of one color so that it overlaps an adjacent color. This overlapping need only be infinitesimal – just enough to prevent white hairline gaps from appearing between colors. Fortunately, many applications support automatic trapping values, so you may not need to do much. Otherwise, you may need to add trapping values to tints manually. This can usually be done by adding a keyline with a thickness of about 0.25 point around a given tint area, making it the same color as the tint it surrounds and specifying that it should overprint the adjacent colors. Your output house is the backstop – if they're good they will fix trapping problems, and may not even tell you.

ORGANIZING WORK ON YOUR MAC There are no hard and fast rules as to how you should organize your work – everyone has their own way of doing it, depending as much on their hardware configuration as on the type of work that they do. Viewing your files "by icon" on the screen looks decorative at first, but dry lists of names make more practical sense when you have hundreds of files to organize.

Naming files It is easy to forget what is in a particular file, so it is important that you adopt a logical, explicit method of naming them. This is particularly important if you share files on a network. Giving a file a number only is of no help to anyone; even if you work alone, it is likely to lead to confusion. It is better to assign a code of, say, three letters to each job and then prefix every file belonging to that job with its code, followed by as explicit a description of the contents of a file as space permits (file names can be up to 31 characters long). If you make your prefix a number, remember to precede it with at least one zero – the Mac will otherwise relentlessly group your 1s with your 11s. Sometimes a date can be helpful as part of a file name, although you will find the dates of both the creation and last modification of a file via the "Get Info" window in the "File" menu.

If you are experimenting on different versions of the same design and are using the "Save As..." command to preserve previous versions, simply keep the same name as

Organizing work A clear and methodical approach to naming and organizing files and folders is essential – the speed at which you create new files that represent variations on a design makes it very easy to lose track of what's where. There are endless permutations of how work can be organized, and this example serves only as a guide. Try to categorize your work as much as possible so that you can create new folders in which to put items – it is much better to have folders within folders ("nested") than hundreds of files loose in a single folder for one job.

1 The hard disk window should contain as few items as possible, which, at this level, are easy to categorize.
2 Give each of your clients a separate folder.
3 Give each job for a client its own folder.
4 Break each constituent of a job into folders – including one for correspondence relating to that job.
5 If much text is involved, give each stage of proofs, prior to layout, a folder.
6 The files at this level should be those you are actually working on – put old ones into a folder or trash them. Give scans and a/w files other folders – don't mix them with layout files.
7 In naming images and a/w, be as explicit as possible and include the file type as part of the name (TIFF, EPS, etc.).

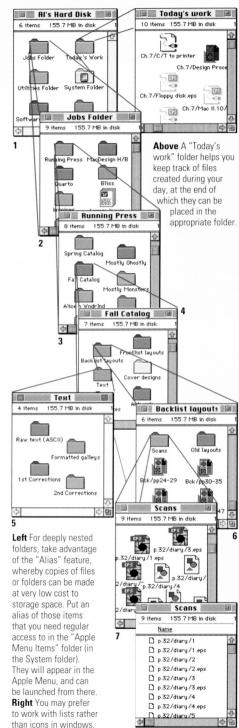

Above A "Today's work" folder helps you keep track of files created during your day, at the end of which they can be placed in the appropriate folder.

Left For deeply nested folders, take advantage of the "Alias" feature, whereby copies of files or folders can be made at very low cost to storage space. Put an alias of those items that you need regular access to in the "Apple Menu Items" folder (in the System folder). They will appear in the Apple Menu, and can be launched from there.
Right You may prefer to work with lists rather than icons in windows.

the original file, but number each new one consecutively. When you've finished experimenting and made a decision, be sure to delete all the other files to avoid confusion.

Organizing folders The simplest way of keeping track of work is to create as many folders as necessary, giving each one a name that identifies the contents. If, for example, you create one folder per job and simply dump every file relating to that job loose in that folder, you may very soon lose track of where you are or, rather, where the files you want are. If you are generating a lot of scanned images, it makes sense to keep them in a folder with the document they relate to. If the scans relate to several different documents, you may decide to keep all of them together in their own folder. The important thing is to create a system that allows you to locate any file at any time with ease.

One useful way of organizing your day-to-day work is to create a folder called "Today's Work" and position it on the desktop or put an Alias of it in the Apple menu. Every document you create during the day and every file relating to those documents gets put in this folder. At the end of the day, you decide how and where you want to keep those files and position them in appropriate folders relating to their job. If you are still working on a document, you put a copy of the document file back in the "Today's Work" folder and work on that version of the document, which replaces the previous version at the end of the day. This gives you an instant view of your progress and of any current files.

If you share your Mac with other users, or if you are networked, it is a good idea to create folders with the names of the people sharing the computer and put everything relating to each person in their respective folder.

BACKING UP The most important aspect of using a Mac is backing up your work frequently *and* systematically. Sooner or later you will be faced with a disaster – either your hard disk will irretrievably crash, your most important file will become irreversibly corrupted or you will join the ranks of those whose computer equipment, including all their disks, has "disappeared". With a backup, you can start over.

My backup policy may seem extreme, but I've lost too many important files and crashed too many disks for it to be otherwise. At the end of each day, I copy each job file in my "Today's Work" folder onto its respective storage disk. I copy the same files into their respective folders on my hard disk, replacing previous versions of the files. I also make duplicate copies of the day's work into another folder on a separate part of my hard disk. To round off the day, I back up the files onto hard disks, using backup software which copies only those files that have changed since the last backup. This routine takes about ten minutes, and it's worth every one of those minutes for the peace of mind it gives.

I keep four sets of backup disks in the form of removable

Backing up Much of the data stored on your hard disk will represent many hours of work and may be irreplaceable. The most reliable disks may fail, and the assumption must always be that one day they will. Even if your disk fails but is repaired and your files are found to be intact, the disk may be out of service for some time. Thus it is of paramount importance that you back up everything that you do. There are many types of backup devices, from floppy disks to very high capacity DAT drives and hard disks, and there are many utility programs to make backup easier. The first backup you make is described as a "baseline" or "global" backup. Thereafter, using a suitable backup utility, you only back up work you have created or modified since your work was last backed up; this is known as an "incremental" backup. Backing up onto floppies is impractical (40Mb uses around 60 disks). Although of limited capacity, removable hard disks give you greater flexibility over what you back up – by creating a folder or two for each backup disk that you have, you only need regularly back up the folders that you consistently work on. Use at least two sets of backup disks (preferably three, one of which you keep in another location) and rotate them alternately at each backup. Some backup utilities replace files that require updating (a good file may be replaced by a corrupt one), so you may like to keep an additional set of work in progress on floppy disks – before putting the current day's work away in the appropriate place in your "Jobs" folder, copy it to a floppy disk, putting it in a folder which you create afresh each day. If a file corrupts, you can return to the last usable version (**5**).

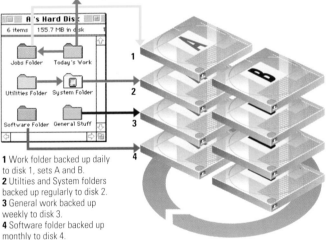

1 Work folder backed up daily to disk 1, sets A and B.
2 Utilties and System folders backed up regularly to disk 2.
3 General work backed up weekly to disk 3.
4 Software folder backed up monthly to disk 4.

media (plus further sets for each large job I am currently involved in), one for each of the folders at the root level of my hard disk – a "Jobs" folder for current work, a "General" folder for my own stuff, a "Software" folder for all my software except utility software, which goes on the fourth backup set, the System folder. Each of these backup disks has its own, second, backup disk (I've been advised not to trust removable media, although I've not yet had a problem with any of my removable hard disks). I keep one set of the disks in a fireproof safe. Although I back up my jobs on a daily basis, I only back up my software and system folders every month since they do not change much during that time.

If your workplace is not totally secure, take a backup set home with you. If your workplace *is* your home, resort to subterfuge. Where is the safest place to hide your most precious possessions? Shift them over to make room for your disks, which are just as precious as your other treasures.

USING SERVICE BUREAUS Unless you intend owning your own imagesetter, you will need to have your files run out by a service bureau (see p.124 for a description of the image-setter's function). Most bureaus can take your files on virtually any kind of media. Your own choice of disk depends on the file size of the documents themselves and of any other accompanying files, such as picture files. (If your documents contain images, such as EPS files of Mac-generated art or TIFF files of scanned pictures, that you want included in the document you must send them to the bureau as well).

Depending on the application that you used to create your documents, you may also need to send some data files with the document. You must always include a proof of the job from your own printer. The bureau is also entitled to know which fonts you have used; it is not legally entitled to ask you for copies of those fonts. Without using the identical fonts, however, they can give no guarantee that the work will come out the way you expect. Common practice and logic prevail – you lend them copies of the fonts to do the job, and they discard them afterwards. Honor is largely satisfied and life goes on.

Many bureaus are also repro houses – the traditional distinction is becoming less clear – and the additional services they offer are outlined in chapter 7.

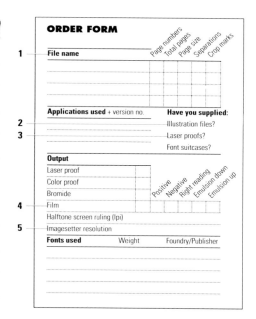

ORDER FORM

	File name	Page numbers	Total pages	Page size	Separations	Crop marks
1						

Applications used + version no.	Have you supplied:
2	Illustration files?
3	Laser proofs?
	Font suitcases?

Output		Positive	Negative	Right reading	Emulsion down	Emulsion up
Laser proof						
Color proof						
Bromide						
4 Film						
Halftone screen ruling (lpi)						
5 Imagesetter resolution						

Fonts used	Weight	Foundry/Publisher

Left Provide your bureau with every detail about a job, or it may be output according to the information specified in the Page Setup dialog box the last time you printed the document. Supply the name of each file to be output (**1**) exactly as it appears on the file (if there are a lot, supply a print-out of the window of the disk you send the bureau). You must supply the illustration files used on the job if you want them to be part of the output (**2**) and also supply laser proofs so that they can check the output (**3**). If you are outputing to film, find out from your printer how it should be presented (**4**). Check with the bureau whether a very high resolution is necessary for your job as this could slow down output (**5**).

7
PREPRESS PRODUCTION
IMAGESETTERS/SERVICE BUREAUS/FILE
FORMATS/TINTS/GATEWAY SYSTEMS/SCANNING
RESOLUTION/PRINTING AND PROOFING

Prepress is a term which will eventually take its place in the historical section of the design dictionary – somewhere between paste-up and projection paper. Current "digital print" systems attempt to remove a whole layer of skills from the process of getting design into print, foreshadowing fundamental changes to the way the whole industry works.

The first of the traditional crafts to fall prey to computers was that of typesetting. Dedicated computer typesetting machines have been used by typesetters since 1963, but because of the sophisticated requirements of designers, typographers, and typesetters alike, and the relative infancy of computer technology, these machines had to be operated by highly trained and skilled craftspeople – the same people, more often than not, who had previously been casting type in metal. The introduction of the desktop computer and, perhaps more important, the laser printer and PostScript, brought a quasi-professional level of print output to a far larger user base. The parallels with prepress are easy to see, though the time scale will no doubt be longer.

Graphic designers who use Macs have largely left the function of high-quality color separation to technicians using high-end scanning machines. But the former huge gaps in hardware and software capability, output quality, capital expenditure, and skill requirements between desktop color scanners and prepress scanners are rapidly being filled. The middle way in all of this is illustrated on page 131, where craft skills are allied with powerful proprietary computer systems.

IMAGESETTERS High quality output, whether it is bromide paper for camera-ready art or fully process-separated final film for imposition and platemaking, is produced on a machine called an imagesetter. Imagesetters work by means of a digitally controlled laser beam passing over a photosensitive material such as bromide paper or film, thus exposing an image onto the material. Imagesetters are either flatbed – in which case the laser beam is projected via a series of mirrors and prisms onto the photosensitive material, which moves forward, one scan line at a time – or drum, whereby the film or paper, wrapped around a glass drum, is exposed by a rotating laser exposure assembly while the photosensitive material remains stationary. Drum imagesetters are thought to create fewer registration problems than flatbed types, because the material remains stationary and because the laser light source remains at a constant distance from the sensitive surface. The process of a light beam raking the surface of the material is known as "rasterizing."

Presented with your job on disk, the imagesetter uses a translator called a "RIP" (raster image processor) to describe the image. This process, naturally called "ripping," takes all the elements of the design, whatever the application, and renders them into a set of commands that the controller of the exposing device can understand. Desktop laser printers have RIPs, albeit less powerful ones, built into them. As a designer, you are only likely to hear about the imagesetter RIP and its capabilities when some complex part of your design trips it up and produces an error.

Imagesetter resolution Although both are laser printers, an imagesetter differs greatly from a desktop laser printer in that it is more precise, it produces a photographic rather than toner-based image, and it possesses greater RAM. Most important, it is able to reproduce an image at much higher resolutions than a laser printer, therefore giving extremely high quality output. Normally, typographic matter will be output from an imagesetter at 1270dpi or 1800dpi (a typical laser printer outputs at 300dpi); the benefits of any higher resolution would be indiscernible on the printed page. Tint and halftone screens, however, will normally be output at resolutions of 2540dpi for screens of 150 lines per inch, or more if the halftone screen is finer. This is because imagesetter resolution only determines the quality of solid black (imagesetters cannot print grays). Imagesetter resolution controls the quality of line and halftone dot – the higher the resolution, the better the quality of halftone dot and thus the opportunity to reproduce the original image with greater fidelity. However, final image quality is determined by the relationship between the input resolution, the imagesetter resolution and the halftone screen ruling prescribed.

Problems with high resolution concern the time it takes to output such files. The higher the resolution, the longer it takes to run out. Documents of smaller sizes, but containing multiple images, may also tie up the imagesetter for hours. Remember that, though this kind of output is normally charged for by the page or linear inch, your demand for very high resolution, and therefore much slower output, may backfire with demands for overtime penalty payments.

Output resolution and fonts Although printer fonts are outlines, printing devices recreate them by generating bitmaps of their shapes. Toner-based laser printers with a resolution of 300 or 600dpi are not able to match the quality of the light-generated shapes from imagesetters, which output at resolutions of up to 2540dpi.

Output resolution and halftones The quality of image output is determined by a combination of input resolution, bit-depth, and output resolution. To achieve 256 grays (the optimum for quality reproduction), an 8-bit scanner must be used to scan originals (24-bit for color – 8 bits each for red, green, and blue). For halftone output, input resolution should allow at least one pixel to be mapped to each halftone dot, but double the halftone screen is normal. Thus a halftone to be printed at 150 lpi should be scanned at 300dpi. Output resolution determines the quality of the dot itself and the number of grays each halftone dot is capable of reproducing. The number of grays is calculated by dividing the output resolution by the desired halftone screen ruling. This figure provides the axes for a matrix, the total number of pixels within that matrix being the number of possible gray levels. Thus a halftone to be printed with a screen of 75 lpi and output at 300dpi will achieve 16 grays (4 x 4 pixels).

Output resolution and lines A drawn, curved, object-oriented line ("path") is made up of straight segments. The number of segments in a path is described as the "flatness" value. Since PostScript limits the number of segments in any one path, and a high-resolution printer requires more segments to print a smooth curve than a laser printer, complex illustrations with low flatness values may cause printing problems.

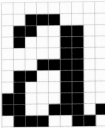

6pt character, 300dpi

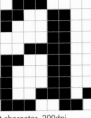

6pt character, 1270dpi

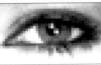

Enlarged detail of 8-bit scan at 300dpi

The same detail printed with a 150 lpi halftone screen

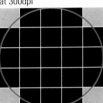

Low-resolution halftone dot (5 x 5 pixels = 25 grays)

High-resolution halftone dot (16 x 16 pixels = 256 grays)

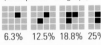

6.3% 12.5% 18.8% 25%   31.3% 37.5% 43.8% 50%

56.3% 62.5% 68.8% 75%   81.3% 87.5% 93.8% 100%

Halftone dot matrix of 4 x 4 pixels, producing 16 grays

[300dpi printer resolution ÷ 60 lpi halftone screen]^2 = 25 grays

[300dpi ÷ 100 lpi]^2 = 9 grays

[2540dpi ÷ 150 lpi]^2 = 286 grays (256 is the PostScript maximum)

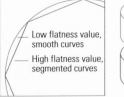

Low flatness value, smooth curves

High flatness value, segmented curves

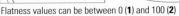

Flatness values can be between 0 (**1**) and 100 (**2**)

SERVICE BUREAUS If you will be using a bureau to output your work, there are a number of factors of which you should be aware. The first consideration is preparing your work for output on an imagesetter, which depends as much upon the application(s) you use as on what you need in terms of output. If you are making four-color film, professional page make-up applications, such as QuarkXPress and PageMaker, are able to pre-separate colors which you have specified on the page, or which exist in imported images placed within the job. Anomalies can occur, however, when the imagesetter discovers, for example, that names of colors have been changed or that colors are not expressed in standard form. These may reproduce incorrectly, crash the machine or even disappear from the film. Your service bureau personnel will no doubt be delighted to share with you a large store of such anecdotes. Curiously, none of them reflects well on the clients involved, but listening attentively can help to avoid similar problems and expense.

When PANTONE colors are specified in an illustration, say, in one application and then exported as a file to be used in another application, it may be necessary to recreate the same PANTONE color in the application finally used to produce the document although, these days, colors are created automatically.

However, the majority of problems encountered when outputting documents through an imagesetter in a bureau concern fonts and typography. Type foundries are constantly tweaking their products, just as software houses do, and a font may go through as many as five upgrades, during which it will have been reconstructed or the data within it changed. The problems occur when the latest version bears no identifying features from the previous versions (although some fonts bear version numbers in the "Get Info" dialog boxes of their printer fonts), and even though the bureau may possess the same font manufactured by the same foundry, it may be a different version – which may cause the text to reflow or run out at a different length.

Sometimes a font used in a document is replaced by an altogether different font when the job is run through the imagesetter. This happens because of a difference in system software configurations between your computer and the bureau's. They may, for instance, have used a utility program to reassign font identification (ID) numbers to avoid conflicts, whereas you did not – the result being that although both your computer and theirs identified fonts with the same ID numbers, they were different fonts.

Fortunately, there is an easy way of avoiding these problems simply by providing a suitcase containing all the screen fonts you used for a job, and, if you use PostScript fonts, copies of the outline printer fonts. *Un*fortunately, however, doing this means that you will almost certainly be

File formats When you save your work for storage on disk, the data that makes up the file is stored within a predetermined structure, or "file format." Many applications offer a choice of format, your decision depending on the intended use of the file. Sometimes the format is unique to an application and, although you may be able to export these files to other applications, it is unlikely that they will be editable outside the original application. The tables on this page show a range of generic file formats which can be imported and exported by most graphics applications. Broadly speaking, there are two kinds of file format, those that handle mainly text-based data (**above**), and those that are used for graphic images (**below**). The type of graphic image – whether it is object-oriented or bitmapped (see p.60) – often determines the file format that can be used, although some formats can contain either.

File formats for storing text and spreadsheet data

ASCII	256 standard character codes used by all computers. Often called "text-only" files. Text loses most formatting instructions.
DBS	Ashton Tate's proprietary database file format.
DCA/RFT	IBM text format for word processing.
DIF	Format for exchanging data supported by some spreadsheet and database applications.
RTF	Microsoft's format for exchanging text documents while retaining text formatting information.
SYLK	Format for spreadsheets, used by Microsoft.
TEXT	Apple's extended version of ASCII for the Mac.
WKS	Lotus's proprietary spreadsheet format.

File formats for storing images

DXF	AutoCAD's proprietary format for storing CAD files.
EPS, EPSF	Encapsulated PostScript Format. Primarily for storing object-oriented graphics files, but can also store bitmapped images (resulting files may be very large). EPS files are in either *ASCII* or *binary* subformats: **ASCII** Text-based description of an image, which contains two versions of it – one for printing on a PostScript device, regardless of resolution, and the other a low-resolution bitmap version for display. Often cannot be edited – even by the application that created it. **Binary** Similar to ASCII EPS format, but uses numbers rather than text to store data. Good format for converting TIFF files for color separation. Smaller file sizes than ASCII EPS format.
GIF	Graphic Interchange Format. CompuServe's format for sending compressed images over telephone lines. Also Transparent GIF for Internet images.
JPEG	Image and video format developed by committee (Joint Photographic Experts Group) to standardize image transfer. Offers range of compression ratios. Don't re-compress compressed JPEG files – the image will suffer irreversibly.
Paint, PNTG	Original and largely obsolete MacPaint low-resolution format.
PostScript	Uneditable text description of a file for printing with any PostScript device. Unlike some formats, PostScript files do not require the originating application.
PICS	Format for storing sequences of PICT and PICT2 images for animations in multimedia and 3D applications. File sizes can be very large.
PICT	Can store combination of bitmapped and object-oriented images. Limited to eight colors. Images copied to the Clipboard may be converted to PICT format.
PICT2	Development of PICT format for storing 8-bit and 24-bit color images. May not maintain resolution of an image when scaled. Not generally used for images requiring color separation, so more suitable where final output is either a screen display or multimedia presentation.
RIB	Pixar's proprietary format for storing rendering and modeling files.
RIFF	Raster image file format. Letraset's own format as an alternative to TIFF.
Scitex CT	Developed by Scitex to link Mac applications, such as XPress and Photoshop, to their prepress system.
Targa/TGA	Used for transferring image files between Mac and PC environments
TIFF	Tagged image file format. The standard format for scanned bitmapped images and used extensively for color separations. There are several versions of the TIFF format, not all of them compatible with every TIFF-supported application. There are four subformats of TIFF 5.0: *TIFF B* for black and white; *TIFF G* for grayscale; *TIFF P* for images which store their color palette with the file; *TIFF R* for 32-bit color. May not maintain resolution when scaled.

breaching the terms of the license agreement between you and the font license holder, but to get the job done by your deadline, and in the most problem-free and cost-effective way, you may have little choice. If it makes you sleep better at night, bear in mind that the likelihood is that your bureau, particularly if it is a large one, in all probability possesses the identical font already – and in any case will entirely delete the folder created for your job, containing your fonts, from their hard disk after a few days.

Another way round the font problem may be to supply your document as a PostScript file (usually an option in the Print dialog box), in which case you elect to "print" your document to disk as a PostScript file rather than to your laser printer. The problem here can be that the resulting file size may be too large to transport if it contains many images or graphic devices (page 68 of this book, for example, occupies 4.4Mb of disk space when saved as a PostScript file).

Some page makeup applications automatically produce a separate "report" file when you assemble the job for output. Details such as variations from the default hyphenation and justification settings will be recorded in order that the bureau version of the application uses your data rather than their own. If you change such things as kerning values, for instance, this information may be stored in the application's data file rather than in the document itself.

If you import image files, such as EPS files, into page makeup documents, you will need to include them with your document when you send it to a bureau, since the information the imagesetter needs in order to output it is contained within the image file rather than in the document into which you imported it. If the imported file contains type, you must also include that font with your disk.

Sometimes, the variable density of printing film produced by bureaus can be a problem, particularly from small bureaus that cater more for the desktop publishing user. Before using a bureau for the first time, establish that they have experience in preparing film for quality printing. This is more likely if, for instance, they make regular use of a densitometer in calibrating their equipment.

Although other problems may occur, these are more or less unique to particular jobs, and your bureau will be able to advise you on what to do to solve them or avoid them altogether. It will save you untold grief if you explain to them the nature of a job *before* you send it, so that they can give you an idea of the best way of presenting it.

There are several ways of getting your files to the bureau. Larger bureaus can accept virtually any form of media. Floppy disks are the most popular way to present small documents, but larger files require the greater capacity of removable cartridges. If you don't have cartridges,

Gradated tints Many applications offer features for specifying gradated tints which can be made up from any mix and any percentage of process colors. However, you should be aware of the limitations imposed by the combination of halftone screen ruling and output resolution. This determines the maximum number of shades of a single color that it is possible to reproduce and thus the rate at which one shade changes into the next (called "stepping" or "banding") in a gradated tint. To achieve a visually smooth blend of shades, there must be as many steps as possible up to the maximum of 256 levels allowed by PostScript. Stepping may become more visible when the percentage values of a single color are very close (e.g. 30%–40%) over a large area, or when the same percentage values are specified at the beginning and end of a gradation comprising two or more colors. To achieve a smooth blend in gradated tints of more than one color, each color should have a different percentage value at one end of the gradation.

Calculating steps To calculate the number of steps in a gradated tint, subtract the end percentage value of the tint from its start value (*note: the start and end values are based on 0–1, where 100% = 1, thus 60% = 0.6 and 30% = 0.3*) and then multiply that figure by the number of grays.

For example, if you specify a gradation starting with 60% and ending with 30%, you subtract 0.3 from 0.6. Multiply the answer, 0.3, by the number of gray levels, say 256, giving 76.8 steps which, over an area 1in. wide would produce a smooth blend with slightly more than one step every point (1in = 72pts).

100% Black	0%

60% Black	30% Black

50% Black	40% Black

50% Black	40% Black

60% Cyan + 60% Magenta	30% Cyan + 30% Magenta

40% Cyan + 60% Magenta	30% Cyan + 20% Magenta

50% Magenta	50% Cyan

30% Cyan + 50% Magenta + 40% Yellow	30% Cyan + 30% Black

20% Magenta + 50% Yellow	40% Cyan + 30% Yellow + 30% Black

100% Magenta + 100% Yellow	100% Cyan + 100% Magenta

file-compression utilities such as DiskDoubler and Stuffit can be used to compress files or even split up single files so that they fit onto floppies. If you have *really* large files, most bureaus will be quite happy to accommodate your external disk drive unit. If you regularly send out considerable numbers of large files, your bureau will soon suggest an electronic hook-up of some kind.

GATEWAY SYSTEMS The diagram below shows a "gateway link" system in which your completed document is passed to the repro house which, having previously scanned your color originals, electronically strip the images into your page. The gateway itself is usually a hardware/software combination which converts your Mac PostScript document into a form that enables the high-resolution repro-scanned images to be placed into your page layout – just as the RIP does in an imagesetter.

SCANNING RESOLUTION When you use a gateway link, an original is scanned at a suitably high resolution, and a low resolution (72dpi) file can be generated automatically; this is returned to you so that you can show the exact crop and final position. The low-resolution scan is replaced by the high-resolution version prior to final output. Using this method still means that you need to know the final size that you want the image to print, since the scan resolution is set at the time of scanning, and any subsequent enlargement may reveal pixelation (though 10 percent enlargement may just about be acceptable). Repro scanner input resolution is

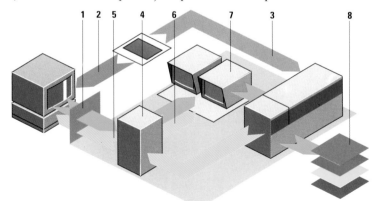

From Mac to film You can combine the power of high-end color scanning equipment and the skills of their operators with the work you do on your Mac by using a "gateway" link (**1**), a hardware/software setup designed to take advantage of appropriate technology at every stage of production, from Mac to final film. You use the originals as low-resolution scans for design purposes (**2**). When you have established image sizes, you send the originals for high-resolution scanning (**3**). Output is stored on high-capacity disks or tape (**4**). A low-resolution version is sent to you for positioning on your layouts (**5**). When you send your layout for output as film, the gateway setup automatically replaces the low-resolution scans with the stored high-resolution versions and converts your layout files to the maker's format of the high-end system (**6**). Cleaning up, if required, is made on an electronic page composition (EPC) system (**7**) before output to final film (**8**).

Input resolution and halftone image quality The quality of a printed color halftone depends on the relationship between scanner resolution, imagesetter resolution, and halftone screen ruling. Theoretically, the higher the input resolution, the better the printed result. However, since normal high-quality color printing rarely uses screen rulings beyond 150lpi, there is little to be gained from scanning images at resolutions of more than double the screen ruling – which is regarded as the rule of thumb for optimum quality. Another factor is the size of file generated – an image scanned at 300dpi will be more than twice the size of one at 200dpi, and yet the difference in printed quality between the two will be very subtle. These illustrations compare different scanning resolutions with halftone screen rulings. They were imageset at 2450dpi.

300dpi scan; 150 lpi screen

300dpi scan; 128 lpi screen

200dpi scan; 150 lpi screen

200dpi scan; 128 lpi screen

150dpi scan; 150 lpi screen

100dpi scan; 128 lpi screen

typically 300dpi; while this may seem very low compared to imagesetter output, remember that the typical halftone screen ruling for color images is only 150 lines per inch, and higher input resolution is really only required for very fine halftone screen rulings, such as those over 200lpi. Confusion may arise when repro scanner operators refer to scanned images as "contones" (continuous tone images) – a relic of the time when mechanical color separations produced continuous tone negatives prior to halftone screening – in fact, the images will already have been digitized.

Some basic principles need to be observed in preparing transparencies and artwork for scanning. First, some limitations. Even with the most sophisticated equipment, the scanner operator cannot enlarge an image to enormous proportions and still satisfy your demand for high quality. Be realistic and stay below 800 percent. If you deal with smaller format transparencies, try to group your pictures according to a select number of enlargement ratios. The operator will take all the 325 percent subjects, for example, tape them to the drum side by side and make one scan. You will keep costs down with a little forward planning. If you've ever seen a glass-mounted transparency smashed in the mail, you'll also agree that un-mounted, untouched-by-human-hand transparencies must be the best for the scanner. On the positive side, the scanner operator can use his

Controlling image quality

When you make modifications to an image, such as rotating and scaling, using an appropriate image-manipulation application, pixel values are constantly being recalculated by the program in a process called "interpolation." Sometimes interpolation causes an image to lose its sharpness – as does "resampling up" (increasing the resolution of an image from its original scanned resolution). In such circumstances it may become necessary to use a filter which sharpens the image and may restore it to somewhere near its original state. This technique is often referred to as "unsharp masking." Care should be taken not to oversharpen an image, since doing so may cause graininess. A wide range of other filters for image enhancement and special effects is also available in image manipulation packages.

Original scanned at 100dpi

Noise filter

Resampled to 200dpi

Diffuse filter

Unsharp masking applied

Emboss filter

or her skill to remove an overall cast from a picture, or use a range of controls to sharpen or otherwise upgrade it. If your scan is to be used in a "gateway" system, the operator will apply a set of parameters which suit that system and the eventual printing machinery; you will get the low-resolution version. However, if you are commissioning the scan for your own further manipulation on the Mac, then just ask for the image to be saved straight away in your chosen format – CMYK or RGB, EPS or TIFF, for example – and you'll spare yourself a lot of tedious re-saving if many images are involved. And insist on them being named on the disk in a way that makes immediate sense to you – not as a collection of numbers. When you get the disks, back them up immediately. The repro house may hold the files on their machines for a while, but don't rely on it.

PRINTING AND PROOFING Further along the production process, the business of printing your design is tending to separate out into three separate areas. First, the established techniques of conventional lithographic and gravure printing remain much as they ever were, but for the fact that the plate films were probably made by an imagesetter rather than a camera. The printing press itself may be equipped with computerised controls. Second is a self-contained "hybrid" press which, when fed with the finished disk, automatically exposes and processes its own plates directly on to the printing cylinders. These plates are good for up to 20,000 impressions on ordinary paper or board using standard printing inks. Remarkably, the used plate surfaces are automatically disposed of – they are withdrawn into the centre of the plate cylinders at the end of the run, whereupon fresh, un-exposed ones replace them from the same location. Third comes a group of machines, some of which have been

Color correction curves

Many applications allow you to make color modifications to a scanned image by manipulating a line which represents the tonal values of the scanned image relative to the screen image. Modifications can be made to the image as a whole, or separately to each of the process colors or RGB colors. Being able to make judgments on subtle color adjustments is only possible with a 24-bit color monitor. The monitor must be calibrated to the specifications of the application in which the corrections are being made in order to establish a direct relationship between displayed and output color. Many applications will calibrate your monitor automatically, but also offer controls for manual calibration. For consistency you should keep your monitor brightness and the ambient light temperature of your workspace constant.

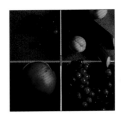

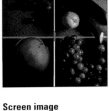

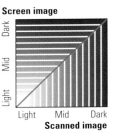

Original image In its unchanged state, the color values of shadows, middle tones and highlights of the displayed image exactly match those which were scanned. In this case the color curve is represented as a straight 45° line.

Increased contrast Increasing the angle of the line squeezes out the extreme shadows and highlights, spreading the middle tones over lighter and darker values. A vertical line would increase contrast to maximum – black and white.

Color proof corrections

Final adjustments to a color image should only be made after it has been proofed on a four-color press. Even if the original transparency was perfect, other factors can affect the outcome. Among these is "dot gain", where the size of halftone dots increases either during the transfer of the image from film to printing plate, or because of the effect of inking. Proofing may also reveal other aberrations which are impossible to detect on your monitor or on a laser proof. One of the most common of these is "moiré" (see p.136).

Correct image

Too much contrast

Detail too soft

Detail too sharp

developed out of copier technology. The printed image may be transferred electrostatically, using toners which are then fused to the printing surface, or by inkjet using quick-drying inks on purpose-made papers. These machines are distinguished by the absence of conventional printing plates: they are driven directly from a disk and the process is known as "digital printing."

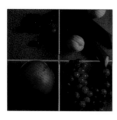

Reduced contrast
Reducing the angle of the line compresses all the tones of the image into the middle tone range of the monitor.

Posterization This technique confines the continuous range of colors to "flattened out" bands.

Color correction To make accurate corrections, it is usually necessary to make adjustments to individual process colors in an image rather than identical adjustments to all the colors. Results must be proofed for final assessment.

Too much yellow

Too much cyan

Too much magenta

Too little yellow

Too little cyan

Too little magenta

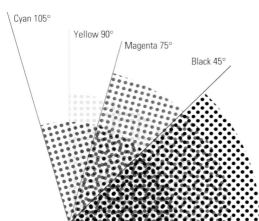

Cyan 105°
Yellow 90°
Magenta 75°
Black 45°

Halftone screen angles
Halftone screens must be set at the correct angles to avoid a picture printing with an undesirable screen clash (moiré, **below**). The screen angles shown (**left**) are common for 4-color printing and are the default angles for most applications.

The differences between the systems from the Mac designer's standpoint are not enormous in terms of design preparation. Plateless systems are, for example, less tolerant of subtle tint changes and only reproduce "spot" special colors with process equivalents. The economics of run length favor the traditional system for large quantities, while flexibility rests with the new machines. The big difference comes at the proofing stage – from film you can get the familiar Cromalin or Matchprint, but if there is no plate there is no film and therefore no proof in the conventional sense, certainly not the old-style "wet proof." What can be provided economically is a "digital proof," which is produced on a separate, probably dye-sublimation, printer. The image should look the same as the pending job – if it's not correct, then the file can be fixed, maybe on the spot. With true plateless systems, the first sheet off the press is the proof – so no problem. If the operator is quick, another file can be sent to print a different job while you're still mulling over your corrections. At every revolution of the plateless press, a completely new image or a change to the existing one can be created. The facility was developed for personalising direct mail shots but it's too attractive to be left there.

Color trapping When two solid areas of color print side by side, imperfections in register sometimes create white hairline gaps. To avoid this, a technique called "trapping" is employed, whereby the edges of an image printing in one color are increased to overlap slightly those of the adjacent color. Conventionally, this would take place during film makeup or platemaking by varying exposures or by the use of "fatties" – interleaved film which causes light to spread, fractionally increasing an image's size. Some Mac applications feature automatic trapping controls, but it may be necessary for you to create your own trapping by adding a rule (**1**) of, say, 0.25pt around a shape (**2**). The rule should be specified in the same color as the area it surrounds and is set to overprint.

1   2

8

TROUBLESHOOTING

PRECAUTIONS/SYSTEM ERRORS/STARTUP ERRORS/
MEMORY PROBLEMS/PROBLEMS WITH FILES/
PRINTING PROBLEMS/FURTHER READING

No matter how well a computer is built – or how well the parts, devices, and programs that serve it are built (or written) – things can go wrong. Problems can occur almost anywhere: a hardware fault, a software bug, a corrupted program or data file, incompatibilities of software, viruses – even operator error (that's you).

You *will* encounter problems, but these can be kept to a minimum if you follow the few simple preventative guidelines listed here. Also listed are remedies for – or at least explanations of – some of the more alarming problems that may occur. The list is not comprehensive, and if you are confronted with a problem that isn't addressed here or in your manuals, contact your dealer or a User Group. Also, individual application problems are not included here; some applications offer you helplines and/or e-mail facilities. Most application problems occur in first releases or upgrades and are usually identified quickly – software "patches" may be issued on disk to registered users or posted on the Internet for you to download. All good software is extensively "beta-tested" by real-world users before the release of the finished article. However, a problem may occur simply because the software developers didn't anticipate the particular string of commands or the action you just made. Of course, *you* won't know if that's the reason, but if it seems to be a recurrent problem – let the developer know. At least then the problem can be fixed for future releases.

PRECAUTIONS

Check that everything is plugged in
This may seem obvious, but even one unplugged item may cause problems. If, in addition, you're not confident about the local power supply because of power surges and spikes, get a surge suppres-

sor, and unplug the Mac when it's not in use.

Never plug in or unplug any item while it is switched on or while the Mac is switched on
While there are exceptions to this rule (modem, printer, and audio ports), it is safest never to plug in or unplug anything while the computer

is live – even the ADB port (mouse and keyboard).

Don't move or jar your Mac or any device containing a hard disk while it is switched on
Doing so may cause a disk to crash, with loss of data. Removeable hard disks continue spinning for a while after you cut the power.

Don't obstruct the cooling vents of your Mac or any piece of hardware

Electrical components, and power supplies in particular, give off a lot of heat.

Always turn off your Mac using the Shutdown command from the Special menu, or the relevant keystrokes

Using the power switch to shut down may damage system files.

Don't keep more than one System folder on your startup disk

Doing so will confuse your Mac and cause system errors.

Turn on peripheral SCSI devices *before* you switch on your Mac

Some (not all) SCSI devices need to be switched on all the time the Mac is on. If you switch on a device *after* you switch on your Mac, it may not be recognized. Turning off a SCSI device while your Mac is in use may cause a system error.

Ensure that no two SCSI devices have the same SCSI address number

Make sure that each device connected to your Mac has a different number before you switch the Mac on. There are eight SCSI numbers (0-7) allowed in most Macs, although number seven is allocated to your Mac's CPU while zero is usually your internal hard disk. Some Macs have two distinct SCSI groups or "buses," one internal, one external. The same rules apply within each bus. The SCSI address number, or ID, is usually located on the back panel of the device, but it may occasionally be allocated by means of software. See the Glossary for more on SCSI and terminators.

Save your work regularly

Get into the habit of saving your work to disk as often as you can (type Command-S). Always Save when you turn away from the Mac. Save at least every 15 minutes – and more frequently unless your document is so large that it takes several minutes to save. Save before you print a document, and save before you hide the application you are working in or switch to another application.

Print out documents before closing them

The unthinkable can happen – a file may become corrupt by the time you open it again. You will at least have a hard copy of the job you may have been working on all day.

Back up your work regularly

Always back up your current work files every day (if not more often) and your complete system every week or so. Keep backup copies of all your original application and font floppy disks. While saving and backing up work will not actually prevent problems from arising, you'll be thankful you did when your hard disk crashes.

Periodically reinstall system and application software

System software and application files may corrupt over time. Replace them if problems occur with increased frequency (frequent system errors may speed up the corruption of system files).

Rebuild your desktop file

This invisible file keeps track of all files on your disk. It also retains information on deleted files, so gets bigger and bigger, eventually causing Finder operations to slow down or even prevent you from opening a file altogether. To clean up the desktop file, "rebuild" it by holding down the Option and Command keys while you start or restart the Mac.

Defragment your hard disk regularly

When data is written to your hard disk, it is placed in the next available – and largest – space, each file side by side (contiguous) to begin with. As you continue working on a file, it outgrows the space it's in, and the new data has to be placed elsewhere on the disk. Soon, all the large free spaces get filled, so even new files must be split and the pieces positioned wherever there is space. Your disk becomes "fragmented." A fragmented disk means a slow Mac, as it takes longer to find the bits of file and retrieve the data. You can use a simple software utility to defragment or "optimize" the disk. Alternatively, you can back up your entire hard disk, reformat it and then restore all your backed-up files to the disk. Either way, the files will be written to the disk contiguously.

Keep a spare startup disk

Your Mac may one day fail to recognize its startup disk so a spare startup disk (a floppy, external or even a CD) will at least let you gain access to your hard disk, identify the problem and rectify it. This assumes that the disk has not suffered a mechanical failure. If it has, you will need professional help to recover the data.

Keep a virus detection program on your hard disk

Computer viruses are deliberately mischievous programs written to create havoc with any computer that they come into contact with. Viruses spread by copying themselves to and from hard disks via floppy disks and also over networks. Use a virus detection utility to check every disk you insert into your Mac and run a regular diagnostic check on your hard disk. Make sure you keep your virus detection program up to date to combat new viruses.

Put your coffee cup somewhere else

Keyboard response is not improved by spilled liquid.

SYSTEM ERRORS

The most alarming problem you are likely to encounter (apart from a hard disk crash) is a system error – a crash, or "bomb" – or an application error. If this happens the first rule is: **keep calm** and don't panic – you *may* be able to do something about it. Before you try any of the remedies below, sit back and look at the screen – try to remember the last time you saved your work to disk. If it was very recently, you may not lose much. If you can't remember, write down or draw everything that you can see on the screen (there's no hurry), such as a layout, or newly defined colors or type specifications, the details of which may be visible on palettes. Next, go through each of the following procedures in turn, always remembering that each of them is a long shot and that the likely outcome is that you will be forced to restart your Mac:

The Mac will not respond to keyboard commands and nothing happens when Menu Bar titles are clicked – even though the pointer moves

Check that the Mac isn't just taking a long time to execute a command – particularly if you are working on a very complex illustration or using an application for 3D rendering. If the pointer has changed its shape to a wrist-watch, you may have to wait. Be aware, however, that the wristwatch often looks active even after the Mac has given up. Try typing Command-period – this may cancel any task that the computer is currently carrying out. If still nothing happens, try the next remedy.

The pointer has "frozen" on the screen and the Mac will not respond to keyboard commands

Check that the mouse and keyboard ADB connections are secure. The error may have occurred within the application rather than the system. Try pressing the Option-Command-Esc keys together. You may get a dialog box asking if you want to forcibly quit the current application and return to the Finder. Clicking Quit may have that result. If it does, your Mac may be in an unstable state, so save any other open documents and restart.

The pointer jumps erratically on the screen

Clean the debris from the internal rollers of the mouse. If you use a graphics tablet as well, make sure you haven't left the stylus lying on it. The Mac can get confused with two sets of incoming signals.

Normal typing produces unfamiliar or exotic characters

You have inadvertently changed the keyboard layout control panel by using a particular keyboard shortcut within an application. This shortcut is shared by the keyboard control panel. Open the panel and revert to the original language layout.

A dialog box appears, saying "Sorry, a System Error occurred"

This is characterized by the bomb icon above. Your Mac has crashed – there's not a lot you can do about it. There are usually two buttons in the dialog box, a Restart button and a Resume button, the latter is rarely enabled and unlikely to work even if it is.

A system error may occur for a number of reasons. Among the most common are:

Application error Many crashes will be for a one-off reason and may never recur under the same circumstances. To check, restart your Mac, open the docu-ment you were working on, and try to repeat the actions you made before the crash. If you Mac crashes again, there is something wrong with the application – either it has corrupted (reinstall it), or it is a bug (notify the publisher). Either way, avoid the sequence of actions which caused the crash.

External hard disk or other SCSI device switched off or disconnected Switching on your Mac before you switch on a hard disk – or switching off a hard disk before your Mac – may cause it to crash. Either way, switch on the disk before restarting the Mac.

Incompatible init files or system extensions Init files are startup documents and may cause system errors during the startup sequence or when called upon while you work in an application. If the problem occurs shortly after installing a new init, remove it and restart. If that solves the problem, your new init is probably to blame. Use the Extension Manager control panel to track down the culprit. You'll be able to make "sets" of inits and extensions which work together, keeping the warring ones apart.

System software corrupted Reinstall the System and Finder files.

Damaged disk The boot blocks (startup information) on your hard disk may be damaged – restore them by reinstalling the drivers on your hard disk (by using the setup program for your hard disk – if it's an Apple disk, use HD SC Setup).

Font conflicts Use a font utility such as Suitcase to prevent damaging clashes.

Hardware failure The Mac's mechanics are normally reliable. Detection and cure of component failure is almost impossible for anyone but a qualified service engineer, but it's expensive. Make sure you've tried all the cures outlined on these pages before you make that call.

STARTUP ERRORS

No hard disk icon on the desktop

If your hard disk fails to mount after an otherwise successful startup, try rebuilding your desktop file. Alternatively, it may be possible to mount your disk using a shareware utility called SCSI Probe (by Robert Pilic). If the disk still doesn't mount, there may be a problem with the hard disk itself; try using a disk repair and recovery utility. If that fails, have your hard disk serviced – it may still be possible to retrieve the data stored on it.

Flashing question mark appears at startup

This indicates that the Mac is asking you to insert a startup disk – either there isn't one, or the Mac can't find it. If you use an external drive as your startup disk, make sure it's turned on. Make sure all your SCSI devices are switched on. You may have switched on your Mac too soon after turning on your SCSI devices – try starting up again. Check that all cables are securely connected and that any required terminator is attached to the right device. Reinstall the system software from the installer disk, or disks. If none of these remedies work, you will have to start up from another disk and run a disk maintenance utility to check and repair your startup disk.

MEMORY PROBLEMS

"Memory low" warnings

You are most likely to get these while working in an application – either the application will warn you, or it will unexpectedly quit,

returning you to the Finder. An application may run out of memory if you are working on a very complex document. If this happens, try resetting the application memory size: quit the application (if it hasn't done so by itself), select the application icon and then Get Info (File menu). Here you can increase the maximum memory size. Remember that the Mac operating system needs quite a lot of memory to function, so don't re-assign all your RAM.

Not enough memory to open an application

If you are presented with a dialog box advising you that there is not enough memory to open the application you just launched, and asking you if you want to try opening it using what memory is left – click "Cancel." This generally happens when you have other applications open – they are all using up memory. Close one of those applications and relaunch the one that failed. If the warning pops up again, you may have to close another or *all* open applications. This is because RAM is allocated in contiguous blocks and can't be split up as can a file on a hard disk. Closing one application may still not free up a large enough block, even though the total memory allocated to open applications mathematically leaves enough memory for the newcomer. The operating system is unable to re-form small remaining blocks of RAM (even though they are not being used) into a usefully large chunk. Find out the size of your largest unused block of memory in About This Macintosh ... item in the Apple menu. If you have no other applications open, you can free up some memory by removing a few fonts or inits from your system folder or by reducing the current size of the application memory (not below its suggested size). Best advice: get more RAM.

PROBLEMS WITH FILES

Document won't open

Any application present on your Mac will have a characteristic icon appear on any file created by that application. It will try to open the file, even if it was created with an earlier version of the same software. If a file won't open in the Finder, launch the application, then try to open the file from within the application. If you don't have the right application installed and the file appears only as an icon-less "document" in the Finder, the Mac may still offer you the chance to open it using a related application. If that doesn't work, there may be a problem with the disk – make a copy of the disk and try to open the file from the copy. If the file has corrupted, you will probably have to revert to an earlier version of the document (thus the reason for frequent backups). Try using a disk maintenance utility to recover the file. If the file contains text, try to recover it using an ordinary word processor. Much of it will be gobbledegook, but some useful text may be embedded in it.

Can't save a document

Try using the Save As... command and giving the file a different name. If the disk is full, save to another disk.

PRINTING PROBLEMS

You may see the words "Limitcheck," or "PostScript Error" appear in dialog boxes. If your document contains EPS files from a drawing application, try applying a higher "flatness" value to its paths and exporting it as a new EPS file. If errors persist while trying to print a long or complex document, try printing it one page at a time. Restart your printer to flush its memory.

FURTHER READING

It may seem strange to recommend printed books as a guide to the most user-friendly computer system ever designed. The reason is simple. Because of the Mac's ease of use, hundreds of industrious enthusiasts set out to see if it could do things that weren't allowed for in the official manuals. They succeeded, and their inventions, shortcuts, tips, and tricks form the core of the best "add-on" Mac books. Just as useful, they discovered what makes the Mac crash and fail – and how to go about preventing it. This is an ongoing process which closely follows both the development of the Mac operating system itself, as well as upgrades to application software. It follows that you should demand the most recent edition of all these books.

GENERAL BOOKS

There are many books published about the Macintosh. They are usually aimed at the general Macintosh user and much of what is contained within them does not directly relate to graphic design. However, the following books are well-written and offer a wealth of technical information and tips. They can often help you when the official Apple manual can't. They all seem to weigh about three pounds!

The Macintosh Bible
edited by Jeremy Judson,
(Peachpit Press)
Updated version of one of the first general Mac books.

The Macworld New Complete Mac Handbook
Jim Heid
(IDG Books Worldwide, Inc.)
Expanded compilation of the Macworld *Getting Started* column.

Macworld Mac and PowerMac Secrets
David Pogue and Joseph Schorr
(IDG Books Worldwide, Inc.)
Enormous and wide-ranging with a CD-ROM included.

Sad Macs, Bombs and Other Disasters
Ted Landau
(Peachpit Press)
Comprehensive problem-solving.

The Macintosh Bible "What Do I Do Now?" Book
Charles Rubin
(Peachpit Press)
Tells you what to do instead of panicking.

APPLICATION GUIDES etc

Visual QuickStart Guides
(Peachpit Press)
A series which offers "get-you-started" tips for the major applications as well as Java and HTML for web-site production.

Macworld Photoshop Bible
Deke McClelland
(IDG Books Worldwide, Inc.)
Full of good information once you become used to the author's unique style.

Real World Guides
(Peachpit Press)
A series of practical guides

for applications such as Freehand and Photoshop. There is also a useful guide to desktop scanning.

The Linotype Color Book
Dominique Legrand
(Linotype-Hell)
A guide to digital color reproduction.

QuarkXPress Bible
Barbara Assadi
(IDG Books Worldwide, Inc.)
Thorough and helpful.

MAC-graphics
Lim Ching San and Gim Lee
(Octogram Publishing/ COMPUTERbooks)
Macintosh type and tint effects, to show what they look like in print, plus very comprehensive process color tint charts.

JOURNALS

MacUser (U.S.)
(Ziff-Davis Publishing Co.)

MacUser (U.K.)
(Dennis Publishing Ltd.)

Macworld (U.S.)
(Macworld Communications, Inc.)

Macworld (U.K.)
(IDG Communications)

X-RAY
(X-RAY Publishing Ventures Ltd.)

INTERNET

Try *alt.sys.mac.newuser-help* for a start. Or download the Mac Net Journal. Be warned, this activity is addictive.

9

GLOSSARY AND INDEX

Here you will find brief definitions both of Macintosh terms and of design terms in the context of the Mac. Italic figures at the end of entries refer to the page number(s) where that topic is discussed in the main body of the book.

Key:
abb: abbreviation
adv: advertising
app: application
fin: finishing and binding
obs: obsolescent

pap: paper/papermaking
pho: photography
pri: printing
rep: reproduction/prepress
typ: typography/typesetting

util: utility program
→   see
●   Apple Menu

A

abort → cancel.

absolute leading → leading.

absolute page number The actual position of a page in a document, relative to other pages, regardless of any other page number.

accelerator card/board An add-on board with a faster central processing unit and/or coprocessor to speed up computer operation. *28, 47*

accent Mark added to a character to denote pronunciation in a given language.

accent characters Type characters that print with accent marks, usually accessed via the Option (or Shift-Option) key on Apple keyboards.

accessory → desk accessory.

access time Of disk drives, the average combined seek time (the time taken for the drive head to reach data being accessed) and latency time (the time taken for the data sector to rotate beneath the head).

Acrobat *(app.) 117*

active icon The currently selected icon, or icons, on the desktop. An active icon is highlighted, usually as a negative of its inactive, or unselected, image.

active window The currently selected window on the desktop, an active window has its title bar highlighted by horizontal lines and is always in front of (or on top of) all other windows.

ADB *abb:* → Apple Desktop Bus.

additive colors The primary colors of light – red, green, and blue (RGB) – that can be mixed to form all other colors in computer monitors and in photographic reproduction.

add-on board → expansion card.

address A number identifying a location in a computer's memory.

address lines Paths on a central processing unit chip used to carry data addresses. The more address lines, the larger the amount of memory that can be used simultaneously.

Adobe Font Metrics A brandname specification for storing font information (metrics) in a file. *91*

Adobe Multiple Master font format *97*

Adobe Type Manager (ATM) *(util.)* A brandname font utility which improves the screen display of PostScript Type 1 fonts by scaling the outlines contained within their printer

files, rather than by using bitmapped screen fonts. *40, 74, 88–9, 91, 94*

Adobe Type Reunion *(util.) 75*

advertising, *software for 71–2*

AFE *abb:* → Apple File Exchange.

AFM *abb:* → Adobe Font Metrics.

After Dark *(util.) 75*

AI *abb:* → artificial intelligence.

airbrush A mechanical painting tool producing a fine spray of paint or ink, used in illustration, design, and retouching.

airbrush tool A tool used in some computer drawing and painting applications, the function of which is to simulate, on screen, the effects provided by an airbrush. *61, 64*

alert (box) A message box which appears unsolicited, usually accompanied by a sound, to pass on information or give a warning.

algorithm A set of precise predetermined procedural steps for solving a specific problem.

algorithmically defined Description of a font which draws each character according to calculations made by a program, the program being unique for each character.

alias A copy of a file's icon – but not a copy of the file itself. The alias icon works in the same way as its original but occupies very little disk space, no matter how many copies are made.

aliasing → jaggie.

aligned left/right → ranged/left, right.

aligning numerals → lining figures.

alphabet (length) A measure derived from the length, in points, of the 26 lower-case alphabet letters. Thus 39 characters have a measure of 1½ alphabets.

alphanumeric set *(typ.)* A full set of letters and numbers, sometimes also including punctuation marks and certain commonly used symbols.

alpha test Early testing of a product, to debug it, by the company developing it.

alpha version First version, for testing, of a program. It is followed by beta and then release versions.

analog computer A computer using a physical variable, i.e. voltage, to represent numbers in arithmetical calculations.

anchor In some applications, the facility to lock, or anchor, one item to another; a picture or rule can be anchored to text so that it flows with it.

Animation A QuickTime compression setting suitable for image sequences which were created in digital form, such as renderings with little or no "noise." → QuickTime.

annotation (**1**) A type label added to an illustration. (**2**) Explanatory notes or names printed in the margin of a text.

anonymous FTP allows access to some Internet sites without a password. → FTP.

antialiasing A technique which reduces the jagged effect of bitmapped screen images by averaging the density of pixels at the edges of images with their background, thus softening the stepped appearance of the image.

antiqua (**1**) Early typeface based on 11th- and 12th-century Italian scripts. (**2**) A German term for roman type.

AOL *abb:* America Online, major US online Internet service provider.

append In some applications, the facility to copy a set of user-defined specifications from one document or library to another.

Apple Desktop Bus (ADB) The standard connection path provided on most Macs (early Macs and the Mac Plus use a different connection) to allow peripheral devices such as keyboards, mice, trackballs, and digitizing tablets to connect to your Mac. *30, 49*

Apple HD SC Setup The standard Apple utility that comes with your Mac which you use for initializing, partitioning, or testing your hard disk.

Apple key → command key.

Apple menu A standard menu, identified by the Apple logo on the left of the menu bar, from which you can access items placed in the Apple Menu Items folder and get information about memory and open applications.

AppleShare The Apple file server on a computer for users of an AppleTalk network, enabling them to share files on that computer.

AppleTalk Apple's local area network (LAN) system, built into every Mac, which you can use to connect your Mac to other Macs or to share printers and other devices. Physical links are made with Apple's LocalTalk connectors and cabling.

application files *22*

application heap The portion of RAM set aside for use by software applications.

Application Memory Size The portion of RAM reserved by each application.

Application Menu A standard menu, located at the extreme right of the menu bar, which lists open applications and is where you can choose to hide or show open windows.

application (program) A program written to create or manipulate data for a specific purpose, such as word processing or page layout, but which is distinct from

nonapplication programs such as system software. *19*

application programming interface → API.

application support file An auxiliary file used by applications for special purposes, such as a spelling dictionary or help file.

ARA *abb:* Apple Remote Access. Program allowing one Mac to be networked to, and controlled by, another Mac.

arabic numerals The numerical symbols 1234567890.

archival backup → backup, archival.

arrow keys The four keys on the keyboard which move the text insertion point, or pointer, left, right, up, or down, or move you through list boxes.

arrow pointer The basic arrow cursor, a left-leaning arrow ( ), used in the Finder and most applications, which is controlled by the mouse.

art(work) (a/w, A/W) Any illustrative matter prepared for reproduction, such as illustrations, diagrams, and photographs, as distinct (usually) from text.

artificial intelligence (AI) A term describing programs that deduce, to a specific set of rules, a solution from original and subsequent criteria provided by you – in other words, the program learns by its own experience.

ascender The portion of a lower-case letter rising above its body, or x-height; i.e. the upper part of the characters b, d, f, h, k, l, t.

ascent The height of text above its baseline, as specified by font designers.

ASCII Acronym (pronounced askee) for the American Standard Code for Information Interchange, a standard by which most computers assign code numbers to letters, numbers, and common symbols. *128*

A-sizes → international paper sizes.

assembled negative *(rep.)* A film negative of combined line and halftone copy used in the conventional preparation of a film positive or printing plate for photolithography.

asynchronous communication A communication protocol by which a start-and-stop signal denotes the beginning and end of each character transmitted, thus allowing two devices to communicate without rigid timing signals. As distinct from synchronous communication.

@ Part of DNS address. Prefixes the hostname. → DNS, host, hostname.

ATM *abb:* → Adobe Type Manager.

attachment Usually an image file "attached" to a text document for electronic transmission → GIF.

authoring programs, *multimedia 72–3*

author's proofs Galley or laser proofs, checked and marked by a proofreader, to be read by the author, who may then mark any necessary correction.

Authorware Professional *(app.) 72*

autoflow The facility, in some applications, to flow text automatically from one page to another or from one box to another.

auto leading → leading.

automated publication Published work of which a copy is kept on disk, tape, or film for future publication with revised matter or format.

automatic font downloading → font downloading.

automatic hyphenation A facility, in some applications, to break a word in a suitable place with a hyphen at the end of a line of text.

automatic text box In some frame-based page layout applications, a text box on an automatically inserted page into which text will automatically flow.

automatic text chain → autoflow.

auto page insertion A facility, in some applications, to add pages automatically when an amount of text greater than the space available to accommodate it is imported into a document.

autotrace A facility, in some applications, to create a freeform path by automatically tracing solid elements of an image. *59*

auxiliary dictionary A user-defined dictionary for checking spelling, which may be based upon the built-in dictionary of the application in which it is created.

A/UX *abb:* Apple/UNIX, Apple's version of the AT&T UNIX operating system.

auxiliary file An application support file.

axis (pl. axes) Imaginary line defining the center of an object around which the object rotates or is symmetrical to on a flat plane.

a/w (A/W) *abb:* → artwork.

B

b/f (**1** *typ.*) *abb:* bold face. Instruction to set copy in a bold face. (**2**) *abb:* brought forward. Copy or matter which has been brought forward from the previous page.

back *(fin.)* The part of a book nearest the fold or the edge at which the pages are bound.

backbone → spine.

backed → back up (**2**).

background Description of a program which runs at the same time as another is running in the foreground, as when two or more programs are open.

background color/tint A color or tint which has been applied to the background of any item, whether it be an illustration, page, or boxed feature.

background printing The facility to print documents and use your Mac at the same time for something else.

background processing The facility of a program running in the background, to process data without interfering with the program operating in the foreground.

back matter → end matter.

back-to-back *(pri.)* Refers to the process of printing on both sides of a sheet.

back up (**1**) To make a duplicate of a disk, application, or document as a precaution against losing the original. *106–7, 121–3, 138* (**2** *pri.*) To print the second side of a sheet of paper. Backed refers to the sheet when it has been backed up.

backup A duplicate of a file, folder, or disk. → back up (**1**).

backup utilities *75*

backup, archival A backup which specifically saves the previous versions of your backups, thus avoiding the possibility of your losing files which may be deleted and rewritten by a mirror-image backup.

backup, global/baseline An exact duplicate of everything on your disk. A global backup is usually the first one you make from a source disk. Thereafter, backups are either incremental or archival.

backup, incremental A backup of only those files which you have worked on or changed since your last backup.

backup, mirror-image A backup achieved by copying the exact contents from one disk to another, thus replacing older versions of files with updated ones.

backup, same disk A backup copy of a document, saved onto the same disk as the original.

backup set A set of backup disks or files containing duplicate, or backed-up, files from a source disk.

Balloon Help A cartoon-like device for giving on-line help about icons and menu commands. The Balloon Help menu is represented in the menu bar by a question mark in a balloon.

bandwidth Measure of a network's ability to transmit information. Restrictions on bandwidth make such systems run slowly when overloaded.

bar code A pattern of vertical lines identifying details of a product, such as country of origin, manufacturer, and type of product, conforming to the Universal Product Code (UPC) – there are several different formats for product coding.

base alignment In computer typesetting, the automatic alignment of type of different sizes on a common baseline.

base artwork/black art Artwork requiring the addition of other elements such as halftone positives before reproduction.

base film *(rep.)* The basic material for contact film in platemaking for photomechanical reproduction, to which film positives are stripped.

base line The last line of space on a page containing type matter.

baseline An imaginary line on which the bases of uppercase letters, and the bases of the x-heights of lowercase letters, rest.

baseline backup → backup, global/baseline.

baseline grid In some applications, an invisible grid to which lines of text can be locked so that their baselines align from column to column.

batch mode The facility of an application to process data processed in batches as distinct from data which is processed as you input it (interactive mode, or real-time); e.g., when you run a spelling check through a whole document.

battery The lithium battery in your Mac, which supplies power to an area of RAM called parameter RAM (PRAM).

baud The unit of measure equating to one unit per second describing the speed of data transfer, e.g. by a modem, sometimes inaccurately referred to as bit rate (two or more bits can be contained in a single event). The greater the baud rate, the faster the transmission of data.

BBS *abb:* bulletin board system/service. → bulletin board.

begin even *(typ.)* Instruction to the typesetter to set the first line of a piece of text without a paragraph indent; i.e., full out.

beta test Testing of a software product by a person designated, although not employed, by the company developing it.

beta version Second version of a program used for testing. It follows the alpha version.

Bézier control handle → Bézier curve.

Bézier curve In object-oriented drawing applications, a mathematically defined curve between two points (Bézier points). The curve is manipulated by dragging,

from an anchored point, control handles which act on the curve like magnets. → object-oriented.

binary code The code by which sets of data are represented by binary digits. → bit.

binary digit → bit.

binary system Numbering system using only two digits, 0 and 1 (binary = of, or involving, pairs), rather than the decimal system of 0-9. *15–16*

binding edge → spine.

binding methods *(fin.)* Methods of securing multiple leaves of a printed item, such as a book. Mechanical binding methods include plastic comb binding, ring binding, and metal clasp attachments. Bookbinding methods include Smyth-sewn, side-sewn, section-sewn, and perfect binding.

BinHex Format for converting binary to ASCII for E-mail transmission.

bit *abb:* binary digit. The smallest unit of information your computer uses. It is expressed as 1 or 0, meaning on or off, yes or no, positive or negative, something or nothing. Eight bits are required to store one alphabet character. *15, 17, 47*

bit density The number of bits in a given area or length; e.g., per inch of magnetic tape.

bit-depth The number of bits used to define a device's capability to reproduce grays or colors – the greater the bit-depth (e.g., 32-bit), the more colors you will have available.

bit map At its simplest, a text character or graphic image comprised of dots. In fact, a bit map is the set of bits that represents the position and binary state (on or off) of a corresponding set of items to form a bit image such as your display screen. *40–1*

bitmapped font A font comprised of bitmapped letters, characterized by their jagged edges, as distinct from the smooth edges of an outline font used by printers. *88–9, 91, 94*

bitmapped graphic An image comprised of dots, as distinct from an object-

oriented graphic. *59, 60* → object-oriented.

bit rate The number of bits per second (data and non-data) carried by a communications channel. Sometimes, inaccurately, referred to as baud rate.

black letter Heavy style of typeface based on broad-nib script, also called Old English (U.S.) and Gothic (U.K.).

black patch/out *(rep.)* A piece of black (or red) material used to mask the image area on base artwork or positive film, leaving a window in the negative for stripping in a halftone image.

black printer *(rep.)* Term for the film which provides the image to print in black ink in the four-color printing process.

blanker → screen saver.

blanking interval The term describing the brief moment of time in which the beam of electrons in a video monitor switches off. This happens when the beam moves from one horizontal line to another (called the "horizontal blanking interval"), and when it moves from the bottom of the screen to the top at the end of each frame (called the "vertical blanking interval").

bleed The part of an image that extends beyond the edge of a page. Images which spread to the edge of the paper allowing no margins are described as "bled off."

blending *59, 61*

blessed folder → system folder

blind folio Page number counted for reference or identification, but not printed on the page itself.

blind P The character ¶, used to indicate new paragraphs. Also called a "paragraph mark" or "reverse P."

block A group regarded as a unit, usually referring to data or memory in which data is stored.

block letter A term used to describe large display sans-serif characters, deriving from letters cut in wooden blocks, which were used for embossing or printing.

blues, blueprint *(pri.)* Low-quality proofs, usually produced by the printer rather than origination house, for a final check before printing. → diazo; Ozalid.

board, circuit board The name given to the support upon which chips and other components are mounted. A printed circuit board (PC board) is one that has been stamped with metallic ink to connect the components. A motherboard, or logic board, is the main board in your computer that bears the CPU, ROM, RAM, and expansion slots. A board that plugs into an expansion slot is often called a card. *29*

body copy/matter Printed matter forming the main part, usually text, of a work.

body type The type used in setting the main part of a text.

bold (face) Type with a conspicuously heavy, black appearance. It is based on the same design as medium-weight type in the same type family.

bomb The name given to an error in your system software of which the net result is that you will almost certainly be forced to restart your Mac. It is often identified by an icon of a bomb in a message box. The term has been extended to mean any condition where your Mac fails to respond to input from the mouse or keyboard, thus requiring you to restart. This is also described by the terms "System error," "crash," "freeze," and "hang." *139*

book face Old term for a particular typeface, but now used to mean any type suitable for the text of a book.

book make-up The collation and identification of copy prepared for printing.

book paper *(pap.)* A general classification of papers suitable for book printing.

book proof *(pri.)* Imposed proofs or page proofs put together in book form for checking before binding.

boot blocks Specifically designated areas on a disk set aside to give your Mac the information it needs to start up, such as the allocation of RAM for different purposes (the number of files that can be opened, for example).

boot disk → startup disk

boot(ing) (up) The process of starting up a computer or any application by loading the necessary program – in the Macintosh's case, the System and Finder – into memory. In Mac parlance, more commonly called "starting up." → cold boot; warm boot.

bottom out To arrange text so there are no unsuitable breaks at the bottom of a page, or so that the page does not end with a widow.

bounding box In some applications, a box enclosing an item.

bowl The curved part of a type character that encloses the counter.

box In some applications, a frame into which text or pictures can be inserted.

box feature/story Information in a book or publication presented separately from the running text and illustrations and either surrounded by a box rule or underlaid with a tint patch. Also called a "sidebar."

boxhead In a table arranged in columns, the heading to each column appearing under the main heading.

box rule A rule or border surrounding an item of type or other graphic matter.

bpi *abb:* bits per inch → bit density.

bracketed type Type in which the serif is joined to the main stem in an unbroken curve.

breve A mark indicating pronunciation of a short vowel (˘).

bridge The most basic hardware and software connection between similar computer networks, from one AppleTalk network to another. → gateway; network.

brightness → HSB.

brightness control A control wheel (and in some cases, a control panel device) on most monitors that allows you to adjust its screen brightness.

bromide (1) A photographic print on paper coated with light-sensitive silver bromide emulsion. **(2)** General term for high-quality output from

an imagesetter, made on photographic paper rather than film.

browser (1) Application for searching the Internet. → Navigator. **(2)** Application for viewing image files on a CD-ROM, for example.

buffer Refers to an area of memory – either in RAM, on a separate cache, or on a hard disk – set aside to undertake a task when required. Buffers are commonly used in output devices to speed up that activity and to free the computer for use. → print spooler.

bug A software program error, made at the time of its creation, which causes the program to behave erratically or incorrectly. Bugged software is not so much a mistake as the result of the complexities of programs being so great that it is virtually impossible to test every possible sequence of commands likely to occur.

bullet A large dot used to precede listed items, separate items of text, or add emphasis to particular parts of a text. It is available in most fonts by keying Option-8.

bulletin board (BBS) A facility for sharing information by using a telephone link from your computer, via a modem, to another computer dedicated to serving that purpose.

bull's eye → hickie.

bundle (1 *pap.***)** Two reams of paper (1,000 sheets). **(2)** A resource used to associate file references and icon lists for the Finder.

bureau → service bureau.

burnout *(rep.)* The masking of copy being exposed in a reproduction process, to make space for new insertions.

bus A series of wires or paths along which information is shared within a computer or between one device and another. → Apple Desktop Bus, NuBus, SE Bus.

button (1) In dialog boxes, any control you can click which allows you to designate, confirm, or cancel an action. A default button is one which is activated by the "return" or "enter" key on your keyboard and is generally identified in dialog boxes by a heavy border. (**2**) The mouse button on top of your mouse which you use for clicking.

by Date (View menu) The command which lets you view the contents of a directory window according to the date on which it was created, with the most recent heading the list.

by Icon (View menu) The command which lets you view the contents of a directory window with full-size icons.

by Kind (View menu) The command which lets you view the contents of a directory window according to whether it is a document, folder, or application.

by Label (View menu) The command which lets you view the contents of a directory window according to an assigned name and/or color which can be changed in the Labels control panel.

by Name (View menu) The command which lets you view the contents of a directory window according to document names, alphabetically. If you want a specific document to head the list, just add a space before its name.

by Small Icon (View menu) The command which lets you view the contents of a directory window with icons of smaller sizes than normal.

byte A unit of information made up of eight bits (0s and 1s), which can represent any value between 0 and 255 (256 is the total number of possible configurations of eight 0s and 1s). One byte is required to make up a single text character. *16, 17*

C

© The mark agreed by the Universal Copyright Convention to signify, when accompanied by the date of publication and copyright owner's name, that an item is protected by international copyright laws. → copyright; Universal Copyright Convention.

c *abb:* → cyan.

C/C++ Programming language commonly used, like Pascal, for compiling Mac applications.

CAD *abb:* computer-aided design. A term describing any design that is carried out with the aid of a computer.

CAD/CAM *abb:* computer-aided design and manufacturing, where computers are used to control, in many cases, the entire production process from design to manufacture. *65*

CADD *abb:* computer-aided drafting and design. → CAD.

callout A piece of explanatory text, separated from the main body and linked, usually by a leader line, to an illustration.

CAM *abb:* computer-aided manufacture. Usually used in the context of CAD/CAM and rarely seen as an abbreviation on its own. → CAD/CAM.

cameo A term for typefaces in which the characters are reversed to show white on a dark ground.

camera-ready art(work) Copy or any material that is ready for photographic reproduction. Also called "mechanicals." → paste-up.

camera-ready paste-up → paste-up.

cancel/abort A button, present in most dialog boxes, giving you the option to cancel the command which generated the box.

Canvas *(app.) 61*

cap, capital The term for an upper-case letter, deriving from the style of inscription at the head, or capital, of a Roman column.

cap height The height of a capital letter measured from its baseline.

Caplin, Steve Case study. *113*

cap line An imaginary horizontal line running across the tops of capital letters.

caps and smalls *(typ.)* Type consisting of capitals for initials and small caps in place of lower-case letters.

caps lock A modifier key that allows all letters (and only letters – numbers, punctuation marks, and symbols are not affected) to be typed to appear as capitals.

caption Strictly speaking, the descriptive matter printed as a headline above an illustration, also called a "cutline," but more generally

used to refer to information printed underneath or beside a picture.

card → board.

caret, caret mark Symbol used in preparing copy and proof correction to indicate an insertion.

carry forward/over → jump; take over.

cartridge, removable hard disk Hard disks that come in cartridge form to make them ejectable from their media, thus making it easier to transport larger amounts of data than a floppy disk will permit. *36*

case (**1** *fin.*) The stiff cover of a book, consisting of two boards, a hollow, and a binding material. (**2** *typ.*) A box with separate compartments in which pieces of type are kept. This is the origin of the terms "upper-case" and "lower-case," referring to the areas of each case reserved for capital and small letters.

cast Term used in multimedia to describe all the elements used in a presentation, such as graphics, sounds, movies, buttons, scripts, etc.

casting off → copyfitting (1).

catchline The temporary heading for identification at the top of a galley proof.

cathode ray tube (CRT) Vacuum tube producing information display electrostatically, the standard video display device. *31*

CCD *abb:* charge-coupled device, a means of translating light into data in a scanner or non-tube video system → scanner. *42*

CCITT *abb:* Consultative Committee on International Telephony and Telegraphy, a data compression standard.

CD *abb:* compact disk → optical disk.

CD-I (*abb:* compact disk - interactive) A multimedia standard allowing you to store sound and video on the same CD.

CD-R *abb:* CD-ROM disk which can be written by a CD writer → WORM.

CD-ROM *abb:* compact disk read-only memory. Non-erasable storage systems of large capacity – around 650MB, which is enough space for a type foundry's entire font library. CD-ROMs are similar to audio CDs, but come in cartridges. *37–9, 98*

CD-ROM-XA (extended architecture) A CD-ROM which runs the CD at high speed, thus enabling the use of real-time video sequences. A CD-ROM-XA drive will read both CD-ROM and CD-I disks.

cdev *abs:* → control panel device.

central processing unit (CPU) Generally used to mean the central computer, built around a CPU chip (itself sometimes referred to as the CPU), that performs the computer's calculating functions and to which other devices are connected. *24, 26, 27, 29*

center-aligned → centered.

centered Description of type which is placed in the center of a sheet or type measure, with both the left and right edges of text being ragged.

CGI *abs:* (**1**) computer-generated image. (**2**) Common Gateway Interface.

chalking *(pri.)* A printing fault caused by ink soaking into the paper and leaving pigment deposited on the surface.

chancery italic A 13th-century style of handwriting on which italic type designs were based.

character An individual letter, figure, punctuation mark, or sign, including, on your Mac, such invisible characters as "space," "return," and "tab."

character assembly *(typ.)* An alternative term for typesetting, especially in reproduction methods not using metal type.

character attribute The complete specification of a character, including font, size, color, style, scale, kern, etc.

character generator A system of hardware or software that provides codes for a computer font.

character set The complete repertoire of letters, figures, and other symbols in a font.

character space The distance between characters, based on the values allo-

cated by the font designer. → kerning; letterspace/fit; tracking.

character width → data bits.

charge-coupled device → CCD.

chase Metal frame for holding individual lines of type. *87*

chat Internet system for near real-time dialogue by typing.

checkbox A square box in dialog boxes that, when clicked on, shows an x , indicating that an option is allowed. When the box is empty, the option is disabled.

Chicago The bitmapped font specially designed for the Mac which appears in dialog boxes and menus. Like Geneva, it is built into your Mac's ROM, so you can't delete it.

chip A small piece of silicon impregnated with miniaturized computer circuits. Chips comprise the basis of computer functions in the form of CPUs or memory chips.

chip family An evolving series of related chips, usually produced by the same manufacturer.

choke A method of altering the thickness of a letter or solid shape by overexposure in processing or by means of a built-in option in some Mac applications.

choose To select a menu entry by clicking on its menu title and dragging the pointer to the desired entry before releasing the mouse button.

Chooser A desk accessory (● menu) supplied by Apple that lets you choose between printers or other network devices by displaying icons of their drivers. The Chooser also allows you to turn background printing on or off.

Chooser documents Files in your system folder that represent devices found as icons in the Chooser. These are known as device resource files.

chroma The intensity or purity of a color.

Cibachrome *(pho.)* An Agfa process for obtaining photographic color prints direct from transparencies.

cicero A unit of the European Didot system of measurement for measuring the width, or measure, of a line of type and the depth of the page. One cicero = 4.511mm (³⁄₁₆in.) or 12 didot points. → pica. *85*

Cinepak A QuickTime compression setting suitable for detailed image sequences which will be played back from CD-ROM disks, with better quality and speeds than the Video codec. → QuickTime.

circuit board → board.

circular screen (rep.) A photomechanical screen that can be adjusted to prevent moiré patterns in color reproduction.

circumflex → accent.

CIX *abs:* Commercial Internet Exchange, an alliance of Internet Service Providers.

Clarisworks *(app.) 74*

clean proof *(typ./pri.)* A typesetter's or printer's proof which is free from correction marks.

Clean Up (Special menu) Available only if you have selected view By Small Icon or By Icon (View menu), this command pigeonholes icons to the nearest available space on your (invisible) desktop grid.

Clear (Edit menu) A command that removes selected items without copying them to the clipboard, thus leaving the contents of the clipboard intact.

Clear key A key on Apple keyboards that duplicates the function of the Delete key, although, in certain applications, such as some spreadsheets, it may have a specific purpose. → Delete key.

CLI *abs:* → command line interface.

click, clicking (on/off) To press and immediately release the mouse button when the pointer is appropriately positioned, for instance, to select an icon. To "click and drag" is to position the pointer as desired and then click and hold down the mouse button while moving the pointer; for instance, to move an item.

client-server A network system in which data is

accessed by "clients" from a central computer, or "server," rather than peer-to-peer in which there is no central server.

clip art Libraries of copyright-free illustrative or design material, of widely varying quality, available either in book form or in various file formats on computer disk.

Clipboard The file used by the Scrap Manager and applications for holding the last item that you cut or copied. Such items can subsequently be pasted into an appropriate place or document. Each process of cutting or copying deletes the previous item from the Clipboard. → Show Clipboard.

clipping Limiting a drawing to within the boundary of a particular area.

clipping path In some drawing applications, a closed path into which an element can be pasted as a fill.

clock speed/rate The number of instructions per second, regulated by the pulses of a quartz crystal, that can be processed by your Mac's central processing unit. The pulse frequency is measured in megahertz (millions of cycles per second) – the more megahertz, the faster the clock speed. Clock speed determines such things as the speed of screen redraw and RAM or disk access.

clone CPU made by another manufacturer under license from Apple and using the Mac OS. → OS.

Close (File menu) A command that closes the active window. If it is a document window, you may be asked whether you want to save any changes. The Close command performs the identical function to the close box.

close box The small box at the top left, in the title bar, of a directory or document window which, when clicked, closes the active window. Also called go-away box. Holding down the Option key while clicking the box closes all windows on the desktop.

close up An instruction to delete a space to bring char-

acters closer together.

closed file A file to which you cannot gain access and which thus cannot be read from or written to.

cloverleaf/pretzel/propeller symbol The symbol used to identify the command key.

club line A short line ending a paragraph, which should not appear at the top of a page or column. → orphan; widow.

CLUT abb: color lookup table. A set of 256 colors which tells the system which colors will be displayed at any one time on an 8-bit monitor.

CMC7 A character set used in magnetic ink character recognition.

CMY abb: cyan, magenta, and yellow. Color model based on the subtractive color theory that is used, in some applications, to produce spot colors which have been mixed from these colors.

CMYK Acronym for the process colors of cyan, magenta, yellow, and black inks used in four-color printing.

Coated paper (pap.) A general term for art, chromo, and enamel papers or similar groups, in which the surface has a mineral coating applied after the body paper is made. It is also known as surface paper.

cocked-up initial → raised cap(ital).

cock-up figure/letter → superior figure/letter.

code The instructions in a program, written by a programmer, that make the program work. The efficacy of a program depends upon how well written its code is.

codec Encoder/Decoder. Generic term for file compression and expansion formats.

codet → color control bar.

cold boot Turning on or restarting your Mac with the power switch. A warm boot is preferable. → warm boot.

collate (fin.) To put the sections or pages of a book or loose-leaf publication in their correct order.

color (typ.) The apparent light or heavy appearance of a particular typeface.

color bar → color control bar.

color break (pri.) The edge between two areas of color in an image.

color control bar/codet (rep./pri.) The standard set of marginal strips placed on each of the four pieces of film used in making the plates for color printing. When printed, they superimpose to form a colored bar in various densities which enables the platemaker and printer to check by eye or instrument the nature of each ink film, the strength and evenness of ink, and the registration of colors.

color correction The adjustment of the color values of an illustration either (**1** pho.) by the original photographer using color balancing filters, or (**2** rep.) by adjusting the color scanner to produce the correct result. Subsequently, corrections can be made on the color-separated films or on a computer by means of an image-manipulation application. 134–5

color filters Thin sheets of colored glass, plastic, or gelatin (**1** pho.) placed over a camera lens to modify the light entering the camera, or (**2** rep.) used in color separation, color correction, or for special effects.

color gamut The range of colors that can be displayed or printed. The human eye can view a greater spectrum than any method of color reproduction.

Color-It! (app.) 65

color library (app.) A text-only document containing predefined colors that can be imported into some graphics applications.

color model In graphics applications, the manner in which colors can be defined or modified. The most common color models are RGB (red, green, and blue); HSB (hue, saturation, and brightness); or HLS (hue, lightness, and saturation); CMY; CMYK (process colors); and PANTONE (spot colors).

color monitors 32–6

color palette (**1**) In graphics applications, the menu (usually tear-off) that contains the colors available for use within that application. (**2**) → file

color picker (**1**) The Control Panel device that allows you, if you have a color monitor, to select colors for your display from a color "wheel." (**2**) A sample book of carefully defined and graded colors from which you can select spot colors and which a printer can use to achieve fidelity.

color positives *(rep.)* A set of positive color separations.

color printers *41*

color rotation/sequence *(pri.)* The order in which the four-color process inks are printed.

color scanner → scanner

color separation *(rep.)* In color reproduction, the process of separating the colors of an image, by means of a scanner or process camera, into a form suitable for printing. *127*

color seps/separations *(rep.)* A collection of images (subjects) that have been, or will be, separated in the color separation process.

color sequence → color rotation.

color swatch A sample of color, usually selected from a color picker, and used as a guide for the reproduction of spot colors.

color temperature *(pho.)* The term describing the color composition of a light source in photography — measured in degrees Kelvin, a system based on a supposed absolute darkness rising to incandescence.

color transparency/ tranny/slide *(pho.)* A photographic image produced on transparent film as a color positive. **color trapping** → trapping.

color value The tonal value of a color, as distinct from a light-to-dark scale of pure grays.

color wheel → color picker.

column (**1**) A section of a vertically divided page, containing text or other matter. (**2**) A vertical section in tabulated work.

column grid → grid.

column inch/centimeter A measure of space used to define text areas or advertising matter in a newspaper or

periodical.

column rule A light-faced rule used to separate columns in a newspaper.

combination line and halftone *(rep.)* Halftone and line work combined onto one set of films, plates, or artwork.

command key A keyboard modifier key which, when used in conjunction with another key, provides a shortcut to menu commands or, in some applications, a method of canceling an operation in progress, such as printing. The command key is identified by a "propeller" symbol or, on Apple keyboards, the Apple logo, or both. → command.

command line interface A user interface in which instructions are given by means of a line of (usually) keyboard commands. The opposite of GUI.

commercial color The term describing color separations produced by desktop scanners as distinct from high-resolution reproduction scanners.

comp (**1**) *abb:* → compositor (**2**) *abb:* comprehensive, a mock-up showing how a finished design or publication will look.

compact disk → optical disk

compatibility, *in modems 47*

compiler Software used in programming that converts high-level program code into machine language. A compiler converts a program in its entirety, as distinct from an interpreter which converts a program a piece at a time.

Component Video A QuickTime compression setting which generates a 2:1 compression ratio and is suitable for archival storage of movies. Limited to 16-bit color depth. → QuickTime.

compose *(typ.)* To set type by any method.

composite artwork Artwork that combines a number of different elements.

composition size *(typ.)* Term used to describe any type up to a size of 14 points, these being the sizes

that, traditionally (in hot metal), could be set on a compositing machine.

compositor *(typ.)* The person who sets type, originally by hand, but now by any method.

comprehensive → comp. (**2**)

compression The technique of storing data, such as applications, images, and movie sequences, so that they occupy less space on disk. Compression methods may be either "lossless," where no data is lost thus achieving maximum quality, or "lossy" in which high compression ratios are achieved, usually at the expense of quality. → QuickTime; JPEG; LZW; codec.

compression, *of files 75*

Compuserve Major US online Internet service provider.

computer A device or machine capable of processing information, expressed in logical terms, according to a predetermined set of instructions.

computer, *choice 105-9*

computer aided design → CAD.

computer aided design and manufacture → CAD/CAM.

computer input device → input device.

computer languages Coding systems developed to deal with specific types of communication with computers.

computer output device → output device.

condensed type A typeface with an elongated, narrow appearance.; a condensed font that will have been specifically designed so that the anomalies of optical condensing (→ horizontal scaling) are eliminated.

configuration, → set-up

connectivity *30-1*

constrain In some applications, the facility to contain one or more items within another item; e.g., a text or picture box within another text or picture box.

constrained item An item that is contained within another.

constraining box An item that has others constrained

within it.

contact screen *(rep.)* A halftone screen made on a film base which has a graded dot pattern. In conventional reproduction, it is used in direct contact with a film or plate to obtain a halftone negative from a continuous tone original.
→ halftone screen.

contiguous Adjoining, next in order. Thus, of memory and storage, contiguous space is that which is not broken up into chunks of data such as programs and files. → fragmented.

continuous tone, contone *(rep.)* An original illustration which contains continuous shades between the lightest and darkest tones without being broken up by the dots of a halftone screen or reduced to a single shade as in a line illustration.

control character A character produced by use of the control key and another character to issue a command. → keyboard equivalent.

control key The key on Apple ADB keyboards that is used by some applications as a modifier key to provide keyboard equivalents.

controlling dimension The width or height of an image taken as the basis for its enlargement or reduction.

Control Panels A folder located in the system folder (and represented in the Apple menu) where you can access programs that allow you to set up your Mac in the way that you want it (speaker volume, mouse tracking, etc.) and to access other, third-party control panel devices.

control panel device (cdev) A utility program which, when dragged to your system folder, is repositioned in the Control Panels folder, which can be accessed via the Apple menu.

control point In some drawing and graphics applications, a point in a line or path by which you can control its shape or characteristics. → Bézier curves; handles.

controls The term describing buttons, checkboxes,

scroll bars, etc., that appear in windows, dialog boxes, and palettes.

coprocessor A microprocessor chip that assists the central processing unit with data-intensive or specific activities, such as large databases or graphics tasks. Also called a floating-point unit (FPU). *27*

copy (**1**) Manuscript, typescript, transparency, artwork, or computer disk from which a printed image is to be prepared. (**2**) To make an exact duplicate of a file or document or of anything within it. Your Mac automatically places the copied item in the Clipboard, from where it can be pasted in the same or any other place. Copy is accessed via the Edit menu or Command-C. → cut and paste.

copyfitting (**1**) Calculating the amount of space typeset copy will fill when set in a specific font, size, and measure. (**2**) Forcing typeset copy to fit within a given area by modifying it; i.e., cutting or adding words, increasing or decreasing character space, horizontal scaling, etc.

copy-protected Description of software that has been produced in such a way as to prevent its unauthorized duplication or use.

copyright The right of the creator of an original work to control the use of that work. While broadly controlled by international agreement (→ Universal Copyright Convention), there are substantial differences between countries, particularly regarding the period for which a work is protected by copyright. In the U.S. copyright of an intellectual property is generally established by registration, whereas in the U.K. it exists automatically by virtue of the creation of an original work. Ownership of copyright does not necessarily mean ownership of the work itself (or vice versa); nor does it necessarily cover rights to that work throughout the world (the rights to a work can be held territory by territory). *54*

copywriting A term applied to the writing of copy specifically for use in advertising

and promotional material.

CorelDraw *(app.)* 61–4

corner marks Marks on original artwork, film, or a printed sheet acting as cut/trim/crop marks during finishing or register marks during printing.

corner radius The roundness of the corners of a round-cornered rectangle expressed in the currently defined unit of measurement.

corporate identity/house style The elements of design by which any organization establishes an appropriate, consistent, and recognizable identity through communication, promotion, and distribution material.
→ letterhead; logotype.

correcting text *118*

counter The enclosed or partially enclosed area of a type character; e.g., the center of an "o" or the space between the vertical strokes of an "n."

cover *(fin.)* The outer layer of paper, board, cloth, or leather to which the body of a book is secured by any binding method.

cpi *abb:* characters per inch. In copyfitting, the number of type characters per inch.

cpl *abb:* characters per line. In copyfitting, the number of type characters per line.

CPS *abb:* characters per second, referring to the output speed of a computer printer or imagesetter.

CPU *abb:* → central processing unit.

CPU chip A silicon microprocessor that is the brain of your computer. It determines the speed of your computer and what software can be run, as well as performing the main information processing tasks.

crash (**1**) → bomb. (**2**) A more-or-less serious breakdown of an electronic system caused by the failure of a component or by a reading head damaging the surface of a disk.

Creator A field in a file containing a four-letter code (signature) that identifies the application that created the file. Creator signatures are registered with Apple Computer so that each is unique.

credit/courtesy line A line of text accompanying an illustration giving the name of an individual or organization which supplied it.

crop To trim or mask an illustration so that it fits a given area or to discard unwanted portions.

crop marks → corner marks.

crossbar/crosshair pointer In some applications, a cross-shaped cursor (+) that, when you click on an appropriate tool, indicates that a certain drawing or selection function is activated. → pointer.

cross-head(ing) Subsection, paragraph heading, or numeral printed in the body of text, usually marking the first subdivision of a chapter.

crossline screen → halftone screen.

cross-section View of an object showing it "cut through" to expose its internal characteristics.

CRT → cathode ray tube.

c/t *abb:* → color transparency.

current startup disk The disk containing the system folder that your Mac is currently using. The icon for the startup disk always appears in the top right-hand corner of the Finder.

cursor → pointer.

Cut (Edit menu, Command-X) The command that removes a selected item from a document and places it on the Clipboard. → Clipboard.

cut and paste The action of removing an item from a document and then, via the Clipboard, pasting it elsewhere in the same, or another, document.

cut dummy *(rep.)* Cut proofs of illustrations used in sequence as a guide to the make up of pages.

cut-line → caption.

cut-marks → corner marks.

cutout (**1** *rep.*) An illustration from which the background has been removed to provide a silhouetted image. (**2** *fin.*) A display card or book cover from which a pattern has been cut by means of a steel die.

cyan (C) The special shade of blue that is one of the four process colors used in four-color printing, sometimes called process blue.

CyberDog Apple's own Web browser, newsreader, and E-mail handler.

cylinder The total number of disk tracks that can be accessed from a single position of the drive's read/write heads. A cylinder is two tracks of a double-sided floppy disk, and four or more tracks of a hard disk. → platter.

D

DA *abb:* → desk accessory.

daisy-chain (network)/daisy-chaining The linking, in sequence, of several peripheral devices to your Mac. Depending on the type of device, daisy-chains may be made to your Mac's ADB or SCSI ports.

dash A punctuation mark usually known as an em dash/rule (—) or en dash/rule (–), as distinct from a hyphen (-). → em; en; hyphen.

data Any information, but in computing usually used to mean information processed by a program.

data bank Any place or computer where large amounts of data are stored for ready access.

database Virtually any information stored on a computer in a systematic fashion and thus retrievable.

data bits Communications bits that contain data, as distinct from the bits that contain instructions. Sometimes called character width. → bit.

data bus The path along which data is transmitted. The wider the bus, measured in bits, the more data that can be transmitted simultaneously.

data compression → file compression.

data file → document.

data fork The part of a Macintosh file that comprises data; that is, the digitized code for the text and graphics generated by you, as distinct from the resource fork, which contains information relating to an application.

data interchange format → DIF.

data transfer rate The

speed at which data is transferred from a disk drive into RAM after it has been read.

Date setting → Alarm Clock.

datum The singular of data, although data is now commonly accepted as a singular noun in computer usage.

daughter board Sometimes used to describe a circuit board that connects to a motherboard. → board.

Day-to-Day Contacts *(app.)* 74

DCA *abb:* document content architecture, a file format for transferring partially formatted text documents.

DCS *abb:* desktop color separation. → color separation; commercial color.

deadline The final date set for the completion of a job.

dead matter Any leftover matter that is not used in camera-ready art or page makeup.

debug To hunt out and correct errors in software programs. → bug.

decimal tab In word-processing and page make-up applications, the facility to align decimal numbers along their decimal points.

decryption The process of removing the protection afforded to a document by encryption. The same software must be used to decrypt a document as was used to encrypt it. → encryption.

dedicated A system or equipment with a unique function that can be used only for that purpose and is not otherwise adaptable, such as a dedicated word processor.

deep-etch halftone *(rep.)* A halftone image from which unwanted screen dots have been removed, so that areas of plain paper will be left on the printed sheet.

deep-etching *(pri.)* The etching of long-run lithographic printing plates to reduce the printing areas of the plate to slightly below the surface.

default The settings of a program in the absence of user-specified settings; in other words, the settings it came with until you change them, e.g., the settings in the Control Panel. → preferences; preset defaults.

default button → button.

default settings → default.

defragment The process of eliminating small blocks of space on a hard disk by rearranging files that have become fragmented, so that they are stored contiguously. → fragmented.

Delete key The key that, in text, moves the insertion pointer back one character, deleting it in the process, or removes a current selection. Items deleted by the Delete key are not placed on the Clipboard. On some Mac keyboards the Delete key is called the Backspace key.

delimit To indicate the end (limit) of a line or to separate one field or record from another by using a specially defined character. The standard characters for some Mac databases are the Tab key to delimit fields and the Return key to delimit records.

densitometer An electronic precision instrument used to measure density and other properties of color and light in transparencies, film, reflection copy, or computer monitors.

density (1) The amount and compactness of type set within a given area or page. (**2** *pho./rep./pri.*) The weight of tone or color in any image. A printed highlight can be no lighter in color than the surface it is printed on, while the shadow can be no darker than the quality and volume of ink the printing process will permit.

descender The part of a lower-case letter that falls below the baseline of the x-height as in g, q, and p.

deselect To deactivate highlighted text or an active item, usually by clicking your mouse. → activate.

designers, *as typesetters* 124–5

design process 108, 114–23

desk accessory (DA) A utility program for system enhancement generally found under the Apple menu, i.e. Alarm Clock, Scrapbook, etc. For use with System 7, the desk accessory application must be removed from its suitcase and dragged to

the Apple Menu Items folder in the System Folder (if you want it to appear under the Apple menu). → suitcase.

desktop The name given to the environment in which you work on screen. *16, 20*

Desktop file The invisible file created by the Finder to record information about the files and folders on your disk. Each disk you use has its own Desktop file.

desktop publishing (DTP) A term coined at the advent of the Macintosh, before the potential of the machine in the professional design and reproduction industries was fully realized. Used to describe the activity of generating text, page layout, and graphics on a computer and then printing, or publishing, the result.

device Short form referring to any peripheral device.

device resource file → Chooser documents.

diacritical mark A mark indicating the particular value or pronunciation of a character. → accent.

dialog box A box that appears on your screen, usually in response to a command from you, requesting information or approval in order to execute an action. Unprompted dialog boxes (often requiring no more from you than to click "OK") are more often called "message" or "alert" boxes. Boxes in which you open or save documents are called Standard File dialog boxes.

dial up To use a modem to contact another computer.

diapositive *(pho.)* A photographic transparency in which the image is positive.

diazo(type) *(rep.) abb:* diazonium. A method of printing from a transparent or translucent original onto paper, cloth, or film. The print may be blue (called blues/blueprints), brown (browns/Vandykes), or black. Also known as Ozalids and dyelines, diazos are widely used in preprint stages for checking imposed film as well as by architectural and engineering draftsmen.

dictionary The file, in word-processing applications, that lets you check words and documents for spelling.

didot point The European unit for type measurement, being 0.38mm (0.0148in) compared to 0.35mm (0.013837in) of the Anglo-American point.

DIF *abb:* data interchange format, a file format for transferring (without text formating) database and spreadsheet data. *128*

differential spacing The spacing of each character of type according to its individual width.

digit Any numeral (0 to 9).

digital typesetting *90*

digitize To convert anything, such as an image or a sound, into a form that can be electronically processed, stored, and reconstructed.

digitizer A peripheral device such as a tablet or camera that digitizes signals so that your computer can understand them.

digitizing fonts *98*

digitizing/graphics pad/ tablet An input device that allows you to draw or write using a pen-like instrument as if you are working on paper. *49, 65*

DIMM *abb:* dual in-line memory module. Standard form of RAM chip. *28, 29*

dimmed command In menus and dialog boxes, if a command is gray, rather than black, it is said to be dimmed and unavailable for use, or disabled.

dimmed icon A dimmed icon indicates that a file or folder is open or that a disk has been ejected.

DIN *abb:* Deutsche Industrie-Norm. The code of standards established in Germany and widely used throughout the world to standardize such things as the size, weight, or speed-rating of certain materials and manufactured items that depend on universal compatibility.

DIN-8 The 8-pin modem and printer port connection on your Mac.

dingbat A decorative font, the modern form of decorations traditionally called printer's flowers, ornaments, and arabesques.

DIP *abb:* dual in-line package. The way in which some chips, such as memory chips, are mounted so that they can be plugged into your Mac.

DIP SIMM A high-profile SIMM.

DIP switch Small toggle switch, usually on peripheral devices, used in combination to set ID numbers → SCSI ID number.

Direct Slot *(obs.)* The expansion slot of the Mac SE/30, incompatible with any other Mac slot. → expansion slot. *31*

directional The term used to describe a word such as "left," "right," "above," and "below," used in a caption to direct the reader to a relevant picture or item.

directory An invisible catalog of information about all the files on a disk. The volume directory contains general information, whereas the file directory logs specific information such as where the files are stored on the disk.

directory dialog box → Standard File dialog box.

directory window The window that displays the contents of a disk or folder.

disabled The condition of an item in a menu or dialog box that is not available for selection, thus it appears dimmed. → dimmed command; dimmed icon.

discretionary hyphen character In some applications, a manually inserted character that indicates a word break.

Disinfectant *(util.)* 75

disk/disc A circular platter coated with a magnetic medium (unless it is an optical disk) on which computer data is stored. Disks may be rigid (hard) or flexible (floppy) and may be permanently installed in your computer, in a peripheral device, or in removable cases. Floppy disks for the Mac are typically 3½in. diameter high density (1.4MB). Floppy disks are also called diskettes. Hard disks also come in a variety of removable cartridges with around 40Mb–2Gb capacity. *36–9*

disk buffer An area in RAM, similar to a RAM cache, where frequently used information from a disk can be stored temporarily → RAM cache.

disk controller Hardware that converts signals from a bus into instructions usable by a disk drive.

disk directory → directory.

DiskDoubler *(util.)* 75, 131

disk drive The hardware that reads data to and from disks. → disk; floppy disk drive; hard disk drive.

disk drive head → read/write head.

disk drive port A port, on some Macs, used to attach external floppy disk drives.

Disk Driver The disk controller for 3½in. (90mm) floppy disks.

diskette → disk.

disk fragmentation *138*

disk icon An icon that indicates the presence of a disk on your Mac. The startup disk icon is always positioned in the top right-hand corner of your screen and subsequent disk icons appear vertically beneath that, in the order in which they mount. → icon.

disk optimizers 75

disk recovery 75

disk window → root directory.

display → monitor.

display matter/type Larger typefaces used for headings, etc., as distinct from the smaller types used for text and captions.

dithering A technique used by some input and output devices to simulate grays by varying the pattern and proximity of black pixels to each other.

ditto mark A symbol (") indicating repetition of the text matter directly above.

DNS *abb:* Domain Name System. Hierarchy for organizing Internet addresses. Names are changed to number sequences for use by servers.

dock To connect one stand-alone computer to another, such as connecting a laptop to your Mac.

document Any file that you create or modify with an application on your Mac, such as a page layout or simply a letter. The document file is created on your disk when you enter text or draw a line and then save it (when you save a document for the first time, a dialog box will appear, asking you to name the document and indicate where you want to put it). *22*

document content architecture → DCA.

document window The window that an application opens to display a document created, or about to be created, with that application.

domain → DNS.

DOS *abb:* disk operating systems. → MS-DOS.

dot (**1** *rep.*) The smallest basic element of a halftone. (**2**) Alternative term for a pixel.

dot area *(rep.)* The pattern of a halftone; that is, both the dots and the spaces in between.

dot etching *(rep.)* The process of reducing the size of halftone dots on negative or positive film, using chemicals, in order to modify the tonal values of a halftone image.

dot for dot (**1** *pri.*) Printing color work in perfect register. (**2** *rep.*) A method of producing printing film by photographing a previously screened halftone image. Generally, on fine-screened images, a maximum limit of 10 percent enlargement or reduction is desirable.

dot gain *(rep./pri.)* An aberration occuring during the reproduction chain from original to printed image, caused by the tendency of halftone dots to grow in size. This often leads to inaccurate results, but if the dot-gain characteristics of a particular printing press are known, compensation can be made during reproduction.

dot loss *(rep./pri.)* The devaluation or disappearance of a halftone dot on a printing plate, the opposite of dot gain.

dot-matrix printer A crude, but usually cheap, printer that uses a grid of pins to create characters, with hammers hitting the correct combination of pins for each letter.

dots per inch (dpi) The unit of measurement that represents the resolution of a device such as a printer, imagesetter, or monitor. The closer the dots are together (the more dots per inch), the better the quality. Typical resolutions are 72dpi for a monitor, 600dpi for a laser printer, and 2450dpi (or much more) for an imagesetter.

dot pitch The distance between the dots, or pixels, on your monitor, measured in dots per inch (dpi).

double burn/print down (rep.) To use two or more negatives to expose an image onto a sensitized plate – often one for line work and a second for halftones.

double-click Clicking of the mouse button twice in rapid succession while the pointer is positioned in an appropriate place. Double-clicking is a short-cut to performing functions such as opening documents or highlighting words in text.

double print down → double burn.

double-sided floppy disk → disk.

double spread/page spread → spread.

double truck → spread.

download To transfer data from a remote computer to your own. Opposite of upload.

downloadable font A font that must be loaded into the RAM of your printer, as distinct from a font that is resident in its ROM.

dpi abb: → dots per inch.

dpsi/dpi² abb: dots per square inch.

drag To carry out an action by holding down the mouse button while you move the pointer, then release the mouse button to complete the action. You use dragging to perform such tasks as selecting and moving items, selecting pull-down menu commands, selecting text, and, in some applications, creating items with an appropriate tool selected,.

DRAM abb: dynamic random access memory (pron. dee-ram) → dynamic RAM.

draw(ing) application/ program Drawing applications can be defined as those which are object-oriented (they mathematically define lines and shapes), as distinct from painting applications which use bitmaps. → object-oriented; bitmapped. 58–64

Drive In appropriate dialog boxes, a button which allows you to select a different volume to the one identified in the dialog box. Sometimes, clicking on the disk on volume name will achieve the same result.

drive → disk drive.

driver An item of software that tells your Mac how to handle or operate a piece of hardware, such as a printer. Drivers are located in your system folder.

drive head → read/write head.

driving out Arranging the spaces in a line of type to fill the measure.

drop (1) A gap, usually at the top of a page or column, before the printed image starts. (2) Of text, the number of lines in a column permitted by the page grid.

drop cap abb: drop capital. A large, sometimes decorative, initial at the beginning of a text or paragraph that drops into the lines of type beneath.

drop folios Numbers printed at the bottom of each page, generally referred to simply as folios.

drop letter → drop cap.

dropout (1 rep.) During reproduction, to use filters or other means to prevent an item from appearing on final negative or positive film. (2) → reverse onto.

dropout blue/color Pencil or other marker, used to write instructions on artwork, which makes a mark that does not reproduce.

dropped initial → drop cap.

dropped-out halftone (rep.) Areas removed from a halftone negative, positive or plate by masking.

dropped-out type Type that is reversed out of its background. → reverse out.

dropping-out The repro house term for the replacement of a low-resolution scan by a high-resolution scan, prior to final output.

drop-shadow An area of tone forming a shadow behind an image or character, designed to bring the image or character forward.

drop tone → line conversion.

DTP abb: → desktop

publishing.

dummy (1) The prototype of a proposed book or publication in the correct format, binding, paper, and bulk, but with blank pages. (2) A mock-up of a design showing the position of headings, text, captions, illustrations, and other details.

duotone (rep.) Technically, two halftones made from the same original to two different tonal ranges, so that when printed – in different tones of the same color – a greater tonal range is produced than is possible with a single color. However, the term is generally used, wrongly, to describe a duplex halftone.

dupe abb: duplicate.

duplex Simultaneous, two-way communication over telecommunication lines. → half duplex.

duplex halftone (rep.) Two halftones made from the same original, but printed in two different colors. Generally called a duotone, although this is technically incorrect. → duotone.

Dvorak keyboard An alternative keyboard layout to the familiar and widely-used QWERTY arrangement found on typewriters and Mac keyboards. Essentially, a Dvorak layout is one where the more frequently typed keys are positioned most comfortably in relationship to your dominant typing fingers

dyeline → diazo.

dynamic RAM (DRAM) Memory that is only active while supplied by an electric current, and is therefore lost when power is turned off. The more expensive static RAM does not lose its memory in the absence of power. DRAM chips for the Mac come largely in the form of DIMMS. → DIMM; RAM; SIMM.

E

Easy Access A system feature to help people who have difficulty typing with both hands, or manipulating the mouse. "Sticky Keys" allows modifier keys to be used without having to press the keys simultaneously, while "Mouse Keys" enables you to manipulate the pointer by using the numeric keyboard instead of the mouse.

edition (pri.) The whole number of copies of a work printed and published at one time, either as the first edition, or after some change has been made (revised edition, second edition, etc).

Edit menu One of the three standard Mac menus, this one contains commands for such actions as Cut, Copy, and Paste.

EDO abb. extended data output. Faster form of RAM device → RAM.

egyptian A collective term for a group of display typefaces with heavy slab serifs and little contrast in the thickness of strokes.

eight-bit The allocation of eight bits of memory to each pixel, giving a screen display of 256 grays or colors (a row of eight bits can be written in 256 different combinations: 0000000, 00000001, 10000001, 00111100, etc). → four-bit color; twenty-four-bit color.

Eject The command found under the File menu when you are in the Finder, or in dialog boxes, that enables you to eject floppy disks or removable hard disk cartridges.

electronic design (ED) Any design activity that takes place with the aid of electronic devices, including computers.

electronic mail → E-mail.

electronic publishing (EP) A term sometimes used as an alternative to desktop publishing.

element In some drawing applications, any object such as a shape, text, or image.

ELF abb. extremely low frequency, referring to the electromagnetic field generated by certain types of electrical current which research has shown to be potentially carcinogenic (cancer-causing), particularly in the event of sustained exposure. Computer monitors emit ELF radiation in greater or lesser quantities, depending on various factors such as the size of the monitor and whether it is mono or color. The sides and back of your

monitor emit greater amounts of radiation than the screen. VLF (very low frequency) radiation is also emitted by monitors, but it is easier to filter and considered to be less harmful than ELF. In any event, you should not sit closer than 28in (800mm) from the front of your monitor. → radiation shield.

ellipse/oval tool In many graphics applications, a tool for drawing ellipses and circles.

ellipsis (**1**) A sequence of three dots (…) indicating that part of a phrase or sentence has been left out. (**2**) The three dots following a menu command indicating that a dialog box will need to be given additional information before the command can be carried out.

elliptical dot screen (rep.) A halftone screen with an elliptical dot, producing more even changes in the mid-tones of a halftone illustration.

em Traditionally, the area (usually a square) taken up by a capital M, but giving rise to a linear measurement equal to the point size of the type being set, so a 6-point em is 6 points wide. A 12-point em is generally called a pica, or pica em, and measures 4.22mm (0.166ins). Half an em is called an en. → pica.

em dash/rule A dash one em wide, the actual width depending on the size of type being set. → em; dash.

em quad (typ.) Alternative term for an em space, being a square of the type size.

em space A space one em wide, the actual width depending on the size of type being set.

E-mail abb: electronic mail. Communication between computers, either locally through a network, or using modems to transmit over telephone lines, usually via a central computer which stores messages until their recipients are ready to receive them.

Empty Trash (Special menu) The command that flushes out the Trash if it has something inside (indicated by a bulging garbage can icon).

emulation The simulation of otherwise incompatible software or hardware in order to make them compatible.

emulsion side (rep.) The matte side of photographic film which holds the emulsion and which is placed in direct contact with the emulsion of another film or a plate when printing down to guarantee a sharp image.

en A measurement equivalent to half the width of an em. → em.

en dash/rule A dash half the width of an em dash.

Energy Saver Control Panel for shutting the Mac down, or sending it to sleep, after a user-determined length of time.

en quad (typ.) A space half the width of an em quad.

en space A space half an em wide, the actual width depending on the size of type being set.

encapsulated PostScript → EPS.

encryption The scrambling of data to protect a file from unauthorized access.

end even (typ.) Instruction to end a paragraph or section of copy with a full line.

end/back matter The final pages of a book, following the main body, such as the index. Also called "postlims."

end-of-line decisions The term used to describe a program's ability to hyphenate words and justify lines of text.

Enter key On the Mac keyboard, the key that duplicates much of the function of the Return key. It confirms an entry or command or may force a carriage return. In some applications, it may have a specific function.

EO abb: erasable optical. An optical disk that can be written to as well as read from. → optical disk. 39

EP abb: → electronic publishing.

EPS(F) abb: encapsulated PostScript (file), a standard graphics file format based on vectors (information giving both magnitude and direction). → object-oriented; PostScript. 128

erase An option in some dialog boxes to erase the

selected volume.

Erase Disk (Special menu) The command to reinitialize or reformat the selected disk on the desktop.

error message A message box that automatically appears when, at its mildest, you have attempted a task that an application won't permit or cannot do, or, at worst, your computer bombs. → bomb.

error/result code The number that often accompanies alert and bomb dialog boxes and sad Mac icons to indicate the nature of the problem.

Esc key *abb:* Escape key. Like the Control key, the function of Esc depends on the application you are using, or you can use it as a modifier key.

E-text Any form of text-only file on the Internet.

Ethernet A local area network hardware standard that offers fast data transfer. *31*

even smalls Small capitals used without an initial full capital at the beginning of a word.

even working *(pri.)* A printed work divided into a number of sections of equal size, such as 16, 32, 48 pages.

event The term used to describe any occurrence that the system or an application may need to respond to, such as a mouse click or a disk insertion.

event-driven Description of a program in which actions are based on events generated interactively by the user.

event manager The part of the System (Operating System Event Manager) or Toolbox (Toolbox System Event Manager) that handles hardware-related events such as mouse clicks.

exception dictionary A list of user-defined word breaks that are exceptions to the standard breaks contained within an application's hyphenation dictionary.

exotic A traditional term for a typeface with characters of a language not based on Roman letterforms, e.g., Hebrew.

expanded/extended type A typeface with a flattened,

stretched-out appearance. An expanded font will have been specifically designed so that the anomalies of optical expansion (→ horizontal scaling) are eliminated.

expansion card/board A circuit board, attached via your computer's expansion slot, which allows you to expand the capabilities of your computer (e.g. an accelerator).

expansion slot The place in your computer where you can add an expansion card. *31* → PCI

expenditure *26, 109*

expert system → artificial intelligence.

export The facility provided by some applications to save a file in an appropriate format for use by another application: a text file may be saved as an ASCII file or an illustration as an EPS file.

extension → system extension.

Extensions Manager A Control Panel that lets you manage other control panels and extensions to cut down the likelihood of system conflicts..

external command/external function (XCMD/XFCN) Extensions to the scripting language of authoring applications, enabling the program to perform specialized commands or functions. *75*

external device → peripheral device.

external disk drive Any disk drive that is not internal – inside your Mac – is said to be external.

extremely low frequency → ELF.

F

face Traditionally, the printing surface of any type character. It now means a group or family to which any particular type design belongs, as in typeface.

face/fade out blue → drop-out blue.

facsimile → fax.

fadeback → ghosting (1).

false double → spread.

family A group of type fonts with a common design, distinguished from each other only by weight – light, roman, bold, etc. – and their corresponding italic styles.

FAQ *abb:* Frequently Asked Question. Answered by ready-made replies in software manuals and on Web sites.

FatBits *(obs)* A magnification of the screen image that lets you edit bitmapped graphics pixel by pixel.

fat face A typeface with extreme contrast in the widths of thin and thick strokes.

fat matter A term for copy with a large proportion of spacing. Dense copy is known as lean matter.

fatty *(rep.)* In conventional reproduction, the name given to the piece of film placed between the negative (or positive) film and a plate in order to create traps – the slight spread of two adjacent colors to achieve perfect registration. → choke; lap; trapping.

fax *abb:* facsimile transmission. The electronic transmission of copy and artwork from one location to another, using telephone lines. Fax cards (→ board) are available to fit into an expansion slot in your Mac to allow you to send and receive faxes direct, without the need for a separate fax machine.

FDHD *abb:* floppy drive high density → floppy disk drive.

feet/foot margin The white area at the bottom of a page between the image and trimmed area.

field In some applications (mainly databases), a self-contained area into which data is entered and which is generally interactive with another field in the same (or another) record, or the same field in another record.

figure (1) A number, as opposed to a letter. (2) An illustration.

figure number The reference number given to an illustration.

file A collection of data to which a name has been given and which is stored on a disk. *19, 22*

file compression The condensing of data within a file so that it is smaller, thus occupying less space on a disk and being quicker to transmit over telecommunication lines. *75*

file creator → Creator.
file directory → directory.
file format The way in which a program saves data. In order to help you work on one job that requires the use of several applications, or to work with other people who may be using different applications to yours, file formats tend to be standardized. *128*
file fragmentation → fragmented.
File menu One of the three standard Mac menus (it appears in the menu bar of virtually every application). The File menu is where you give commands to, among other things, create, open, save, print and close files, quit applications, and eject disks.
filename The name given – or that you give – to a file. Macintosh filenames can be up to 31 characters long, although most dialog boxes show fewer than that. *119, 121*
file partition → partition.
file, *problems 140*
file recovery The act of resurrecting a file after you have deleted it. A deleted file remains on a disk (only its name is erased from the directory) and, until the space it occupies is used by your computer for something else, it can sometimes be recovered. Many utilities are available for recovering deleted files.
file server A computer on a network, with special software so that all the network users can access the applications and documents stored on it. Also describes very large capacity systems run by Internet Service Providers to handle clients' E-mail and Internet access.
file sizes *43, 45*
file tag Information relating to data stored within each sector of a disk, designed to enable you to recover deleted files.
file transfer To send a file from one computer to another over telecommunication lines, using a modem.
file type The four-letter code assigned to every Mac file when it is created, to identify its format, i.e., APPL for an application, TEXT for text files, MPNT for

MacPaint, and so on.
fill In most graphics applications, the color, tone, or pattern applied to the inside of a closed path or shape.
fill character In some applications, the user-defined character that is inserted between specified tab stops.
film assembly/stripping *(rep.)* The process of assembling film negatives or positives in correct positions for the preparation of printing plates.
filmsetting → phototypesetting.
film speed *(pho.)* The rating given to photographic film so that an exposure can be calculated.
Filmstrip A commercial file format for displaying high-speed animations from PICT files, suitable for animated "buttons" in multimedia presentations.
filter (1) → import/export filter. **(2)** A feature in many paint and image-editing applications that lets you apply predefined (but sometimes editable) visual effects to an image.
final draft Copy ready for typesetting.
final film *(rep.)* The positive or negative used for platemaking, incorporating all corrections and in which the halftones are made with a hard dot.
Finder The program that provides the desktop, file, and disk management and the ability to launch applications. The Finder is one of the three basic components of the Mac's operating system (the others are the System file and the ROM chips). → desktop; System; system folder. *16, 18, 52*
Finder desktop → desktop.
Finder flags Attributes, such as locked, invisible, busy, etc., for every file on your disk.
Find File An Apple-supplied application to enable you to find any file or folder on the selected disk by entering full or partial file names. Searches can also be made by creation date and other parameters.
fine rule → hairline rule.
fine tuning, *of designs 115–16*

Finger *(app.)* Searches the Internet for subscriber information.
finished artwork → artwork.
finished page area The area on your monitor that will form the page after it is printed and trimmed, or the area on a printed sheet that will form the page after the sheet is trimmed.
→ trimmed page size.
finished rough → mock-up.
finishing *(fin.)* All operations after printing.
firewall System for preventing direct Internet access, and offering protection from virus attack. Part of security system at Internet Service Provider.
firmware The term given to the permanent software contained within your Mac's ROM, which forms an integral part of your computer's hardware.
first generation copy A copy of a photograph or other item made directly from the original, as distinct from a copy made from another copy of the original.
fit (1) → letterspace/letterfit. **(2** *rep.)* The alignment and register of individual areas of color or images within a printed page, as distinct from the register of the colors on an entire printed sheet. Errors of fit occur in film stripping, whereas errors of register occur in printing.
fit in window The facility of some applications to enlarge or reduce a page to the size of the window within which you are working on your monitor.
fixed-size font → bitmapped font.
fixed word spacing A standard space between characters and words, used for unjustified typesetting, as distinct from the variable spacing required for justified setting.
F-key A term (derived from "function keys") used to describe the keyboard equivalents for basic functions like ejecting disks (shift-command-1).
flame, flaming Violent or abusive response on the Internet. → newsgroup.
flash *(rep.)* A second expo-

sure in conventional halftone processing that reinforces the dots in dark areas. These would otherwise run together and print solid.

flat (**1** *pri.*) An assembly of composite imposed film, used in preparing plates for printing. (**2** *rep.*) A halftone of insufficient contrast.

flatbed scanner → scanner.

flat-file database A database program in which each file is self-contained and cannot exchange data with another file, as distinct from a relational database in which files can exchange data.

flatness In object-oriented drawing applications, a term that refers to the number of straight lines, or segments, that make up a curve (which is how PostScript treats curved lines) to be printed on a PostScript printer – the lower the number, the smoother the curve.

flat plan A diagrammatic plan of the pages of a book used to establish the distribution of color, chapter lengths, etc. Also called a flowchart.

flat-tint halftone A halftone printed over a background of flat color.

flicker Image vibration on your monitor, caused by a slow refresh rate. Also called a "strobe" effect.

flip → flop.

floating palette A palette which you can position anywhere on your screen by dragging its title bar. → palette.

floating point unit (FPU) → coprocessor.

flop To reverse an image from left to right (horizontal flop) or top to bottom (vertical flop). Sometimes called flip. → lateral reverse.

floppy disk → disk.

floppy disk drive A hardware device for reading and writing data from and to a 3½in. (90mm) floppy disk. An internal floppy disk drive is standard on every Mac (some Macs have a slot for an optional second drive).

flowchart → flat plan.

flowers → dingbat.

flush → Clear.

flush left, right → ranged left, right.

flush paragraphs Paragraphs in which the first word is not indented, but which aligns with the left edge of the text. → full out.

foil Clear, stable film used as a backing during film assembly.

folder A place on your Mac, represented by an icon of a folder (which it emulates), where you keep your documents and applications. Folders form the basis for the organization of all your data on your Mac. *20–1, 22, 121*

folder bar In Standard File dialog boxes (such as Open and Save), the bar above the scrolling list that, when clicked on, reveals a list of the folder hierarchy. → HFS.

folio (**1**) Technically, the number of a leaf of a book when it is not numbered as two separate pages. However, a folio number is generally said to mean a page number. (**2**) The size of a book that is formed when the sheet containing its pages is folded only once, thus making the pages half the size of the sheet. A folio-size book is generally said to mean a large-format book.

follow copy *(typ.)* Instruction to a typesetter to follow the spelling and punctuation of a manuscript, even if unorthodox, in preference to the house style.

follow on → run on.

FOND *abb:* font family descriptor. The log of a font family (all the sizes and styles of a typeface) kept in a suitcase or in your System file.

FONT → font ID conflict.

font/fount Traditionally, of metal type, a set of type of the same design, style, and size. On the Mac, a font is a set of characters, including letters, numbers, and other typographic symbols, of the same design and style – although some definitions of the term include, wrongly, all styles: light, roman, bold, etc. → outline font; printer font; screen font; TrueType. *73, 84–5, 88–9, 91, 98, 99, 127–9*

font downloading The process by which a printer font file is downloaded, or sent, to your printer. A font may be available in your printer's built-in ROM chips, on its hard disk, manually downloaded into its RAM, or automatically downloaded when it is needed, by the printer driver. To download PostScript fonts automatically, the printer font files must be in your system folder or, if you are using a font management utility such as Suitcase, the printer font files may be kept in the same folder as any open suitcase file. → suitcase.

font effects, *diagram 81*

font family The set of all the characters of a typeface design in all sizes and styles.

font file The file of a screen font, called a suitcase. *91*

font ID conflict An aberration that may occur as the result of an Apple-imposed limit (in the early days of the Mac) of 128 identity numbers (actually 256, but the first 128 were reserved), called (confusingly) FONTs, for all PostScript fonts you may have installed on your Mac. This results in such anomalies as a screen font that you specified in a document being different from the one that prints. The problem was partially solved with the introduction of NFNTs (new font numbering table) which allows for some 16,000 ID numbers. Utilities such as Suitcase and MasterJuggler both resolve ID conflicts. Adobe Systems Inc. maintains a registry of unique font ID numbers and names for PostScript Type 1 fonts. *97, 127*

font ID number → font ID conflict.

font names, *table 99*

Fontographer *(app.) 73, 96*

font organization *88, 97–8*

font/type series The identification of a typeface by a series number, i.e. Univers 55.

font substitution A facility of LaserWriters to substitute outline fonts for the basic system bitmapped fonts: Geneva (for which Helvetica is substituted) and Monaco (Courier).

font usage In some applications, a facility that lists all the fonts used in a document.

foolscap Standard size of printing paper in Europe 13½ x 17in. (343 x 432mm).

foot The margin at the bottom of a page or the bottom edge of a book.

footer (1) In some applications, particularly word processing programs, the facility to place text and numbers automatically at the bottom of printed pages. (**2**) A running headline that appears at the bottom of a page.

footnotes Short explanatory notes, printed at the foot of a page or at the end of a book.

footprint The exact space on a surface occupied by a piece of hardware.

foreground application The application that is currently active and whose menu bar occupies the top of your screen.

foreign file A document created in a different application to the one you are using, and one which you may wish to import.

format (1) The size of a book or page or, in photography, the size of film. (**2** *typ.*) To attribute type characteristics such as font, size, weight, tracking, leading, etc., to a text. (**3**) The arrangement of sectors and empty directories on a disk in preparation for its initialization. (**4**) In some applications, to specify paragraph, and other, attributes such as indents, hyphenation and justification, tabs, etc.

formatting The process of preparing a new disk for use on your Mac. When a disk is formatted, sectors, tracks and empty directories are created, and the disk may be verified (a test of the integrity of the data blocks).

for position only (FPO) An instruction on layouts and artwork that an item is displayed only as a guide for positioning.

forward delete key A key found on extended keyboards which deletes characters to the right of the text insertion point rather than to its left, as with the delete key of standard keyboards.

fount → font.

four-bit color The allocation of four bits of memory to each pixel, giving a screen display of 16 colors (a row of four bits can be written in 16 different combinations: 0000, 0001, 1001, 0110, etc.). → eight-bit color; twenty-four-bit color.

four-color process *(rep./pri.)* The printing process that reproduces full-color images by using three basic colors – cyan, magenta, and yellow plus black for added density.

FPD *abb:* → full-page display.

FPO *abb:* → for position only.

FPU *abb:* floating-point unit → coprocessor.

fractions, *table 96*

fragmented The condition of disk storage space when, in time, tracks get broken into non-contiguous chunks, leaving only small blocks of free space into which new files can be written, thus making it necessary for the new files to be split apart so that they will fit onto the disk. This means that both the disk and the files on it become fragmented. The result can be a dramatic increase of access time. *138*

frame A decorative border. → box rule.

frame-based A term sometimes used to describe applications which require you to create text or picture boxes in a document before text or pictures can be added.

FrameMaker *(app.) 58*

frame rate → refresh rate.

freeform tool In graphics applications, any tool which allows you to draw free shapes.

FreeHand *(app.) 61, 62–3, 94*

freehand tool In graphics applications, the tool that allows you to draw a line as you click and drag the mouse.

free line fall → unjustified.

free space A memory block that is available for allocation.

freeware Any software that is declared to be in the public domain and free of copyright restrictions, as distinct from shareware. *74*

freeze → bomb

front matter The pages of a book preceding the main text, usually consisting of the half title, title, preface, and contents. Also called "prelims."

FTP *abb:* File Transfer Protocol. Established method of transferring electronic files using standard commands. Also used as a verb.

fugitive color *(pri.)* A colored ink that is not stable and may change or fade when exposed to certain conditions of light or atmosphere.

full color Term usually used synonymously with "four color." → four-color process.

full out Description of type set to the full measure, without indents.

full-page display (FPD) Name given to a 12in. (300mm) monitor (measured diagonally). → monitor.

full word wrap The transfer of a whole word to the following line to avoid a word break.

function key A key on an extended keyboard that can be assigned to a specific function. Not to be confused with F-key.

FYI *abb:* "For Your Information."

G

galley proof *(typ.)* A proof of typeset text before it is laid out into a page design. The term derives from the days when metal type was proofed from a long, shallow, metal tray called a galley.

gang up (1 *pri.)* To print two or more jobs on the same sheet, which would then be divided appropriately. (**2** *rep.*) To place a group of originals of the same proportions together for reproduction.

gateway (link), router A hardware/software connection between dissimilar computer networks. → bridge; network. *131*

Gb *abb:* → gigabyte.

General Controls The basic Apple control panel device that lets you modify the desktop settings, such as the time and date, that are stored in your Mac's parameter RAM (PRAM).

generic disk drive A disk drive with a mechanism that is common to many brands.

Geneva A system font that

is a bitmapped version of the typeface Helvetica. Like Chicago, it is built into your Mac's ROM, so you can't delete it.

Get Info (File menu) Invoking this command, having first selected a folder or file, produces a window that gives you information about that folder or file, such as its size, when it was created, and to which disk it belongs. You can also lock or unlock a file (but not a folder), and you can make a file into a template (→ stationery). You can make comments in the box provided, although those comments will be lost if you rebuild the desktop. If the selected file is an application, you will also be able to see which version it is (unless the application is open) and adjust its memory heap.

ghost icon The term for the grayed icon of a disk (or its contents, if it was open) left on the desktop after it has been ejected, as distinct from the grayed icon indicating that a file or folder is open.

ghosting (**1** *rep.*) To decrease the tonal values of the surrounding parts of an image in order to make the main object stand out more clearly. (**2**) In illustration, particularly technical illustration, to depict parts of an image that would not normally be visible, such as parts of an engine covered by its casing.

GIF *abb:* graphic interchange format developed by CompuServe. A file format often used for transferring graphics files between different computer systems via the Internet. *128*

gigabyte (Gb/gig) A unit of measure to describe 1,024 megabytes. → byte; kilobyte; megabyte.

gigo *abb:* garbage in – garbage out. A principle, particularly in computer programming, that poor quality input produces equally poor quality output.

global backup → backup, global/baseline.

glossary (**1**) An alphabetical list giving the definition of terms, usually related to a particular subject. (**2**) In

some word processing applications, the facility to insert frequently used text by means of a keyboard shortcut.

g/m²/gsm/grams per square meter *(pap.)* A unit of measurement indicating the substance of paper on the basis of its weight, regardless of the sheet size.

go away box/region → close box.

golden section A formula for division of a line or area supposed to give harmonious proportions. If a line is divided unequally, the relationship of the smaller section to the larger section should be the same as that of the larger section to the whole. It is in practice a ratio of about 8:13.

Gopher *(app.)* Internet search system.

gothic → black letter.

grabber (**hand**) **tool** In some graphics applications, the tool which lets you either move a picture around inside a box, or move the page around in its window.

gradated fills *59, 61*

gradated tints *130*

gradation/graduation (**1**) The smooth transition from one tone or color to another. (**2**) The range of values between black and white.

graphic (**1**) A typeface originating from drawn rather than scripted letter forms. (**2**) A general term describing any illustration or design.

graphical user interface → GUI.

graphic interchange format → GIF.

Graphics A QuickTime compression setting which is suitable for maintaining good picture quality on 8-bit displays. → QuickTime.

graphics tablet → digitizing pad.

grayed command → dimmed command.

grayed icon → dimmed icon.

grayscale (**1**) A tonal scale printed in steps of no-color through to black and used for quality control in both color and black-and-white photographic processing. (**2**) Of monitors, the ability to display a pixel in a range of grays from white to black. (Monochrome monitors can

only display black pixels, in which case grays can only be achieved by the varying density of black pixels to white pixels. → dithering)

greek(ing) To indicate type by substituting rules or a gray tint for the actual letters. This is common practice when preparing rough visuals, or scamps. On a Mac, this is a feature of some applications (some even allow pictures to be greeked by substituting a flat gray tint) and using it speeds up the process of screen redraw.

grid (**1**) A measuring guide used in book and magazine design to guarantee consistency. The grid usually shows such things as column widths, picture areas, trim sizes, etc. (**2**) In some applications, a background pattern, usually invisible, of equidistant vertical and horizontal lines to which elements such as guides, rules, type, boxes, etc., can be locked, or "snapped," thus providing greater positional accuracy.

group In some applications, the facility to combine several items so that a single command can be applied to all the items in the group, or so that all the items can be moved around together.

GSM *abb.* global system for mobile communications.

GUI *abb.* graphical user interface. The feature of a computer system, such as a Mac, that allows you to interact with it by means of pointing at graphic symbols (icons) rather than by typing coded commands. Also called WIMPs or pointing interface. *17, 19*

guides In some applications, visible but non-printing horizontal and vertical lines that help you to position items with greater accuracy.

gutter Strictly speaking, the space on a sheet, imposed for printing, comprising the foredges of the pages, plus trim. Commonly, however, the term is given to the margin down the center of a double-page spread, or to the vertical space between adjacent columns on a page.

gutter bleed An image

allowed to extend into the fold, or to extend unbroken across the central margins, of a double page spread.

H

H&J, H/J *abb:* → hyphenation and justification.

hairline rule Traditionally, the thinnest line that it is possible to print. In applications that list it as a size option for rules, it is about 0.25 point thick.

hairlines The very thin strokes of a typeface.

hairspace Traditionally used of letterspacing, the term generally refers to a very narrow space between type characters.

half duplex Communication, over telecommunication lines, between two devices but in one direction at a time. → duplex.

half up A term that describes artwork prepared at one-and-a-half times the size at which it will be reproduced. Artwork that is drawn half up will need to be reduced by one third, to 66 percent, to print at its intended size.

half-title (1) The title of a book as printed on the recto of the leaf preceding the title page. **(2)** The page on which the half-title appears.

halftone (1 *rep.*) The process by which a continuous tone image is simulated by a pattern of dots of varying sizes. **(2** *rep.*) An image reproduced by the halftone process. *126, 132*

halftone screen Conventionally, a sheet of glass or film crosshatched with opaque lines. Also called a crossline screen or contact screen, it is used to translate a continuous tone image into halftone dots so that it can be printed. → contact screen; elliptical dot screen; moiré. *136*

handles (1) In applications which feature drawn lines and boxes, text boxes or picture boxes, the small black squares positioned at each corner (and sometimes also at other places) that allow you to resize those items. → control point. **(2)** → Bézier curve.

handshake The term given to the procedure that two

networked computers or other devices go through when initial contact is made, so that they can establish data transmission protocols.

hang → bomb.

hanging cap/capital An initial character that is larger than the text to which it belongs and which is positioned outside and to the left of the paragraph.

hanging indent An arrangement in typeset text where the first line of each paragraph is set out to the column measure and the remaining lines are indented to the right of the first line.

hanging punctuation Punctuation marks allowed to fall outside the measure of a piece of text.

hard copy (1) A copy of matter prepared for printing, used for revision or checking. **(2)** A printout of a computer document.

hard disk → disk; hard disk drive.

hard disk drive A hardware device for reading and writing data from and to a hard disk. The term "hard disk drive" – or even just "drive" – is often used to mean an external device, as distinct from "hard disk" which usually refers to the disk inside your Mac, even though both are drives. Most connect to Macs via a SCSI port. The disk itself may be non-removable and may be made up of several platters, depending on its storage capacity, or it may be removable, in which case it will consist of a single platter housed in a rigid plastic case, or cartridge. *30, 38, 106–7, 108*

hard dot *(rep.)* A halftone film produced either directly from a scanner or as final film and which, being dense, has a dot that can only be minimally retouched or etched.

hard hyphen The term sometimes given to a hyphen that will not permit the hyphenated word in which it appears to break at the end of a line.

hard space The term sometimes given to a space that will not permit two words between which it is placed to separate at the end of a

line. A hard space can sometimes be generated by pressing Option-Spacebar.

hardware A term for equipment. It generally applies to the physical apparatus of a computer environment, as distinct from firmware (built-in programs) and software (programs). *26–49*

hardware, *case studies 110–13*

hardware, *choice 105*

Hayes-compatibility *47*

HD SC Setup → Apple HD SC Setup.

HDTV *abb:* high-definition television.

head → read/write head.

head crash The breakdown of a disk drive caused by a read/write head coming into contact with, and damaging, the surface of a platter.

header (1) In some applications, particularly word processing programs, the facility to place text and numbers automatically at the top of printed pages. **(2)** details at top of E-mail file with sender's ID, date and subject.

heading The title introducing a chapter or subdivision of text. A crossheading, or crosshead, appears in the body of the text.

headless paragraph A paragraph set apart from other text, but without a separate heading.

head to head/foot/tail *(pri.)* In page imposition, the placement of the heads and tails of pages on each side of a sheet to suit the requirements of binding.

heap The portion of memory set aside for use on demand by the System or by applications. → application heap; system heap.

heavy Of type, an alternative term for bold or, sometimes, type heavier than bold.

help A feature of most applications to provide on-line explanations and advice.

help balloon → Balloon Help

hertz (Hz) The measurement of a unit of frequency. One hertz is one cycle, or occurrence, per second.

hex *abb:* hexadecimal, meaning the use of the number 16 as the basis of a counting system.

HFS *abb:* hierarchical file system. The name given to the way you and your Mac organize and store files and folders so that they can be accessed by any program: you organize your files inside folders which may, in turn, be inside other folders, thus creating a hierarchy. This is the hierarchy in which you move up or down within Standard File dialog boxes. Files or folders bearing the same name may exist on the same disk, but only if they are not at the same level in the same folder.

hickie/hickey/bull's-eye *(pri.)* A common printing defect, visible as a spot surrounded by a blank halo, caused by a speck of dirt pushing the paper away from the printing plate.

hierarchical file system → HFS.

hierarchical menu A menu that contains items which, when highlighted, generate their own menus, called submenus. The presence of a submenu is indicated by a (▶) symbol to the right of the menu item. → menu.

high density → disk.

high key *(pho.)* A photographic image exposed or processed to produce overall light tones.

high-level language Any programming language that is based as closely as possible on English rather than machine code.

highlight (1 *pho./rep.)* The lightest tone of a photograph or illustration. (**2**) To mark an item, usually text or a menu command, to indicate that it is selected or active. The form in which an item is highlighted depends upon what type of monitor you have (color, grayscale or monochrome) and what application you are using.

high-profile SIMM → SIMM.

high-resolution printer → imagesetter.

hinting, hints The set of instructions contained within Type 1 fonts which modifies character shapes so that they appear better when displayed or printed at low resolutions

HLS *abb:* hue, lightness and saturation → HSB.

holding line → keyline (1).

hologram An image created by lasers to give an illusion of three dimensions.

home page The first page of a web site, but not necessarily the first one accessed.

horizontal blanking interval → blanking interval.

horizontal scaling In some applications, the facility to condense or expand type. By retaining the exact attributes of the source font, horizontal scaling distorts its appearance and, while the facility can be a bonus, you may prefer to use a specially designed condensed or expanded version of the font. → condensed type; expanded type. *104*

host A computer connected permanently to the Internet.

hostname Identity of Internet participant. Commonly in three parts thus: myname.servername.co. Suffix can indicate country location e.g. us, uk etc.

hot spot The specific place on the pointer that activates the item on which it is placed.

house organ A publication produced to give information about a company to its own employees or customers.

house style (1) The style of spelling, punctuation and spacing used by a publishing house to maintain a consistent standard and treatment of text throughout its publications. (**2**) → corporate identity.

HSB *abb:* hue saturation and brightness. A color model based upon the light transmitted in your monitor, hue being the spectral color, saturation the intensity of the color pigment (without black or white being added) and brightness representing the amount of black present. Called HLS (hue, lightness, and saturation) in some applications.

H/T *abb:* → halftone.

HTML *abb:* Hypertext Markup Language. Programming language for creating Web sites.

HTTP *abb:* HyperText Transport Protocol. System allowing rapid transfer of documents between Web servers and browsers.

human interface → inter-

face.

HyperCard An Apple-supplied application with which you can design your own programs or modify the models provided.

HyperTalk The "scripting" language used in HyperCard to create programs.

hypertext A programming concept that links any single word of text to an unlimited number of others.

hyphen A mark (-) used to divide broken words or to link two words.

hyphenate To divide a word between syllables at the end of a line of text or to create a compound form from two or more words, using a hyphen.

hyphenation and justification (H&J; H/J) The routines of an application that distributes spaces correctly in a line of type to achieve the desired measure in justified text. When this cannot reasonably be done without breaking words at the end of a line, hyphens will be introduced at a position determined by the application's built-in dictionary or H&J rules. *100–1*

hyphenation exceptions The facility, in some applications, for you to modify, add or delete words that can be hyphenated.

hyphenation zone In some applications, a (sometimes) user-definable area, at the right of the column in which type is being set, in which words can be hyphenated.

Hz *abb:* → hertz.

I

IAC *abb:* interapplication communication architecture. A protocol used by applications developers to allow their programs to share and exchange data.

IAP *abb:* Internet Access Provider.

I-beam pointer The shape the pointer usually adopts (I) when it is used to edit text, as distinct from the insertion point. Sometimes called the text tool.

IBM PC → PC.

icon A graphic representation of an object, such as a disk, file, folder, or tool, or of a concept or message. *18, 20–1*

ideal format *(pho.)* A size of photographic film measuring 2.3 x 2.7in (60 x 70mm).

ID number (1) A number sometimes given in bomb alert boxes, indicating the likely cause of the system error. → bomb; error code. **(2)** → SCSI ID number. **(3)** → font ID conflict.

Illustrator *(app.)* 60–1, 94, 112

image The subject to be reproduced as an illustration on a printing press. *132–3*

image area (1) In design, the space within which a particular image is to fit. **(2** *pri.)* The printing or ink-carrying area of a litho plate.

image, *editing* 64-5, 68-9

image, *handling* 118–19

image master *(typ.)* A film-based font.

image, *storage, file formats 128*

imagesetter *(typ.)* A high-resolution output device that is used to produce reproduction-quality copy for printing, either as camera-ready artwork on photographic paper or as film negatives or positives. *115, 124–5*

imagesetter, *and bureaux 127, 131–3*

import To bring text, pictures, or other data into a document. Some applications allow you to import material in a variety of file formats such as ASCII or EPS.

import/export filter In some applications, a file that allows the translation of a file format to or from another application.

impose/imposition *(pri.)* To arrange pages – in the correct sequence and with the appropriate margins for folding and trimming – before printing.

imposed proof *(pri.)* A proof of imposed pages prior to the final print run.

imprint The printer's imprint is the name of the printer and the place of printing (a legal requirement in many countries if the work is to be published). The publisher's imprint is the name of the publisher, usually printed on the title page of a book.

imprint page The page of a book carrying details of the edition, such as the printer's imprint, copyright owner,

ISBN, catalog number, etc.

incremental backup → backup, incremental.

incremental leading → leading.

indent Of type set to a narrower measure than the column measure, the term given to the distance that the beginning or end of the line is from the left or right edges of the column.

index The section of a publication giving an alphabetical listing of subjects, proper names, etc., mentioned in a book, with page number references.

index letter/number A character or number used to key a reference between an illustration and the caption or text.

Indexed color A palette of a maximum of 256 colors, either applied to an image using the System palette, or extracted from the image so that the colors displayed are as close as possible to the original. Colors are stored in a "color lookup table." → CLUT; palette (2).

inferior character Letters or numbers set smaller than the text and set on or below the baseline, as H_2O. In most Macintosh applications, inferior characters are called "subscript."

information agent *(app.)* Generic type of program for Internet database searching. Works independently without user intervention.

information bar/palette/ window In some applications, an area or window containing information, such as measurements, about the document you are working on.

information service A commercial service that provides a facility, via telephone lines, for information, messages, and sharing software. → bulletin board.

init *abb:* initialization program. A small utility program that runs automatically when you start up and which modifies the way in which your Mac operates. An init is activated by placing it in your system folder and restarting your computer. → system extension.

init conflict A problem caused by some inits being

incompatible with other inits, system files, or applications, which may cause your Mac to crash. An init conflict may be resolved by renaming the offending init, thus changing the startup loading order (inits load alphabetically), although be warned that some inits must not be renamed.

initial cap/capital (1) Instruction to set the first letter of a word or phrase as a capital. **(2)** The initial letter of a paragraph that may be enlarged and set as a drop, hanging, or raised cap.

initialization file/resource → init.

initialize To create or clear the directory of a disk so that new data can be stored. When a hard disk is initialized or reinitialized (which you can do again and again), its directory is emptied of file information, but the data itself remains (although it is invisible) until written over by the new files. When a floppy disk is initialized, the disk is formatted as well as initialized, thus the files stored on it, if any, as well as the directory, are deleted. → formatting.

inline lettering Any typeface with a white line inside the shape, that follows the outline of the character.

in pro *abb:* in proportion. **(1)** Individual subjects for reproduction that are to be enlarged or reduced in proportion to each other, either all together or separately. **(2)** An instruction that one dimension of an item is to be enlarged or reduced in proportion to the other.

input Any data entered into a computer, by whatever means.

input device Any hardware device capable of entering data into a computer; i.e., keyboard, scanner, digitizer, etc. *48–9*

input resolution *132*

insertion point The point, indicated by a blinking vertical line, where the next action you type on the keyboard will appear. The insertion point can be positioned in an appropriate place by using the I-beam pointer and clicking.

install To add new system

files or resources to the system folder of a startup disk.

Installer The Apple-supplied program for installing system software onto your hard disk. The Installer should also be used for installing system upgrades rather than simply drag-copying the files to your system folder.

installer programs The programs that come with many applications, particularly those that occupy several floppy disks, to enable you to install the application onto your hard disk. Installer programs will also put the application files in their appropriate places, creating folders for them and putting files, if necessary, into your system folder.

integrated circuit The electronic circuit embedded in a microchip.

interactive Term describing the immediate and reciprocal action between person and machine.

interactive mode The facility of an application to process data as you input it, as distinct from processing data which is processed in batches (batch mode), say when you are interrupted by a spelling checker as soon as you make a spelling mistake. Also called "real-time" processing.

interface The physical relationship, or point of interaction, between systems and/or machines, or between person and machine (which is called "user" or "human" interface). → GUI. 18-*19*

Interleaf *(app.) 58*

interleave ratio The numbering order of track sectors on a disk. A ratio of 1:1 means that the sectors are numbered consecutively, whereas 3:1 means that the numbers run consecutively only in every third sector. This ratio is an indication of how many times a disk must rotate in order for all data in a single track to be read – a computer with a slow data transfer rate requires a disk to spin more times so that it has time to absorb all of the data in a track (so a 3:1 interleave ratio requires a disk to rotate three times

because it only reads every third sector). A ratio of 1:1 is the fastest, since all the data in a track will be read in a single revolution of the disk. If your disk has the wrong interleave ratio, reading and writing data may become very slow – even if your computer has a fast data transfer rate.

interleaving (1 *pri.)* Sheets of paper placed between newly printed sheets in order to prevent ink transfer. Also called slip-sheeting. (**2**) Blank pages between the printed pages of a book, provided for handwritten notes. (**3**) → interleave ratio.

interlinear spacing → leading.

interlock To run type characters into each other by reducing character space.

internal disk drive → floppy disk drive; hard disk drive.

internal modem A modem that is manufactured as an expansion card to fit inside your Mac.

international paper sizes *(pap.)* The standard range of metric paper sizes laid down by the International Standards Organization. The papers are designated A, B, and C series and are available in proportionate sizes, divided in ratio to the largest sheet, A0 (trimmed – untrimmed sizes are prefixed with R, or SR for bled work), which is one square meter in area (841 x 1189mm): the shortest dimension of a sheet is equivalent to the longest dimension of the next size down.

internet with a lower-case "i" denotes any network that is connected to another: The Internet is the whole collection of worldwide networks.

interpolation The term describing the technique of recreating the color values of pixels in bitmapped images which have been modified (i.e. by rotating or skewing).

interpreter Software used in programming that converts program code into machine language. An interpreter converts a program one piece at a time as distinct from a compiler which converts a program in its

entirety.

intranet a closed network, in an office for example

invisible character/invisibles The term used to describe characters that may be displayed on screen, but do not print, such as spaces (·), paragraphs (¶), etc.

invisible file A file that exists, but is not visible on your desktop; i.e. desktop file.

I/O *abb:* input/output.

IP *abb:* Internet Protocol. The principal protocol for Internet systems.

IP number Numerical translation of the alphabetical Internet address.

ISBN *abb:* International Standard Book Number. A unique ten-figure serial number that appears on every book published and which identifies the language in which it is published, its publisher, its title, and a check control number. An ISBN is often included in the bar code on a book.

ISDN, ISDN2 *abb:* Integrated Services Digital Network. A high-speed telephone network for data transmission. *48*

ISO *abb:* International Standards Organization. A Swiss-based organization that has been responsible for standardizing many elements common to design, photography, and publishing.

ISP *abb:* Internet Service Provider.

ISSN *abb:* International Standard Serial Number. A unique eight-figure number that appears on magazines and journals and which identifies the country of publication and the title.

ISOC *abb:* The Internet Society, administrators of the Internet.

italic The specially designed sloping version of a roman typeface deriving from handwriting and calligraphic scripts, intended to be distinctive from, but complementary to, that face. A version of italic, often called oblique or sloped roman, can be generated electronically on your Mac by slanting the roman style to the right.

ITC *abb:* International Typeface Corporation, a type foundry.

item tool In some applications, the tool that selects, modifies or moves items.

J

jaggie/staircasing The term, technically called aliasing, given to the stepped appearance on monitors of bitmapped images and fonts, particularly when they are enlarged, caused by pixels consisting only of straight, square sides.
→ antialiasing.

Java Cross-platform Internet application by Sun Systems Inc.

jobbing (pri.) Description of general printing, not specializing in any field (such as book work) and usually comprising short runs.

JPEG abb: Joint Photographic Experts Group, a data compression standard for reducing file sizes of continuous tone images.

jump In a publication, printed matter carried over to continue on a succeeding page.

jump line The reference on a page indicating that matter is continued elsewhere; i.e., "continued on page X."

justification The spacing of words and letters so that the beginning and end of each line of text share the same vertical left and right edges.
→ H&J. 87, 100–1

K

K abb: key, used to describe the process color black, deriving from the key, or black, printing plate in four-color process printing. Using the letter K rather than the initial B avoids confusion with blue, even though the abbreviation for process blue is C (cyan).

K(b) abb: → kilobyte.

Kbit abb: → kilobit

kern The part of a type character that overhangs the next.

kerning Adjusting the space (usually reducing it) between a pair of type characters to optimize their appearance. Traditionally, in metal type, kerned letters were those that physically overhung the metal body of the next character and were particularly important in italic typefaces

– the roman versions of most metal fonts being designed so that they did not require kerning. As distinct from tracking, which is the adjustment of space over several characters.

kerning pair Any two characters that normally require kerning or to which a kerning value has been applied.

kerning table In some applications, the table describing the automatic kerning values of a font, which you can modify.

kerning value The space between kerning pairs.

key (1 rep./pri.) Any printing plate (traditionally the black, called the key plate) or piece of artwork that provides a guide for the position and register of other colors. (2) To input matter via a keyboard.

keyboard 48–9, 106–7

keyboard characters, table 92–3

keyboard command
→ keyboard equivalent.

keyboard equivalent/command/shortcut A command made via the keyboard rather than by the mouse, as distinct from a menu command ("equivalent" meaning equivalent to the menu). Typical keyboard equivalents, or keyboard combinations, are command-O for Open, command-S for Save, command-P for Print, etc.

keyboard event The action generated by pressing a key on your keyboard. This action will occur either at the moment you press down the key ("key down") or when you release it ("key up"). If you hold down a key so that an action is repeated, it is called an "auto-key event."

keyboarding (typ.) A term referring to the first procedure in typesetting, that of inputting copy. 116

keyboard shortcut → keyboard equivalent.

keyboard special character → special character.

Key Caps The Apple-supplied desk accessory that allows you to preview the entire character set of a font.

key combination → keyboard equivalent.

key frame Movie frame that

marks key positions in a movie sequence.

key letters/numbers Letters or numbers forming a reference link between elements of an illustration and their description in a caption.

keyline (1) An outline drawing on artwork, that may or may not form part of the artwork, indicating an area that is to be filled by a mechanical tint. (2) A line drawing on a page layout indicating the size and position of an illustration or halftone. (3) The outline on artwork that, when transferred to a printing plate, will provide a guide for the register of other colors.

keyline view/preview In some graphics applications, the facility to view an outline of an item without showing any fills that may have been applied.

keypad → numeric keypad.

key plate (pri.) The plate that prints black ink in four-color process printing.

Key Repeat Rate The speed at which a character is repeated if you hold down a key.

keystroke The action of pressing a key, or group of keys, at a single time, whether or not it generates a character.

kilobit 1,024 bits.

kilobyte (K, Kb, Kbyte) A unit of measurement representing 1,024 bytes, which is used to describe the amount of memory a computer or disk may have. Since one byte represents a single character, one kilobyte is roughly equivalent to 170 words.

knockout (rep.) The term describing an area of background color that has been overlaid, or "knocked out" by a foreground object, and therefore does not print.

L

LAN abb: → local area network.

landscape/horizontal format An image or page format in which the width is greater than the height.

lap abb: overlap, of two colors to avoid registration problems. → choke; fatty; spread; trapping.

laptop computer A small portable computer.

Larger Print Area An option (File menu - Page Setup - Options), in many applications, to increase the print area of a page printed on a LaserWriter – but at the expense of the number of fonts that can be used.

laser The acronym for light amplification by stimulated emission of radiation, meaning an intense, fine beam of highly integrated light, sometimes generated with considerable energy. It is used widely in computer hardware such as printers and scanners, and for various commercial printing activities such as platemaking and engraving.

laser font A scalable outline font.

laser imagesetter *90, 124–5*

LaserPrep The file that provides a data link between a PostScript laser printer and your Mac's QuickDraw language.

laser printer A printer that uses a laser to prepare computer output data for printing onto paper. A laser printer may or may not be PostScript compatible, and if not, uses your Mac's QuickDraw language for scaling bitmapped fonts. *39–41*

LaserWriter Apple Computer's own, widely used, model of laser printer.

lasso The lasso-shaped tool used by many drawing applications to select an item by holding down the mouse button and drawing around the item.

latency time → access time.

lateral reverse The transposing of an image from left to right, as in a mirror reflection. → flop.

lathing Method of creating a 3D object by revolving a 2D profile about an axis.

latin (1) The standard alphabet used in most European languages, consisting of the upper- and lower-case characters from A to Z. The exceptions are Greek and Cyrillic (Russian, etc.). Oriental languages, including Arabic and Hebrew, are usually classified as "exotics." **(2)** A term sometimes given to typefaces derived from letterforms common to western European countries, especially those with heavy, wedge-shaped serifs.

launch To open, or start, a software application. You do this normally by double-clicking on the application's icon, by highlighting the icon and choosing Open from the File menu, or by using either of these techniques to open a document created in that application.

layer In some applications, a level to which you can consign an element of the design you are working on.

layout Visualization which gives the general appearance of a design, indicating, for instance, the relationship between text and illustrations. The term is more properly used in the context of preparing a design for reproduction. Also called tissues, deriving from the transparent paper often used for drawing layouts.

lc; l/c *abb:* → lower case.

LCD/lcd (1) *abb:* liquid crystal display. An electronic method of display commonly seen on calculators, clocks, and computer displays, particularly on portables and laptops. **(2)** *abb:* lowest common denominator, meaning the most basic level that is common to all concerned.

lead(ing) Space between lines of type, originating from days when strips of lead were placed between lines of type to increase the space. In some applications, leading can be specified as: "absolute," meaning the specific value given to spaces between lines of text; "auto," the value given to automatic line spacing by means of a user-definable preference; or "incremental," a value given to line spacing totaling the largest character on the line plus or minus a user-defined value.

leaded Type which is set with space, or leads, between the lines.

leader A row of dots (usually) or dashes, used to guide the eye across a space to other relevant matter. In some applications, leaders are specified as a "fill" between tab stops in text, and may be any character that you want.

leader line/rule A line on an image, usually keying elements of that image to annotation.

lean matter → fat matter.

left-aligned/justified Ranged left. → ranged left/right.

left indent → indent.

legend The descriptive text printed below an illustration, more often called a caption.

letterhead(ing) Strictly speaking, the heading – a name, address, and telephone number of a business or individual – on any item of stationery, but sometimes used to describe the item of stationery specifically used for writing letters.

letterpress *(pri.)* The original relief method printing process, whereby the surface of a raised, or relief, image or piece of type is inked and then pressed onto paper or other surface.

letterspace/letterfit The adjustment of space between type characters from that allocated by the font designer, by kerning or by increasing or decreasing the tracking. → character space; kerning; tracking. *87–90*

lhp *abb:* left-hand page.

library A feature of some applications to provide a facility for storing frequently used items or attributes (such as colors) that you have created so that you can access them immediately from within any document.

lifted matter *(typ./pri.)* Text, already typeset, that is taken from one job to be used in another.

ligature Two or three type characters tied, or joined together, to make a single type character, as in fi, fl, ff, ffl and ffi. *96*

light, light face Type with an inconspicuous light appearance. It is based on the same design as medium, or roman, weight type in the same type family. The opposite of bold face.

lightfast/colorfast *(pri.)* A term describing ink or other material whose color is not affected by exposure to light, atmosphere, or chemicals.

lightness → HSB.

light table/box A table or box with a translucent glass top lit from below, giving a color-balanced light suitable for viewing color transparencies and for color-matching transparencies to proofs.

Limitcheck error An error you may encounter when printing a complex document, caused by an illustration containing too many line segments for PostScript to handle. Some applications may allow you to reduce the number of line segments (→ flatness) in an illustration for printing purposes.

line → rule.

line and halftone → combination line and halftone.

line art(work) Artwork or camera-ready copy consisting only of black on white, with no intermediate tones and thus not requiring halftone reproduction.

line conversion The photographic or electronic method of eliminating the middle tones from a continuous tone original so that it can be treated as line artwork.

line copy → line art(work).

line gauge → type scale.

line increment The smallest allowable increase in the basic measure between typeset lines.

line original → line art(work).

line pattern The sequence of dots, dashes, and spaces in a rule.

line tool In graphics applications, the tool that you use to draw lines and rules. If the tool can only draw horizontal and vertical rules, it will usually be called an "orthogonal" line tool.

line up The arrangement of two lines of type, two illustrations, or a line of type and an illustration, to touch the same imaginary horizontal line.

line weight The thickness of a line or rule.

lines per inch (lpi, although often described as, say, "150 line") The measurement used to describe the resolution, or coarseness, of a halftone, being the number of rows of dots to each inch. The range in common use

varies between around 85lpi for halftones printed on newsprint, to 150lpi or more on art papers. The default setting on laser printers is usually around 60lpi.

lining figures/numerals A set of numerals aligned at top and bottom. Sometimes called "modern" numerals. *96*

lining up/lineup table *(rep.)* A table used for preparing and checking paste-up, flats, etc. It will generally be comprised of a gridded, illuminated surface with movable scales.

linking In some frame-based page layout applications, the facility for connecting two or more text boxes so that text flows from one box to another.

Linotype Hell A German type foundry and manufacturer of typesetting equipment (such as the Linotronic series imagesetters), supplying PostScript and TrueType fonts. The original Linotype machine was the first keyboard-operated composing machine to employ the principle of a "matrix," and cast type in solid lines, or "slugs." It was invented by the German-born American engineer Ottmar Mergenthaler and patented in 1884. The Monotype machine was invented almost simultaneously, in 1885. *87, 90*

list box The scrolling box in standard directory dialog boxes that lists the contents of the disk or folder displayed above it.

literal → typo.

lith *(rep.)* A high contrast and high quality photographic emulsion used in graphic reproduction.

lithography *(pri.)* A printing process, invented in 1798 by the German Aloys Senefelder, that produces an image from a dampened, flat surface, using greasy ink, based on the principle of the mutual repulsion of oil and water. → offset lithography.

Live Picture *(app.)* 65

local area network (LAN) A network of hardware devices confined to a small ("local") area — one room, say — using appropriate connections and software. At its

simplest, a LAN can be set up so that several Macs have access to a single printer or a centralized hard disk.

LocalTalk The hardware connections used for AppleTalk networks.

lock In some applications, the facility for securing, or anchoring, an item so that it cannot be moved or modified.

locked floppy disk A floppy disk which is write-protected.

logic board → board.

logical volume A volume created by software, as distinct from a physical volume such as a disk.

logo/logotype Traditionally, any group of type characters (other than ligatures) such as company names or emblems cast together on one metal body. The term is now used to describe any design or symbol for a corporation or organization which forms the centerpiece of its corporate identity.

log on To connect to, or announce your presence on, a network.

long page A page with the type area extended by one or two lines to avoid an inconvenient break.

look-/see-/show-through *(pap.)* The term used when describing the opacity of a paper, as indicated by the degree to which an image or type on one side of the sheet may be visible on the other.

lookup field A field in a database file that shows the same information as in a specified field in another file.

low-profile SIMM → SIMM.

lower case Description of the small letters in a type font, as distinct from capitals, which are called upper case.

luminance A term used to describe the strength of a grayscale video signal.

LZW *abb:* Lempel-Ziv-Welch Compression method for TIFF images, in which no data — thus no detail — is lost. → TIFF; compression.

M

M *abb:* → magenta.

M, **MB**, **Mb**, **Mbyte** abb:
→ megabyte.
MacBinary A file transfer
protocol that allows
Macintosh files to be properly transferred to non-Mac
computers.
machine code The lowest
level of programming lan-
guage. It is the least like
English, but it is the most
efficient, as a computer
finds it the easiest to understand.
machine proof (pri.) A final
proof made on a machine
similar to the one on which
it will be printed (if not that
actual machine).
Macintosh, the box 26–7
and designers 50–1
models and properties 30–1
organizing work 119–21
set up 105, 106–7
typesetting with 90
**Macintosh Operating
System** The basic software
and firmware in your Mac,
combining disk- and ROM-
based routines that handle
very basic tasks such as
startup, input, and output to
peripheral devices, and the
management of RAM space.
→ operating system.
Mac RenderMan (app.) 71
Macintosh User Groups
(MUGs) 51
macro Literally, macro
(deriving from the Greek
"makros" = long, large)
means large or large-scale,
prolonging. Macroscopic
means large units as distinct
from microscopic, which
means small. Thus, when
applied to computers, a
macro refers to a single
command which contains
several other commands –
one large unit made up of
smaller units. A macro program is a small application
with which you can build or
record a sequence of
actions, carried out on your
Mac, into a single keyboard
equivalent.
Macromedia Director
(app.) 72
MacTCP Macintosh control
panel. → TCP/IP
MacWrite Pro (app.) 74
magenta (M) The special
shade of red that is one of
the four process colors used
in four-color printing, sometimes called process red.
Theoretically, magenta contains no blue (cyan) or yel-

low.
magnetic disk → disk.
magnetic ink characters
Characters printed using a
magnetized ink which are
readable both by humans
and by appropriate
machines, using a process
called MICR (magnetic ink
character recognition).
magnetic media/storage
Any material coated with a
magnetic oxide and used for
storing computer data, such
as disks, tapes, cards, etc.
36–7
magnifying glass, **mag-
nify tool** A tool in many
applications that will
enlarge a document, usually
when (having selected the
tool) you click anywhere in
the screen (the place where
you click will become the
center of the enlarged view),
or by "drawing" a "mar-
quee" (box) around the portion that you want to
enlarge.
main exposure (rep.) The
first exposure in the conventional processing of a
halftone image.
main memory Installed
memory (usually RAM), as
distinct from virtual memory.
→ RAM.
make ready → making
ready.
make-up (**1**) The sheet indicating the positions of various items on a page. →
layout. (**2** rep.) The final preprint assembly, whether on
paper, film, or on a com-
puter, of all items to be
printed. 54–8
making ready (pri.) The
term describing the process
of preparing a printing press
before a new run, to establish register, evenness of
impression, size, etc.
Manual Feed button The
option in LaserWriter Print
dialog boxes (File menu)
that, when checked, will
only print the paper in the
special single-sheet manual
feed guide on top of the
paper cassette of your
printer. (If you put a sheet of
paper into the manual feed
guide, but forget to check
Manual Feed, it will print on
that sheet anyway.)
manual font downloading
→ font downloading.
manuals, for the Mac 52
manuscript (MS/MSS) An

author's text submitted for
publication.
margins The blank areas of
a printed page which sur-
round text or illustrations.
margin guides In some
applications, nonprinting
guides used to indicate the
edges of a predefined text or
image area.
marked proof (typ.) A proof
that has any necessary corrections marked on it before
it is given to the author.
mark-up (**1**) To specify, to
anyone in the reproduction
process, every detail of a job
that the person may require
to carry out the job properly.
(**2**) The actual item produced
to put (1) into effect.
marquee In some applications, a moving dotted line
drawn using the pointer or
some other tool, to select
the area within it.
mask (**1**) A material used to
block out part of an image in
photomechanical reproduc-
tion, photography, illustration, or layout. (**2** rep.) A
photographic image modi-
fied in tone or color.
masking (**1** pho./rep.)
Blocking out part of an
image with opaque material
to prevent reproduction or to
allow for alterations. (**2** rep.)
A technical method of
adjusting the values of color
and tone in photomechanical
reproduction.
(**3**) A protective layer applied
to an illustration to cover an
area while other parts are
painted or airbrushed.
master directory block
The block on a disk that contains the disk directory,
which is put into RAM when
you start or insert the disk.
→ directory.
master page In some applications, the page to which
certain attributes, such as
the number of text columns,
page numbers, type style,
etc., can be given, which can
then be applied to any other
page in a document. 116
master proof (typ.) A
marked proof with client's,
editor's, and author's comments combined.
mat(rix) (typ.) Traditionally,
the name for the copper
mold from which hot metal
type was cast; the term was
later applied to the photographic negative on photo-

typesetting machines from which type characters are generated. *90*

math coprocessor
→ coprocessor.

mathematical signs/symbols Type symbols used as a shorthand for mathematical concepts and processes, i.e. + (add), ÷ (divide), √ (radical, or square root).

matter Traditionally, manuscript or copy to be printed, or type that has been set.

Mbit *abb:* → megabit.

Mbps *abb:* megabits per second, a measure of the speed of data transfer.

mean line The imaginary line showing the top of the x-height of lower case letters. → x-height.

measure The length of a typeset line, used to indicate the width of a text column, usually measured in picas or points, and sometimes in inches or millimeters.

measurements window/palette A window giving information about various items, such as the position of the pointer, size of box, type attributes, etc., in the document you are working on, depending on which item is selected and the application you are using. → palette.

mechanical → camera-ready art(work); paste-up.

mechanical tint The term used to describe a tint, usually flat color, consisting of a line or dot pattern that can be laid down during conventional reproduction or by applying a percentage tint to a selection in some graphics applications.

media (1) A plural term, now accepted as a singular, used to describe any information or communications medium such as television, radio, newspapers, etc. **(2)** A plural term generally accepted as a singular, used to describe to the actual item on which computer data is stored, such as a floppy, hard, or optical disk, as distinct from the devices in which they are used. → disk.

medium (1) A synonym for a catchline. **(2)** The substance which binds the pigment of

paint or ink, also called the "vehicle." Printing ink medium is usually linseed oil. **(3** *pri.*) A standard size of printing paper, 18 x 23in. **(4)** A weight of typeface halfway between light and bold, often being the roman version.

meg *abb:* → megabyte.

megabit (Mbit) 1,024 kilobits, or 1,048,576 bits.

megabyte (M, Mbyte, MB, meg) 1,024 kilobytes, or 1,048,576 bytes, or roughly 175,000 words. *17, 23*

megahertz (MHz) One million cycles, or occurrences, or instructions per second, generally used to describe the speed of a computer's central processing unit, or its "clock speed."

memory The faculty of a computer to recall data and remember it, as distinct from storing the data, for which you use media such as disks. Your Mac has two types of memory: RAM, which memorizes the activities that take place on screen until they are written to disk and which exists only as long as your computer is switched on; and ROM, which is a memory chip that permanently stores data vital to your computer's operation. → DIMM; RAM; ROM; SIMM. *22–5, 28–9*

memory allocation
→ application heap; heap; RAM cache; system heap.

memory-management coprocessor → PMMU.

memory, *problems 140*

memory upgrade To increase the RAM of your computer. → DIMM; SIMM.

menu A list of commands available to you, depending on the application you are using. *18, 20–1*

menu bar The horizontal strip across the top of your screen containing the titles of menus.

menu box A box, usually with a drop-shadow, and containing a menu title, that displays a menu when you click on it.

menu command A command made via a menu, as distinct from one made via the keyboard.

menu indicator Symbols in a menu that give information regarding menu commands.

An ellipsis (…) means selection of that command will display a dialog box before the command can be executed; a check-mark indicates a command is active; a right-pointing triangle indicates a submenu; and a down-pointing triangle indicates more to come.

Menu Manager The part of the System Toolbox that handles the setting up and use of menus. → hierarchical menu.

menu title The title of a menu, as displayed in the menu bar or in a menu box.

merge A facility in some applications to combine data from two documents.

message box An unprompted dialog box, giving information. → alert (box).

Meta Tools *(app.) 65*

metrics Font information, such as character width, kerning, ascent, and descent.

MFS *abb:* Macintosh file system. The original method of file organization, now superseded by the hierarchical menu system.

MICR *abb:* magnetic ink character recognition. → magnetic ink characters.

microchip → chip.

microprocessor → CPU; coprocessor; 68000 series chip. *27*

MIDI *abb:* musical instrument digital interface, a communication standard used by computers to control musical sound.

millisecond (ms) One thousandth of a second.

MIME *abb:* Multipurpose Mail Extensions. Standard Internet format for non-text E-mail.

minuscules An alternative term for lower-case letters.

minus leading/linespacing → negative leading.

mips *abb:* million instructions per second.

mirror-image backup
→ backup, mirror-image.

mock-up A visualization of a publication or pack design showing its size, shape, type, color, etc.

modal dialog box A dialog box that will not allow any activity to take place other than that within its box. Even desk accessories are rendered inaccessible until the dialog box is closed.

modem *abb:* modulator-demulator. A device for transferring data from one computer to another across telephone lines, using appropriate software. *46–7, 117*

modern face A typeface characterized by vertical stress, strong stroke contrast, and thin, unbracketed, serifs.

modern numerals → lining figures/numerals.

modifier key Any key that, when pressed in combination with a character key, changes the typed character. Pressing Option-Z produces Ω. Other modifier keys are Control, Shift, Command, and Caps Lock.

modular Mac Any Macintosh computer that does not incorporate the monitor in its case.

module A self-contained element of a program that connects with other elements.

moiré *(rep.)* An aberration occuring in halftone reproduction when two or more colors are printed, giving a halftone image an appearance rather like that of watered silk. This is caused by two or more dot screens being positioned at the wrong angles or, sometimes, by the re-screening of an image to which a halftone screen has already been applied. The angle at which screens should be positioned depends upon the number of colors being printed, but the norm for four-color process printing, and thus the default setting for most Mac applications that support four-color separation, is: cyan 105°; magenta 75°; yellow 90°; black 45°. *136*

monetary symbol A symbol denoting a unit of currency. There are four currency symbols available on Apple keyboards, but the keys you press to get them depend upon which nationality version of the System you are using. The symbols are: $ (Shift-4); ¢ (Option-4); £ (Option-3); ¥ (Option-Y).

monitor The screen on which you view what you do on your computer. A monitor may be able to display in color, grayscale, or monochrome, and is either built into the same case as the computer, as with compact Macs, or is a separate unit. Monitors are available in a variety of sizes from 9in. (229mm) (measured diagonally) to 21in. (534mm) or more. Although most monitors use cathode ray tubes some contain liquid crystal displays, particularly portables and laptops. Monitors are variously called "screens," "displays," "VDUs," and "VDTs." *26–7, 31–6, 106–7*

Monitors cdev The control panel device that – depending on what monitor you have – allows you to select the number of grays or colors, check the convergence pattern (to make sure that the red, green, and blue beams of light are suitably adjusted), and, if you have more than one monitor connected to your Mac, to adjust their physical positions in relation to each other. The same results are achieved in later Macs by the Monitors and Sound application.

monochrome (1) Any image or reproduction made in a single color. **(2)** Of monitors, description of those which display pixels only as either black or white, as distinct from grayscale monitors, which display pixels in a range of grays.

monospaced Description of typewriter-like fonts in which all the characters are of equal width, as distinct from the more usual proportionally spaced fonts.

Monotype A type foundry and manufacturer of typesetting equipment, supplying PostScript and TrueType fonts. The original Monotype process, invented in 1885 by Tolbert Lanston of Ohio (only a year after the invention of the Linotype machine), employed a keyboard-operated composing machine to cast type as individual letters, using large numbers of matrices (which was only feasible due to the invention, by L.B. Benton, of a mechanical punch cutter).

montage The assembly of several images, or portions of them, to form a single original. → photomontage.

motherboard → board.

mouse The mechanical device that sits on your desk which you manipulate to navigate the pointer on your screen. *49, 106–7*

mouse button → button (2).

Mouse cdev The control panel device that allows you to select the tracking speed and clicking rate of your mouse.

mouse event The action generated by pressing the button on your mouse. This action will occur either at the moment you press down the button ("mouse-down") or when you release it ("mouse-up").

Mouse Keys → Easy Access.

mouse pad/mat A small mat specially designed to help your mouse move efficiently. By being easy to clean, it also helps to keep bits of grit out of your mouse.

MPEG *abb:* Motion Picture Experts Group. Compression format for video files.

ms *abb:* → **(1)** millisecond. **(2)** manuscript.

MS-DOS *abb:* Microsoft disk operating system. An operating system used on non-Mac personal computers, sometimes called PC-DOS → Windows.

MS(S) *abb:* → manuscript.

MUG *abb:* Macintosh user group. → user group.

Multi-Ad Creator *(app.) 71*

MultiFinder *(obs.)* A pre-System 7 Apple-supplied application that allowed more than one application, including the Finder, to run at the same time.

multimedia The activity of integrating text, graphics, sound, and video for (mostly) presentation purposes, and the applications that let you do this with a Mac. *72–3, 76–7*

multiple screens The attachment to a Mac of two or more screens. Their relative positions can be modified via the Monitors program in the Control Panels folder (● menu).

multiple-selected items In some applications, the selection of two or more items, so that they can be modified or moved as one.

multitasking The facility to run two or more applications at the same time, when the central processing unit will appear to work on them simultaneously by switching very rapidly from one to the other (sometimes called "time-slicing").

multi-user (1) Description of any hardware or software that can be accessed by more than one person at the same time. (2) Of software licenses, those which permit copying and use by more than one user, usually with a predefined limit.

music program Any application by which music can be composed and played, either with or without a musical keyboard or other audio equipment.

N

naming files *119, 121*
nanosecond (ns) A measure of speed, being one billionth of a second – the fewer ns, the faster.
native file format → file format.
Navigator application for searching the Internet and organizing E-mail transmission and reception.
neg(ative) (**1** *pho./rep.*) A photographic film or paper in which all the dark areas appear light and vice versa. Negatives are used extensively in the reproduction process and are either made direct from originals or from a positive, or produced by an imagesetter. (**2**) The facility (sometimes called "inverting"), in many applications, to reverse the screen bit map so that the black pixels appear white and vice versa.
negative leading/line spacing In text, a line interval smaller than the point size of the type.
nested folder A folder that is placed inside another folder, in which case, it may be described as being "two layers deep."
network The interconnection of two or more computers and peripheral devices, and the hardware and software used to connect them. → Ethernet; local area network. *108, 109*

new line character In some applications, a character that you can insert (by pressing Shift-Return) to start a new line without starting a new paragraph.
newsgroup Group of Internet participants interested in a single subject → Usenet.
NFNT *abb:* new font numbering table → font ID conflict.
nibble/nybble Half a byte (four bits).
nickname Shortened form of an E-mail address.
Nisus Writer *(app.) 74*
NLQ *abb:* near letter quality, describing a type of low-quality printer.
node (**1**) Any network device. (**2**) Internet name of an individual computer.
nodename → node (**2**)
noise A term used to describe undesirable fluctuations or interference in a transmitted signal.
nonbreaking space → hard space.
noncontiguous selection The facility, in some word-processing applications, to select unlimited disconnected pieces of text.
None A QuickTime setting in which data is not compressed, so there is no degradation of quality. However, much more disk space is required to store the movie. → QuickTime.
nonimpact printing Print work produced without a plate or cylinder, i.e. by the writing head of a plotter.
nonlining figures/numerals A set of old-style numerals designed with descenders (3, 4, 7, 9) and ascenders (6, 8), therefore not of a standard height and alignment, as are lining figures.
nonprinting characters → invisible character/invisibles.
Norton Utilities *(util.) 75*
np *abb:* new paragraph. A mark used in editing and proof correction.
ns *abb:* → nanosecond.
NuBus *obs.* The bus "architecture"of the Macintosh II family. → bus.
NuBus slot *obs.* The expansion slots in the Macintosh II family to which expansion cards, or boards, were added

to enhance performance.
nudge A facility of some applications to move items, usually in increments of one pixel or one point (or even a fraction of a point), by using a keyboard command. Even if the application you are using does not have a nudge command, you can invoke one by using Easy Access's Mouse Keys feature.
null modem cable A communications link between two computers, usually over a short distance, without using a modem (null = nonexistent).
numbering format A term generally used to describe the style of numbering used for page numbers: 1, 2, 3; I, II, III; etc.
numerals, *table 96*
numeric coprocessor → coprocessor.
numeric keypad The cluster of number keys with a few calculator functions situated (normally) to the right of the keyboard.

O

object-oriented Of graphics applications, those that allow the selection and manipulation of individual, but self-contained, portions of an illustration or design, as distinct from bitmapped graphics which are edited by modifying pixels or turning them on or off. An object-oriented application uses mathematical points, based on vectors (information giving both magnitude and direction), to define lines and shapes. Strictly speaking, these points are the "objects" referred to here (as distinct from an illustration, or graphic, as an object) – an object in computer programming is a database of mathematical formulae. The data for each shape is stored in these points, each one a database, which in turn pass information from one to the other on how the paths between them should be described – as straight lines, arcs, or Bézier curves. This means that the quality of the line between each point is determined entirely by the resolution of the output device – a line produced by an imagesetter will be very much smoother than the same line output on a LaserWriter. *59, 60, 64*

OCR *abb:* → optical character recognition.

OEM *abb:* original equipment manufacturer. The manufacturer of an item which may form part of another piece of equipment and is marketed under a different name, as happens with generic disk drives.

off-line Work done in relation to a computer or network, but not actually done on the computer or while connected to the network. The opposite of on-line.

offset lithography *(pri.)* A method of lithography, developed separately in the U.S. in the early 1900s by Ira Rubel, Alex Sherwood, and the Harris brothers, in which the image is printed indirectly by "offsetting" it first onto a rubber-covered cylinder, called a "blanket," from which the image is printed. It is the most widely used commercial printing process and is sometimes called photolithography. This book was printed by the offset lithography process.

OK press → pass for press.

old face/style A typeface characterized by diagonal stress and sloped, bracketed serifs. Garamond is an example of an old face.

OmniPage *(app.) 74, 116*

one-and-a-half-up Artwork prepared at one-and-a-half times the size at which it will eventually be reproduced. It will need to be reduced by one third or to 66 percent, to be the correct size.

on-line Work done on a computer or while connected to a network.

on-line help In some applications, a file that gives help and advice, which is always available while that application is open.

Open A command (File menu) that lets you reveal the contents of a file or folder or launch an application.

open architecture The provision, in the design of a computer, for modification and improvement of that computer and its system.

Open button The button in

the Open dialog box that opens the highlighted file or folder in the directory list. Double-clicking on that file or folder, or (sometimes) double-clicking on the icon of the file or folder while you are in the Finder, achieves the same result.

Open dialog box The Standard File dialog box that appears when the Open command is invoked.

OpenDoc Apple's own system for cross-platform computing.

open/standing time Unused production time due to a break in the schedule.

operating system The software and firmware that provides the environment within which a computer user operates. In the case of the Macintosh, this environment is made up of the Operating System ROMs, System file, Finder, and related system software.

optical alignment An arrangement of (usually curved or pointed) characters allowing a degree of projection beyond the margin when vertically aligned, to give an overall appearance of alignment between the main vertical strokes. Horizontal optical alignment is normally already designed into a typeface.

optical center A point within a rectangle, slightly higher than the actual geometric center, at which an object or image appears to be centrally placed.

optical character recognition (OCR) A means of inputting copy into it, by using software which, when used with a scanner, converts typescript into editable computer text. *74, 116–17*

optical disk/media A medium for storing digitized data by means of minute pits (the size of which represents a 1 or a 0) imbedded into the disk. They are "read" by an optical pickup using a laser which is reflected off the disk's surface by a shiny metallic layer. Usually referred to as CDs (compact disks), optical disks are widely used for audio and video recording and computer data storage, and are

capable of holding large amounts of data. CDs are more resilient to damage than magnetic media, but are also much slower. → CD-I; CD-R; CD-ROM; CD-ROM-XA. *37-9*

optical(ly) even spacing The adjustment of the spaces between characters to create an even appearance to a line of type.

optical type font A font used in optical character recognition.

option Any button, checkbox, menu, or command that allows you an alternative choice.

Option key A keyboard modifier key which, when used in conjunction with another key, provides a special character or a shortcut to menu commands, or carries out some other action, depending upon the application or utility you are using.

organizing folders *121*

organizing work *119–21*

origin The fixed, or zero, point of horizontal and vertical axes or of the rulers displayed in some applications, from which measurements can be made.

original Any image, artwork, or text matter intended for reproduction.

origination *(rep.)* A term used to describe any or all of the reproduction processes that may occur between design and printing. *108, 124–36*

ornament → dingbat.

orphan A short line, usually the first line of a paragraph, that falls at the top or bottom of a page or column. → club line; widow.

ortho(chromatic) *(rep.)* Photographic emulsion used extensively in conventional reproduction, being sensitive to all colors except red.

orthogonal line tool → line tool.

OS *abb:* Operating System. The Mac OS, for example, controls all the basic functions of the Macintosh.

outline font A typeface formed from an outline which can be scaled or rotated to any size or resolution. Outline fonts, often called printer fonts or laser fonts, are generally used for printing by laser printers and imagesetters, but both PostScript and TrueType font outlines can also be used for screen display. As distinct from bitmapped fonts which are comprised of dots. *91*

outline letter A type design in which the character is formed of outlines rather than a solid shape.

outliner A word-processing application used for organizing headings and text.

out-of-memory message Any message which tells you that there is not enough memory available to perform the task that you require.

out of register → fit (2); register.

output device Any hardware device capable of displaying or producing data from a computer in a visible form, such as a monitor, printer, plotter, imagesetter, etc.

output resolution *126*

overflow In some applications, the term given to excess text when it will not all fit into its allocated space. Traditionally called "overmatter."

overhead A term describing space in a document that is occupied by formatting data rather than by the actual content you have created or need to access.

overhead projector A presentation device for projecting onto a flat surface images that have been created or output on transparent cellulose acetate.

overlay (1) A transparent sheet used for preparing multicolor artwork. **(2)** A translucent sheet covering a piece of original artwork on which you write instructions for reproduction.

overmatter *(typ.)* The traditional term for typeset matter which will not fit within the space allocated for it. → overflow.

overprint (1 *pri.)* To make a second printing, or "pass" (not always in an additional color), on a previously printed sheet. **(2** *pri.)* To print two or more colors so that they overlap, thus producing more colors. The opposite of "knockout."

overrun The term describing words that move from one

line to the next, possibly for several successive lines, as a result of a text insertion or correction. The opposite of run back.

overs *(pri.)* The term describing printed copies beyond the number ordered. This is normally deliberate to allow for copies that may be ruined during finishing or lost or damaged during shipping.

Ozalid *(rep./pri.)* A brand name describing a copy made by the diazo process and often used to refer to the prepress proofs of an imposed publication.
→ blues; diazo.

P

p, **pp** *abb:* page, pages.

page A contiguous segment of memory.

page break In continuous text, the place between two lines where the text is interrupted so that it fits on a page.

page description language (PDL) A type of programming language used to describe image and font data to a printer so that the printer can construct and print the data to your specifications. PostScript is the most widely used PDL. *40, 90*

paged memory management unit → PMMU.

page guides In some applications, nonprinting guides that show you the width of margins, position of columns, etc.

page layout → layout.

page layout/makeup application Any application that assists you to carry out all (and more) of the functions normally associated with layout and make-up.

PageMaker *(app.) 55, 56, 58*

page make-up → make-up.

page makeup applications *54–8, 129*

Page Mill *(app.) 78*

page preview A facility to view a page before it is printed, necessary in some applications such as word processors and databases.

page proofs *(rep./pri.)* Proofs of pages which have been paginated. Traditionally, the term refers to the secondary stage in

proofing, after galley proofs and before machine proofs, although there may be other stages of proofing both before and after page proofs, such as the "blues" used to check imposition.

Page Setup A dialog box (File menu) in which you can select various options for printing, such as paper size, enlargement or reduction, paper orientation, inversion, etc. The options offered depend on the printer you are using, as selected in the Chooser (● menu) or on the Desktop.

pages to view Refers to the number of pages visible on one side of a sheet that will be, or has been, printed on both sides.

pagination *(rep./pri.)* Strictly speaking, the term given to the numbering of book pages, but also commonly used to describe make-up of material into pages after typesetting and origination.

paint (PNT(G)) A standard bitmapped graphics file format, sometimes called a MacPaint format. PNTG files will only support an image resolution of 72dpi. → EPS; PICT; TIFF. *128*

Painter *(app.) 65, 66–7*

paint(ing) application/program Painting applications can be defined as those which use bitmaps as distinct from drawing applications which tend to be object-oriented, although some applications combine both. → bitmapped; object-oriented. *61, 64–5, 66–7*

palette (1) window, often movable, or "floating," that contains features such as tools or patterns which you select, or measurements which you modify, during the course of your work within an application. **(2)** A set of colors used to display an image. → CLUT. **(3)** → file

PANTONE Pantone Inc.'s check-standard trademark for color standards, control, and quality requirements. It is a system in which each color bears a description of its formulation (in percentages) for subsequent use by the printer. It is also a system that is used throughout the world, so that colors specified by any designer can be matched exactly by any printer. Computer VDU simulations, supported by some graphics applications, are unlikely to match PANTONE-identified solid color standards, and you should always use current PANTONE color reference manuals to match colors accurately. Pantone, Inc., are, quite rightly, extremely vigilant about protecting their system, and conditions for specification and reproduction are very stringent – you must, for instance, follow their rules and regulations before using PANTONE identification numbers in, say, a corporate identity manual. They will not permit the use of their trademark PMS, the initials of PANTONE MATCHING SYSTEM, and note that in all the references contained in this book the word PANTONE appears in capitals – this is another requirement. If you have any doubts about the way in which you want to specify colors – particularly if you are actually reproducing a reference to a PANTONE color – fax the Trademark Control Department at Pantone, Inc. on 201-896-0242. *57, 59, 62, 127*

paper size *41*
paragraph format → format (4).
paragraph mark → blind P.
parallel interface A computer interface, not found on Macs, in which eight bits (or more) of data are transmitted simultaneously in the same direction along a single cable. As distinct from serial interface.
parameter RAM (PRAM) The area in your Mac's RAM which maintains Control Panel (● menu) settings, such as time and date and startup volume, when your Mac is switched off. The PRAM chip is provided with a continuous power supply from its own lithium battery so these settings (with the exception of the desktop pattern) do not change if you startup from another disk. *25*
parity bit An extra bit added to a unit of communications data, used to verify that the

bits received by one device match those transmitted by another.
parked Description of a drive's read/write heads when they are at rest, allowing you to move the drive or to remove a disk without damage to disk or head.
partition(ing) To divide up a hard disk into smaller volumes, each one treated as if it were a separate disk and represented on the desktop by its own icon. Partitioning is particularly useful if you have a very high capacity hard disk, since, among other things, you only need to regularly back up the volumes that you use frequently. There are two kinds of file partitions – SCSI (real partitions) and file partitions, the latter being large files rather than proper mountable volumes.
Pascal Programming language originally used for compiling Mac applications.
pass for press *(rep./pri.)* Endorsement that a job has had all corrections made and is ready for press. Also called "OK press."
Paste (Edit menu, Command-V) The command that copies an item on the Clipboard and places it in a document. → Clipboard.
pasteboard In some applications, the nonprinting area around the page on which items can be stored or modified. *56*
paste-up *obs.* A layout of a page or pages incorporating all the design elements such as text, illustrations, and rules. A paste-up may be either "rough," in which case, while including all the design elements, it will not be used for final reproduction (except, perhaps, as a guide), or it may be "camera-ready" (also called "mechanicals"), in which case it will be photographed to make negatives or positives for reproduction. → camera-ready art(work).
patch A piece of program code used to upgrade software or fix bugs. Patch code is also used in System upgrades for overriding some ROM routines.
path (1) The hierarchical trail from a file, through fold-

ers, to a disk. (**2**) A line, or segment of a line, drawn in an object-oriented application.
pathname The name given to identify the path taken by a file to a disk, such as jobdisk:jobfolder:jobfile (the file named "jobfile" is inside the folder named "jobfolder" which is on the disk called "jobdisk"). Note that colons are used to separate each name in the path, which is why you cannot use colons to name files.
PC *abb:* personal computer, usually used to describe IBM PCs and other personal computers that are IBM-compatible.
PC board *abb:* printed circuit board → board.
PC Exchange Control Panel for managing input from applications running in PC environments. Imported files are assigned to be opened and translated by resident Mac applications.
PCI *abb.* peripheral component interconnect. Internal slot design for Mac expansion devices
PCMCIA *abb.* Personal Computer Memory Card International Association. Also used to describe the communications cards produced in this format.
PD *abb.* → public domain.
PDF *abb.* Portable Document Format, a file format used by Adobe Acrobat for viewing documents on Mac, Windows, DOS, and UNIX operating systems.
PDL *abb.* → page description language.
PDS *abb.* (obs.) → processor direct slot.
peculiars → special sorts.
peer-to-peer A network system in which data is spread around different users, who access it directly from each other, rather than from a central "client-server."
peripheral (device) Any item of hardware that is connected to a computer, such as a printer, scanner, hard disk drive.
peripheral cable A cable for connecting a peripheral device to your Mac. → SCSI (daisy-) chain
permanent font An "official" term, although a mis-

nomer, for fonts that are manually downloaded to a printer – they are only permanent until you switch off your printer, meaning you have to download them again when you switch on. As distinct from a "transient," or automatically downloaded, font, which only lasts in memory while a document is being printed.

perspective The art of describing three-dimensional objects on a two-dimensional plane, giving the same impression of their relative positions and size as the objects themselves have when viewed from a particular point.

Persuasion *(app.)* 74

phonogram A symbol designed as the written equivalent of a spoken sound, which may or may not correspond to the International Phonetic Alphabet (IPA).

phosphor The coating on the inside surface of cathode ray tubes, and thus computer monitors, which glows briefly when hit by a bombardment of electrons, thus creating an image.

Photo (JPEG) A QuickTime compression setting which is suitable for image sequences which do not contain high levels of detail. Achieves high compression ratios, but does not work well for playback. → QuickTime.

photocomposition → phototypesetting.

photogravure *(pri.)* An intaglio printing process in which a photomechanically prepared surface holds ink in recessed cells. Widely used for long runs like magazines.

photolithography → offset lithography.

photomechanical (1 *pri.)* A method of making printing plates that involves photographic techniques. (**2)** The full version of the term "mechanical" → art(work); camera-ready art(work); paste-up.

photomechanical transfer (PMT) *(rep./pri.)* A method of photographically transferring images onto paper, film, or metal litho plates. An image produced by this method is commonly called a PMT.

Also called diffusion, or chemical transfer, or "velox."

photomontage The use of images from different photographs combined to produce a new, composite image. → montage.

PhotoShop *(app.)* 65, 68–9, 112

phototypesetting/photocomposition *(typ.)* Strictly speaking, typesetting produced on photographic paper or film from a film matrix, but now extended to include, by virtue of the output medium being photographically based, computer typesetting produced on an imagesetter.

pica A unit of typographic measurement, one pica comprises 12 points, and, in true typesetting values, one inch comprises 6.0225 picas or 72.27 points. However, computer applications use the PostScript value of exactly six picas, or 72 points, to the inch. → point.

PICS animation A standard file format for combining individual PICT images into an animation sequence.

pi character → special sorts.

PICT *abb:* picture. A standard file format for storing object-oriented images. The PICT format uses QuickDraw routines and thus will support bitmapped images, since QuickDraw routines are what your Mac uses to draw on its screen, and is supported by virtually all graphics applications. Originally PICT only accepted eight colors, but now, as PICT2, it will support 32-bit color, and is thus unlimited. → EPS; paint; TIFF. *128*

pictogram/pictograph A simplified, pictorial symbol representing an object or concept.

picture → PICT.

picture box In frame-based applications, a box created for a picture, as distinct from a text box.

picture skew → skew.

pixel *abb:* picture element. An individual dot of light on your monitor which contributes to forming an image. The more pixels there are per inch, the higher the resolution of your monitor (the

Mac standard is 72dpi). In its simplest form (monochrome), one pixel corresponds to a single bit in RAM: 0 = off, or white, and 1 = on, or black. On color or grayscale monitors, one pixel may correspond to several bits; i.e., an 8-bit pixel can be displayed in any of 256 colors (the total number of different configurations that can be achieved by eight 0s and 1s). *32, 33, 34, 42–3*

pixel depth A term used to describe the number of colors or grays a single pixel can display. This is determined by the number of bits used to display a pixel. Thus 1-bit equals 1 color (black), 4-bits (any permutation of four 1s and 0s, i.e. 0011 or 1001) equals 16 colors or grays, and so on, up to 24-bits which can produce 16.7 million combinations of twenty-four 0s and 1s, thus 16.7 million colors.

pixellization/pixelation A term used to describe the effect of an image that has been broken up into square blocks, resembling pixels, to give it a "digitized" look.

Place The command used by some applications to import an image file.

planographic *(pri.)* Any method of printing from a flat surface, such as lithography.

plate (1 *pri.)* A sheet of metal (usually), plastic or paper from which an image is printed (or transferred, in offset litho, to a blanket and then printed). (**2)** Strictly speaking, a book illustration printed separately from the text and then tipped or bound into the book, but sometimes erroneously used to describe a full-page illustration printed in a book. (**3** *pho.)* A size of photographic film, a whole plate measuring 6½ x 8½in. and a half plate measuring 4 x 6½in.

platter A circular, rigid disk which is incorporated, either singly or severally, into a hard disk drive. *36, 38*

plotter An output device that uses an inked pen, or assembly of pens, to produce large format prints. Plotters are used mostly in the CAD/CAM industries.

PMMU *abb:* paged memory management unit. A microchip which enables the use of virtual memory, among other things. 27

PMS → PANTONE.

PMT *abb:* → photomechanical transfer

PNT(G) → paint.

point The basic unit of the Anglo-American typographic measurement system. Historically, printing has always been an inexact science, and no two printers could agree on a standard system of type measurement, which meant that type cast in one foundry was incompatible with that cast in another. In the mid 18th century, the French typographer Pierre Simon Fournier proposed a standard unit which he called a "point," which was further developed by Firmin Didot into a European standard which, although their systems were based upon it, was not adopted by Britain or the U.S. The Anglo-American system is based on the division of one inch into 72 parts, called points; mathematically, one point should equal 0.013889in. but, in fact, it equals 0.013837in., meaning that 72 points only make 0.996264in. The European didot point equals 0.0148in. and 12 of these form a unit measuring 0.1776in. There is no relationship between the Anglo-American point and the didot point, and neither of them relate to metric measurement. On the Mac, one point measures 0.013889in., and 72 points really do equal one inch. It is no coincidence that the basic Mac screen resolution is 72dpi. → pica. 85–6

pointer A general term that refers to any of the many shapes of marker on your monitor which identifies the current screen location of your mouse, your current position in a piece of text, or that your Mac is undertaking a particular activity. Typical pointer shapes are the arrow pointer, vertical bar, I-beam, crossbar or crosshair, and wristwatch. Sometimes called a "cursor." 18

pointing interface → GUI.

polygon tool A tool in some applications with which you can draw polygonal, to which text, pictures, or fills may be applied.

POP *abb:* (**1**) Point of Presence. The local server of your Internet Service Provider, giving you worldwide contact at local call rates. (**2**) Post Office Protocol. E-mail storage and retrieval system.

pop-up menu A menu in a dialog box or palette that appears when you click on it. Pop-up menus are usually identifiable as a rectangle with a drop shadow.

port Sockets in a Mac, or peripheral device, into which other devices are plugged. Typical ports on a Mac are the ADB, SCSI, and serial ports. 30–1

portrait monitor A monitor with a screen in an upright format, as distinct from the more usual landscape format. The Radius "Pivot" monitor is rotatable to portrait or landscape formats.

portrait/upright Description of an image or page in a vertical format.

Poser *(app.)* 70

posterize To divide a continuous tone image into a predefined or arbitrary number of flat tones.

postlims → end matter.

PostScript Adobe Systems Inc.'s page description language for image output to laser printers and high-resolution imagesetters. → page description language. 40, 74, 84, 88, 90–4, 95, 97, 128, 129

PostScript dictionary A file, such as LaserPrep and Aldus Prep, containing definitions of PostScript terms, for use by the printer.

PostScript font → outline font

PostScript interpreter The built-in code that printing devices use to understand PostScript commands.

PostScript printer Any printing device using Adobe-licensed PostScript page description language.

PowerPoint *(app.)* 74

PPC *abb:* program-to-program communication. → IAC.

PPI *abb:* pixels per inch.

PPP *abb:* Point-to-Point Protocol. One of several methods for connecting a Mac to the Internet.

PRAM *abb:* → parameter RAM.

PRAM chip → parameter RAM.

precautions, *on machines* 137–8

prepress → origination.

preferences An option in many applications to enable or disable features of the application (such as the unit of measurement) and to modify the program default settings. Preferences can be modified for a single document or, sometimes, all documents – if none are open when you make the modifications. → default; preset defaults.

prefs file An application file that records your preference settings so that when you reopen a document you don't have to reset the preferences.

prelims, preliminary matter → front matter.

PRES → Chooser documents.

presentation visual → comp (2); dummy (2); mock up.

preset defaults Preprogrammed settings of an application that remain in use until you change them. → preferences.

press proof → machine proof.

pretzel/cloverleaf/propellor symbol → command key.

preview → keyline view.

primary colors Pure colors from which theoretically, although not in practice, all other colors can be mixed. In printing they are the so-called "subtractive" primaries: cyan, magenta, and yellow. The primary colors of light, or "additive" primaries, are red, green, and blue.

primitive Basic geometric element from which a complex object can be built.

Print A command (File menu) that, when selected, displays the Print dialog box.

print buffer A hardware device that intercepts data on its way to be printed and stores it until the printer is available, thus allowing you to continue working. As distinct from a print spooler.

Print dialog box The dialog box, invoked by the Print command, in which you select the options offered by the application you are working in. The most basic Print dialog box will allow you to select the number of copies you require and which pages.

printed circuit board (PC board) → board.

printer *(rep./pri.)* The film or plate of a single color produced for four-color process printing.

printer driver → driver.

printer file A file containing a font that can be downloaded to a printer.

printer font A font used for printing, as distinct from a font used for screen display. → font downloading.

printer port A serial port via which you can connect your Mac to a printer, network, or modem.

printing-in-progress Printing activity as described in a dialog box. In addition to advising you of the printing status of a document, this normally allows you, by providing a Cancel button, to cancel printing.

PrintMonitor The Apple-supplied print spooling application that allows you to print while you carry on working. → background printing; print spooler.

print origination → origination.

print spooler Software that intercepts data on its way to be printed and diverts it to disk until the printer is available, thus allowing you to carry on working. Apple's PrintMonitor is a print spooler. As distinct from a print buffer.

process blue → cyan.
process color → CMYK.
process color printing *(rep./pri.)* The printing that uses the four process color inks – cyan, magenta, yellow, and black – to recreate full-color images. Halftone screens are used to break up continuous tone images into tiny dots which, when printed in each of the process inks overlap to form most colors, although by no means all.

processor chip → central processing unit; coprocessor.

processor direct slot *obs.* (PDS) The slot for expansion cards included on a Mac SE or SE/30, although a card for one model cannot be used in the other.

process red → magenta.
process yellow (Y) The special shade of yellow which is one of the four process colors used in four-color printing.

program A set of coded instructions that controls the operation of a computer. → application; software.

program defaults → default; preferences; pre-set defaults.

programmer Someone who writes computer programs, as distinct from someone who uses them.

programmer's switch *(obs.)* A plastic switch included with some Macs (although you may have to attach it yourself), having two buttons: a reset button (the frontmost) that does the same thing as the Restart command (Special menu); and the interrupt button (rearmost) which is used by programmers for accessing various programming and debugging software. → interrupt button; reset button.

programming language A specially devised vocabulary used to write computer programs. Programming languages are either "high-level," which are based as closely as possible on English, or "machine code," the lowest level, being the least like English but the easiest for a computer to understand. The languages most frequently used for writing Mac software are BASIC, C++, and FORTRAN → compiler; computer languages; interpreter.

progressive proofs *(rep.)* Proofs used in color printing to show all colors both separately and in combination.

PROM *abb:* programmable ROM.

prompt In some applications or in special circumstances, a symbol, i.e. >, indicating that the computer is waiting for you to enter an instruction.

proof *(typ./rep./pri.)* A representation on paper, taken from a laser printer or imagesetter, inked plate, stone, screen, block, or type, in order to check the progress and accuracy of the work. Also called a "pull."

proof correction marks A standard set of signs and symbols commonly understood by all those involved in preparing copy for publication.

proofreader A person who reads proofs for corrections and who marks them accordingly.

proportional spacing A method of spacing characters so that letters and numbers occupy an appropriate amount of space for their design, to accommodate, for example, the difference in width between m and i.

protocol A set of mutually agreed rules that hardware and software must observe in order to communicate with one another.

ProView *(app.)* 73

public domain (PD) Description of any item of "intellectual property" that is free of all copyrights, thus freeing it for use by anyone for any purpose, either because its copyright period has lapsed or because, as is sometimes the case with computer software, its creator has deemed it so.

publish and subscribe A Mac system facility, supported by some applications, to automatically update a document ("subscriber") with information created or modified in another ("publisher").

pull → proof.

pull-/pop-/drop-down menu The menu that appears when you click on a menu title in the menu bar along the top of your screen.

push button A round-cornered rectangular button in a dialog box which, when you click on it, you invoke the command specified on the button. If the button rectangle has a thick rule around it, this means that it is the default button and will respond to the Return or Enter keys being pressed. → button.

Put Away (File menu) The command that you use to return a file or folder on the desktop (or in the trash) to whence it came.

Q

quad (typ.) In conventional typesetting, a space whose width is normally that of its height, thus "to quad," or "quadding," is to fill out a line with quad spaces.

QuarkImmedia (app.) 73

QuarkXPress (app.) 55–8, 90, 96, 112, 115

QuickDraw The part of the Mac system that performs all display operations on your screen. 40

Quicken (app.) 74

QuicKeys (util.) 75

QuickTime Apple system extension which provides several methods of compressing and decompressing digitized movie sequences.

Quit (File menu) The command by which you "shut down" an application and return to the Finder, as distinct from closing a document within the application, in which case the application remains open. Pressing Command-Q usually achieves the same thing.

qwerty The standard typewriter-based keyboard layout used by most, although not all, devices that require the use of a keyboard. The name derives from the arrangement of the first six characters of the top row of letter keys. → Dvorak keyboard.

R

® The mark attached to a trade mark indicating that it is registered and cannot be used by any other person or organization.

RA paper sizes (pap.) The designation of untrimmed paper sizes in the ISO A series of international paper sizes. → SRA paper sizes.

radial fill A fill pattern made up of concentric circles of gradated tints.

radiation shield A wire mesh or glass filter that fits over your monitor screen to reduce the level of emanating radiation. → ELF.

ragged left/right → ranged left/right.

RAID abb: Redundant Arrays of Independent Disks. Hardware system for enhanced security where data is recorded simultaneously on two or more hard disks.

raised cap(ital) A bold-face capital that projects above the line of type. Also called a "cocked-up initial."

raised point/dot A full point (period) printed at half the height of capitals rather than on the baseline.

RAM abb: random access memory. The working space instantly available to you every time you use your Mac. When you launch an application or open a document, it is loaded into RAM and stored there while you work with it. However, an item only stays in RAM for as long as your Mac is on (→ dynamic RAM) or until you write, or "save" it to disk. To carry out even basic graphic design work efficiently, you will need at least 16 MB RAM, but you'll probably find you need more, especially if you work with scanned images. → DIMM; SIMM. 23–5, 28–9, 36

RAM cache A piece of RAM that you set aside (via the General icon in the Control Panel) which stores the most recent actions you have carried out so that when you need them again, they do not have to be retrieved from disk.

RAM chip → DIMM; SIMM.

RAM disk A part of RAM that is temporarily "tricked," by certain utility software, into thinking that that particular portion is a disk drive. Because the process of retrieving data from RAM is so much faster than from disk, operations performed by items stored in a RAM "disk" will speed up. This "disk" is represented on the desktop by its own icon, which is erased when you switch off.

ranged left/right A style of typesetting in which lines of unequal length line up on either the left or right of a column of text so that they are vertically flush with each other, leaving the opposite ends of the lines uneven or "ragged."

ranging figures → lining figures/numerals.

raster The method of display (and of creating images → RIP (**1**)) used on video screens, and thus monitors, whereby the screen image is made up of a pattern of several hundred parallel lines created by an electron beam "raking" the screen from top to bottom at a speed of about one sixtieth of a second ("raster" comes from the Latin word rastrum, meaning "rake"). An image is created by the varying intensity of brightness of the beam at successive points along the raster. The speed at which a complete screen image, or frame, is created is called the "frame" or "refresh" rate. → refresh rate. 125, 127

raster image processor → RIP.

Raw Image file format for transferring files between applications and computer platforms, although some knowledge of using file-editing programs, such as Norton Utilities, may be required.

Ray Dream Designer (app.) 71

raytracing Rendering algorithm which simulates the physical and optical properties of light rays as they reflect off a 3D model.

RDEV → Chooser documents.

Read Me A file that accompanies many programs, giving important information or revisions to printed documentation. The files will usually be in SimpleText format or in a popular word-processing format such as Word.

read only Of disks, memory, and documents, those that can only be read from, and not written to.

read-only memory → ROM.

read/write head The part of a disk drive that extracts (reads) data from, and deposits (writes) data to, a disk. One read/write head is positioned above each side of every disk platter (a hard drive may consist of several platters). These move, on rails, over the surface of the platter while the platter rotates at speed. Also called a "disk drive head."

real time The term used to describe the actual time in which events occur, thus on your computer, an event that corresponds to reality. For example, at its very simplest, a character appearing on screen the moment you type it, is said to be real-time, as is a video sequence that corresponds to actual clock time.

reboot To restart your Mac. → boot; cold boot; restart; warm boot.

rebuild desktop To renew the desktop file in order to speed up Finder operations. The desktop file records not only new files, but deleted ones as well, so the more files you add and delete, the more the desktop file keeps growing. Rebuilding it gets rid of obsolete information. You rebuild the desktop by holding down Option-Command while you restart the computer.

record A total set of related fields in a database, comprising an individual entry.

rectangle tool → square-corner tool.

recto The right-hand page of a book.

redraw rate The speed at which an application renders an image on screen after a change has been made. Sometimes erroneously confused with refresh rate. → refresh rate.

reduction glass/tool → magnifying glass.

reflection copy *(rep.)* Any flat item which is reproduced by photographic means, using light reflected from its surface. → camera-ready art(work).

reflection tool In some applications, a tool by which you transform an element into its mirror image, or make a mirror-image copy of an element.

reflow The term describing the automatic repositioning of running text as a result of editing.

refresh rate The frequency, measured in hertz, with which a screen image, or "frame" (a single pass of an electron beam which "rakes" the screen several hundred times from top to bottom) is redrawn. A refresh rate of 71.3Hz means that the image is "refreshed" 71.3 times every second. A screen with a slow refresh rate may produce unacceptable flicker. → raster. *34–5*

register *(rep./pri.)* The correct positioning of one color on top of another or of the pages on one side of a sheet relative to the other (called "backing up") during printing. As distinct from "fit."

register/registration mark *(rep./pri.)* The marks used on artwork, film, and printing plates which are superimposed during printing to make sure that the work is in register.

relational database A database program which allows different files to exchange data with one another, as distinct from a flat-file database in which files are self-contained and cannot exchange data.

release version The version of a program that is released for general sale, following the alpha and beta tested versions.

relief printing *(pri.)* Printing from a raised surface, as in letterpress printing.

removable hard disk → disk; hard disk drive.

rendering *65, 70–1*

repro(duction) *(rep.)* The entire printing process from the completion of artwork or imagesetter output to printing. Also called origination. *124–36*

reproduction copy → camera-ready art(work).

ResEdit An Apple-supplied resource editing application, used for modifying any Mac program, system, or otherwise.

reset button *obs.* One of two buttons on the programmer's switch, the reset button is the frontmost and is an alternative way of restarting your Mac, more particularly after bombs. → interrupt button; programmer's switch.

resident font A font stored in ROM (usually in the printer ROM).

resolution The degree of precision – the quality, definition, or clarity – with which an image is represented or displayed, such as by a scanner, monitor, printer, or other output device. → pixel.

resolution, *and imagesetters 125, 126, 129 and laser printers 40–1 and monitors 32, 34–5 and reproduction 125, 126 of scanners 43, 44, 118, 131–2*

resource The term describing a system file that provides information to the central processing unit so that it can communicate with a peripheral device.

resource fork The part of a Macintosh application file that contains resources, that is, the information it uses for menus, fonts, and icons, as distinct from the data fork which contains data generated by you.

Restart A command (Special menu) that lets you reboot your Mac without switching it off (shutting down) and switching on again.

Restart button The rarely invokable button that appears in some bomb alert boxes. → bomb.

restart To reload your Mac's operating system from disk, but without switching it off (shutting down) and switching it on again. You restart your Mac if you have installed or removed certain system files (such as inits and cdevs) so that they may be activated or flushed out of the system, or after it has "bombed." Any work that you have not saved will be lost when you restart.

rest in pro(portion) → RIP (**2**).

restore To return backed-up files to disk if the originals are damaged or deleted.

result code Macspeak for "error code." → error/result code.

retouching *(pho./rep.)* Altering or correcting an image, artwork, or film by hand to make modifications or remove imperfections. Scanned images are usually retouched electronically using appropriate software. *65, 68–9*

Return key The key that operates much like a typewriter "carriage return" key in that it moves the text insertion point to the beginning of the next line, usually creating a new paragraph as it does so. In most applications and dialog boxes, it also duplicates the actions of the Enter key.

reverse b to w *abb:* reverse black to white. Instruction to reverse out an image or type. → reverse out.

reverse indent → hanging indent.

reverse l to r Instruction to reverse an image from left to right. → flop; lateral reverse.

reverse out *(rep.)* To reverse the tones of an image or type so that it appears white (or another color) in a black or colored background. Also called "drop-out," "save out."

reverse P → blind P.

reverse reading → wrong reading.

reversed type → reverse out.

RGB *abb:* red, green, blue. → additive colors; color model.

rich text format → RTF.

RIFF *abb:* raster image file format, Letraset's brand-name file format for storing images. *128*

right-aligned/justified Ranged right. → ranged left/right.

right reading *(rep.)* Description of positive or negative paper or film on which the text, if any, can be read as normal, that is, from left to right.

right-reading, emulsion-side-down *(rep.)* Description of negative film on which the text, if any, can be read as normal, i.e. from left to right, and in which the photographic emulsion is on the underside.

RIP (1) *abb:* raster image processor, a device that converts a page description language such as PostScript into a form which can be output by a high-resolution imagesetter. → raster. *127*
(2) *abb:* rest in pro(portion), an instruction to reproduce an image or artwork, giving only one dimension – the rest to be reduced or enlarged in proportion. *125, 127*

RISC *abb:* reduced instruction set computing. A micro-processor that provides high-speed processing by accepting only a limited number of commands, without – due to advances in memory technology – loss of efficiency.

river An aberration in typeset text, in which a series of word spaces form a linked or continuous stream of white space down a page. Often caused by badly justified type.

ROM *abb:* read-only memory, memory which can only be read from, and not written to. ROM resides in a chip on the Mac's motherboard and is where the "firmware" part (meaning software that's permanently built in and cannot be changed) of the operating system is kept. The data stored in ROM can only be updated by changing the ROM chip, which is why the constantly changing part of the operating system is provided as disk-based software. *23, 24*

roman The standard characters of a font in which the characters are upright, as distinct from italic.

root directory/level The term that describes the first level at which files and folders are placed, represented by the window that appears when you double-click (open) on a disk icon.

rotation tool In some graphics applications, a tool which, when selected, allows you to rotate an item around a fixed point.

rough A preliminary drawing showing a proposed design. Also called a "scamp." *114–15*

router → gateway.

routine A piece of programming code designed to perform a specific task.

RS *abb:* receive-send, a standard laid down by the U.S. Electronic Industries Association (EIA) for data transfer connections between computers or devices. The letters prefix a number, as in the RS-422 printer and modem port on Macs.

RTF *abb:* rich text format, a Microsoft file format for transferring formatted text documents. *128*

rule A line. The term derives from the Latin *regula* meaning "straight stick" and was used to describe the metal strips, of type height, in various widths, lengths, and styles, which were used by traditional typesetters for printing lines. *94–5*

ruler In some applications, the feature of a calibrated ruler, in your preferred unit of measure, at the edges of a document window.

ruler guide In some applications, a nonprinting guide which you obtain by clicking on the ruler and dragging to the desired position.

ruler origin → origin.

runaround Text that fits around a shape, like an illustration. Also called "text wrap."

run back The term describing words that move back from one line to the previous line, as a result of a text deletion or correction. The opposite of overrun.

run-in → run on.

running text The main body of a text which runs from page to page, although it may be broken up by illustrations or other matter.

run-in heading A heading leading into the text starting on the same line, as distinct from a heading placed above the text.

run on (1 *pri.)* Sheets printed in addition to the specified quantity. **(2** *typ.)* An instruction that two paragraphs are to be set as one as indicated.

run ragged Ragged right. → ranged left/right.

S

sad Mac icon The unhappy fellow who appears in place of the smiling icon at startup, indicating that something has gone wrong during the internal diagnostic tests that your Mac performs during startup. The sad Mac icon is accompanied by various sounds (or a number, depending on your model of Mac) which are different from the normal startup chord, and which indicate (to a trained ear) the nature of the problem.

SAM *(util.)* 75

same disk backup → backup, same disk.

sampler A device that digitizes sound so that it can be

manipulated by computers.

sans serif Description of a generic type style without serifs and usually without stroke contrast.

saturation → HSB.

Save (File menu) The command that writes data from RAM to disk, thus ensuring that your work is preserved. Get into the habit of saving your work as frequently as possible – all you have to do is press Command-S. *138, 140*

Save As… (File menu) The command with which you can save a document under another name in the same or another location (or it can have the same name if it's in another location). Some applications will also let you save a document in another file format.

Save dialog box The dialog box that appears the first time that you save a document, asking you what you want to call it and where you want to put it.

save out → reverse out.

sc, s caps *abb:* → small caps.

scale/scaling To determine the degree of enlargement or reduction required to obtain the desired reproduction size of an image.

scaling text → horizontal scaling.

scamp → rough.

scanned image *(rep.)* An image that has been converted by a scanner to a suitable file format that you can import into an application. To designers, the size of the file is important, since a single high resolution four-color scan for high-quality reproduction may create a file of many megabytes, thus reducing the practicality of working with any quantity of scanned images. On jobs containing multiple images, it is more usual for designers to work with low resolution scans and use them for position only. → scanner.

scanner *(rep.)* An electronic device which converts artwork and transparencies into digital form so that they can be manipulated by a computer and/or output to separated film. A scanner may be a relatively simple "desktop" flatbed type or a very sophis-

ticated reprographic device used for high-quality color separation. *41–6, 106–7, 118, 131–3*

scatter proof *(rep.)* A proof of illustrations in which all the images are positioned at random and as closely packed as possible, without reference to their final page position. This is done in order to cut proofing costs, particularly when large numbers of illustrations are involved, such as in illustrated book work.

Scrapbook An Apple-supplied desk accessory where you can permanently store text or images, as distinct from the Clipboard which only holds items temporarily. To use the Scrapbook, you select an item you are working on, copy or cut it, open the Clipboard, and then select Paste from the Edit menu. The item will automatically appear on its own "page" in the Scrapbook.

Scrap Manager The part of the Toolbox that handles copying and pasting between applications and/or desk accessories.

scratch A term describing disk space that you may not need for normal Mac use, but which you have set aside by creating a partition, in case a non-Mac (or Mac) application requests it for temporary storage.

screen (1) → monitor.
(2) → halftone screen.
(3) → radiation shield.

screen angle *(rep.)* A term referring to the angle at which halftone screens of images printing in two or more colors are positioned, to minimize undesirable dot patterns when they are printed. The angle at which screens should be positioned depends upon the number of colors being printed, but the norm for four-color process printing, and thus the default setting for most Mac applications that support four-color separation, is: cyan 105°; magenta 75°; yellow 90°; black 45°.
→ halftone screen; moiré.

screen clash → moiré.

screen dump → screen shot.

screen filter → radiation shield.

screen font A file containing a bitmapped font that your Mac uses to render a typeface on your screen – or at least, that was how a Mac originally displayed a font on screen. Graphic design on the Mac was once a very frustrating occupation because of the vagaries of the bitmapped on-screen display of type – the notorious "jaggies." Fortunately, the advent of outline font technology has made it possible for screen rendering of typefaces to be much more accurate – the outline printer font can be "borrowed" for screen display. Unless you are using TrueType fonts, you will need Adobe Type Manager to make this work with PostScript fonts. Even with ATM, you still need to install at least one size of the bitmapped screen font – so that its name appears in menus.

screen printing *(pri.)* Also known as "silkscreen" printing, a printing process whereby ink is forced through a fine mesh stretched across a frame. The image is formed by means of a hand-cut or photographically generated stencil, which is bonded to the screen. Commercially, screen printing is generally used for printing onto difficult surfaces, for display work and small print runs.

screen resolution (1) → pixel; resolution.
(2 rep.) Of halftone screens, the number of lines, or rows of dots, per inch. The greater the number of lines per inch, the finer the resolution – until the dots start filling in (which is dependent on the printing process and on the quality of paper). → halftone screen.

screen ruling → halftone screen; screen resolution (2).

screen saver, blanker A utility program (usually a control panel device) for preserving the phosphor coating on monitors by dimming the screen image, or by putting up a moving pattern, after a preset (by you) time of inactivity. *75*

screen shot/grab/dump/ capture A "snapshot" of

part or all of the current screen image. Several utility programs are available for this purpose.

screen size (**1**) → monitor. (**2**) → screen resolution.

screen tester (rep.) A device used for identifying the screen resolution of a printed halftone image.

screen type (rep.) Of a halftone screen, its pattern, such as dot, line, etc.

script The name given to programming languages that certain applications, such as HyperCard, allow you to write.

scroll, **scrolling** To move the contents of a window (or directory listing) up or down, or sideways, so that you can view a part of a document that was hidden beyond the edges of the window. You do this by means of scroll bars, scroll boxes, and scroll arrows.

scroll arrow The arrows at each end of a scroll bar that, when you click on one, move the contents of the window up, down, or sideways.

scroll bar The bars on the sides and/or (usually) bottom of a window (or directory listing) in which sits the scroll box. If the bar contains a gray fill, it indicates that there are portions of the document that go beyond what is displayed in the window.

scroll box The box that sits within the scroll bar of a window (or directory listing). It can be moved either by using the scroll arrows, or by clicking on it and dragging it up or down (or sideways) along the scroll bar. The position of the window image in relation to the whole document is indicated by the relative position of the scroll box to the scroll bar (if the scroll box is halfway up the scroll bar, the part of the document displayed in the window is halfway through the document).

SCSI/SCSI 2 (pron: skuzzy) abb: small computer system interface. A computer industry standard for interconnecting peripheral devices such as hard disk drives and scanners. The internal hard disk drive in your Mac is also

a SCSI device. *30*

SCSI bus A term sometimes used to describe a chain of devices linked to a Mac SCSI port.

SCSI (daisy-)chain The linking, in sequence, of several peripheral devices to a SCSI port. There are various factors to bear in mind when setting up a SCSI chain: the maximum number of devices you can add to those already there (your internal drive and the Central Processing unit) is six; the total combined length of cabling between all the devices must not exceed 23 feet (7 meters), but an upper limit of 16 to 20 feet (5 or 6 meters) is safer; no two devices should have the same ID number (→ SCSI ID number); there must be no more than two terminators in the entire chain (→ SCSI terminator); the actual position of a device, or order of devices, in the chain relative to other devices may be important – refer to the manufacturer's instructions.

SCSI device A peripheral device that attaches, or is attached, to a computer by means of a SCSI connection.

SCSI device, *problems 138*

SCSI ID number The number, or "address," assigned to each SCSI device connected to a Mac. There are eight numbers on the internal SCSI chain, though the Mac's CPU occupies number 7 and the (principal) hard disk takes number 0. There are a further eight locations on the external chain, again from 0–7. Remaining numbers are available to any other device in the chain, but each device must have a unique number. The numbering order of devices is arbitrary, but the device with the highest number takes priority if a situation demands it. The method of changing the number of a device varies; it may be by means of a "push-wheel" button, a dial, software, or it may even be preset internally.

SCSI partition → partition.

SCSI port The point where a SCSI cable connects to a SCSI device, using one of two varieties of SCSI connectors – 25-pin or 50-pin.

Permutations of cable connections depend not only on the number of pins in the connector, but also on whether it is male or female. The SCSI port on your Mac is a 25-pin female bus.

SCSI Probe (util.) *140*

SCSI terminator A device that protects a SCSI cable from "signal echo." A terminator may be internal within a device, or it may be a plug, resembling a SCSI connector, which you fit to the SCSI port of a device. On some devices, termination may be turned on or off by means of switches. Internal drives are already terminated, but if you add another device, that too must be terminated – the first and last devices in a chain must be terminated and your internal drive counts as the first (physically the first, regardless of SCSI ID number).

.sea *abb:* Self Extracting Archive. suffix of a compressed file which needs no extra software to be expanded.

search path The route taken by your Mac when it looks for a file. → path (1).

SE Bus *obs.* The data path from the expansion slot to the Central Processing unit, unique to the Macintosh SE (but not the SE/30, which has its own, called the "Direct Slot"). → bus; expansion slot.

secondary color A color obtained when two primary colors are mixed.

sector A segment of a track on a disk, containing space for 512 consecutive bytes of data, and being the smallest contiguous space in which data can be stored. → cylinder; track (2).

sector interleave factor → interleave ratio.

seek time → access time.

see-through → look-/see-/show-through.

segment A portion of an application. An application may be made up of several segments, not all of which need to be in RAM at the same time.

Select All (Edit menu) A command by which you can, in the Finder, select the entire contents of a window. It is also a command in some applications which allows you to select the entire contents of a document, page or an active box.

select(ing) To choose a thing (such as an icon or a piece of text) so that you can do something to or with it. To alter the state of any item, it must first be made active, or selected. If nothing within a window is active, but the window itself is, it may be understood by some applications that the entire document is selected; i.e., a spelling check may be applied to a portion of text if that is selected, or to the whole document or text chain if it is not. You select something by clicking on it or dragging across it, depending on the current circumstances.

selection rectangle/box A dotted line forming a rectangle, drawn using the pointer or a "selection" tool, and which either disappears once the desired selection is made, or becomes a marquee. → marquee.

separation → color separation.

separation artwork Artwork in which a separate layer is created for each color to be printed.

serial interface A computer interface which transmits data bits sequentially, one at a time, in the same direction along a single wire or channel inside a cable. As distinct from a parallel interface.

serial ports The sockets on your Mac where you plug in devices which use a serial interface, such as printers and modems. *30*

serif The small terminal counterstroke at the end of the main strokes of a type character.

server → file server.

set In traditional type design, the width of an individual character. The width, or set, of the widest character (an em) is measured in points and subdivided into units, the set of each other character being a multiple of these units.

service agreement *109*

service bureau A company that provides general computer services from disk con-

version to color scanning. The main use of a bureau by designers is for high resolution imagesetting – typesetting to bromide or film from your disk. *123, 127, 128, 131–3*

set solid A term describing type set on its own body size without any leading: 10pt on 10pt.

service provider → ISP

set-up *105–9*

set-up, *case studies 110–13*

set-up, *cost 109*

SGML *abb:* standard generalized markup language, a mark-up coding structure suitable for converting PC word-processor documents to conventional (non-Mac) computer typesetting systems.

shaded letter (1) → shadow font. (**2**) A letterform filled with crosshatched lines rather than solid tone.

shadow font Letterforms given a three-dimensional appearance by heavy shadows beside the main strokes.

shared disk A hard disk, attached to a networked computer, which can be accessed by other computers on the network.

shareware The term describing software that is freely available through user groups, bulletin boards, etc., and which you pay for only if you decide to continue using it. Unlike public-domain software, shareware is protected by copyright (not to be confused with "copy protected" – shareware, by its nature, is never copy-protected). *74*

shift-clicking To make multiple selections by holding down the Shift key while you click on the item.

Shift key The modifier key used to generate capital letters and other characters displayed on the keyboard. It can also be used for a variety of specific functions (→ shift-clicking) as well as serving as a general modifier key.

short page A page containing text to a length shorter than the usual length on other pages, adjusted to improve the layout or accommodate a break.

Show Clipboard A command in most applications allowing you to view the contents of the Clipboard, or in other words, to see the last item that you cut or copied.

show-through → look-/see-through.

shuffling In some page make-up applications, a term describing the re-ordering of the pages of a document while retaining a logical numbering sequence.

Shut Down (Special menu) The command that lets you turn off your Mac "safely" – that is, by first saving open documents, and ejecting any inserted disks.

shut down To turn off your Mac or a peripheral device, having saved and closed all open documents and ejected all disks.

sidebar → box feature/story.

side bearing The letterspace assigned to each side of a PostScript type character that, if an application permits, can be adjusted to provide greater or less kerning.

SIG *abb:* special interest group.

signature (1) → Creator. (**2** *fin.*) The consecutive number, letter, or other mark at the tail of each section in a book, which serves as a guide for binding. (**3** *fin.*) A numbered section prior to binding.

SIMM *abb:* single in-line memory module, a small plug-in board containing RAM chips on early Macs. SIMMs are still available in densities (capacity) of 256K, 1MB, 4MB, and 16MB. SIMMs may be either low- or high-profile (referring to physical height), depending on the model of Mac. *28, 29*

SimpleText An application that allows you to read "plain text" documents. These are documents that frequently accompany application files to provide instructions for installation, corrections to the documentation, etc.

single-sided floppy disk *obs.* → disk.

.sit *abb:* Suffix of a file which has been compressed using StuffIt.

68000 series chip *obs.* The series of microprocessor chips made by Motorola for early Macs.

size/sizing up
→ scale/scaling.

size box The box in the lower right-hand corner of a window that allows you, by clicking on it and dragging, to alter the size of the window.

size, *of monitor 32*
of type 85–7

skew, skewing In some applications, a feature allowing you to slant an item, such as a picture or word.

slab/square serif Description of typefaces with square serifs of almost the same thickness as the uprights, used in most "egyptian" typefaces.

slash → solidus.

slide presentation software *74*

SLIP *abb:* Serial Line Internet Protocol. One of several methods for connecting to the Internet.

slip-sheeting → interleaving (1).

sloped roman A term describing an italic version of a font that is an optically or digitally distorted version of the roman design, as distinct from being a separate, specially designed italic.

slot → expansion slot.

small capitals/caps (sc, s caps) Capital letters which are smaller than the standard size, usually being about the size of the x-height. Traditionally, small caps were a specially designed and cut font, rather than just being a smaller size of type. However, on the Mac, small caps are generated by scaling a single outline printer font, resulting in small caps that are lighter in weight than the upper and lower case. More and more fonts are becoming available which have a specially designed version for providing small caps, giving a much more even "color" to text setting. *96*

small computer system interface → SCSI.

small icon → by Small Icon.

smart quotes The term sometimes given to the facil-

ity provided by some applications to convert quotation marks from straight "pecks" (" ') to typesetting, or "curly" ones (" ').

smoothing A term describing the refinement of bitmapped images by rounding off the corners of the square dots, or pixels.

SMTP *abb:* Simple Mail Transport Protocol. Mail transfer system on the Internet.

snailmail The ordinary postal system.

snap to A facility provided by some applications to exercise a sort of "magnetic pull" on items by guides and rulers, thus making positioning of items more accurate.

softback → paperback.

soft copy (1) A copy of a file or document supplied on a disk, as distinct from a "hard" copy of the file or document as a printout on paper. (2) Text matter appearing on a computer monitor. (3 *typ.*) Typeset copy used for checking a text before camera-ready art is produced.

soft dot (*rep.*) A halftone dot on film that is less dense at the edge than at the center and is thus easier to etch for correction purposes.

software The term used to describe specially written collections of data, called programs, that make it possible for a computer or any other item of computer-related hardware to perform its tasks. *50–83*

software, *for graphic designers 74–5, 82–3, 111-12*
for set-up 107
training 52–3
upgrading 53–4

solidus A type character in the form of an oblique stroke, used as a fraction slash (/) and generated on a Mac keyboard by pressing Shift-Option-1.

sort (1 *typ.*) A single character of type. (2) A feature provided by some applications to arrange data in any chosen order.

Sound and Displays Control Panel for managing monitors, alerts, and sound input and output.

sound-in/sound out ports *31*

Sound Manager The Macintosh device driver that generates sound.

source (1) Used of files, folders, and disks to mean the original being copied, as distinct from the copy, or duplicate. (2) Used of files, folders, and disks to mean the one something came from, as distinct from the target, the one it is going to.

source document A document from which items have been copied, as distinct from the document an item is being copied to – the "target," or destination document.

source volume Used of files, folders, disks, and devices to mean the place you are copying something from, as distinct from the "destination" – the place it is going to.

space An invisible, graded unit for spacing out a line of text.

Spacebar The key for creating spaces between type characters.

spam, spamming Unfriendly posting of large numbers of similar messages to newsgroup sites.

spec(ification) A detailed description of the components, characteristics, and procedures of a particular job, product, or activity.

special character A type character supplied as part of a font, or character set, but generated by pressing modifier keys.

special effects *65, 70–1*

Special menu One of the standard Finder menus, containing commands for such things as emptying the Trash and shutting down.

special sorts Type characters not normally included in a font, or character set, such as fractions, musical notations, etc. Also called "peculiars" or "pi characters." *96*

specimen page A proof of a page as an example of a proposed style of design, paper quality, printing, etc.

speed, *of computers 27–8*
of modems 47

spell checker A means of checking a document for spelling errors by way of a special dictionary, built in to most word-processing applications, but also available as stand-alone utilities. Spell checkers may be of batch or interactive mode varieties.

SPH *abb:* sheets per hour.

spike suppressor → surge suppressor.

spine *(fin.)* The center of the case of a book, which runs down the back of the book when it is cased in. Also called a "backbone."

split dash/rule A rule used as a traditional decoration. It is a rule that is thick at its center and tapered toward the ends, and which is split at the center by a bullet, star, or other ornament.

spooler → print spooler.

spot color *(rep./pri.)* The term used to describe any printing color that is a special mix of colors, and not one of the four process colors.

spread (1) In general usage, two facing pages of a document or publication. Technically, a double truck or double-page spread occurs when matter crosses the gutter to occupy the two center pages of a section. Otherwise, it is a "false double." **(2)** → trapping.

spreadsheet An application that, using a grid system of rows and columns which create interacting rectangles, called "cells," makes it possible to carry out complex calculations. *74*

square-corner/rectangle tool In most graphics applications, the tool that enables you to draw a rectangular box or shape.

squared(-up) (halftone) *(rep.)* A halftone image that has been trimmed to a square or rectangular shape.

squares *(fin.)* The portion of the inside of a case which projects beyond the cut edges of a book.

square serif → slab serif.

SRA paper sizes *(pap.)* The designation of untrimmed paper for bled work in the series of international paper sizes.
→ international paper sizes; RA paper sizes.

s/s *abb:* same size, an instruction to reproduce an item at its original size.

stacking order In graphics applications, the position of an item relative to other items in front of or behind it.

staircasing → jaggie.

standard character set → character set.

Standard File dialog box The dialog box you get when you select Open or Save As from the File menu, or when you open or save documents within an application. Also called directory dialog box.

Standard File Package The routines for providing the standard Macintosh user interface when a file is opened or closed.

standard generalized markup language → SGML.

standard menu One of three menus (Apple, File, and Edit) that appear as standard in almost all applications.

standing time → open time.

starburst (1 *pho.)* A photographic effect of radiating lines from a highlight, provided by a filter that diffuses light from a strong, concentrated source. **(2)** In some applications, the name given to the shape that the pointer assumes when certain transformation tools are selected.

star network A network configuration in which the the central processing unit node has a number of other nodes radiating from it in a star shape.

start bit A bit used in data communication to indicate the start of data transmission. → asynchronous communication; stop bit

start(ing)/startup → boot(ing) up.

startup disk/device Any disk – internal or external, hard or floppy – that contains, at the very least, the System and Finder files which your Mac needs in order to boot up. *138*

startup document/file → init.

startup errors *140*

startup items a folder within the system folder. Items (applications, files, or aliases) stored in this folder will be opened automatically when the Mac starts up

startup screen The image displayed at startup – the default screen shows the Mac OS icon. You can replace it with your own design which must be titled

StartupScreen and placed in the system folder.

startup sheet The printed test sheet that a LaserWriter produces each time it is switched on, telling you, among other things, how many sheets have been printed on that particular printer.

static RAM → dynamic RAM.

stationery A document which serves as a template – when opened, it is automatically duplicated, leaving the original intact.

stem The most distinctive vertical stroke, or that closest to vertical, in a type character.

step and repeat To produce multiple copies of an image at different sizes in defined increments.

stet A Latin word meaning "let it stand." It is used when marking up copy and correcting proofs to cancel a previous instruction or correction.

Sticky Keys → Easy Access.

stop bit A bit used in data communication to indicate the end of one byte. → asynchronous communication; start bit.

storage The term used to describe data that is preserved for future use or modification, as distinct from memory, in which data is merely "in transit." → disk. *24, 25, 29–30*

storage media *36–9*

straight matter A body of text without break for headings, illustrations, etc.

StrataVision 3d *(app.) 67, 71*

stress The apparent direction of a letterform, given emphasis by the heaviest part of a curved stroke.

string A given sequence of characters, including spaces and special characters.

stripping (1 *rep.)* Assembling two or more images to produce a composite for making final film in photomechanical reproduction. **(2** *typ.)* To insert a typeset correction in film or on camera-ready art. **(3** *fin.)* To glue a strip of cloth or paper to the back of a paperback book or pad as a reinforcement.

stripping up as one *(rep.)* Assembling two or more images or items of film to combine them as a single piece of film in photome-chanical reproduction.

strobe → flicker.

stroke (1) The outline of any shape or type character, as distinct from the inside area, called the "fill." (**2** *typ.*) A straight, diagonal part of a type character.

StuffIt Deluxe *(util.)* 75, 131

Style (sheets) In some applications, the facility for applying a range of frequently used attributes, such as typographic and paragraph formats, to elements in a document by using specially assigned commands. 116

style The term used to describe a stylistic modification of a font, such as italic, shadow, outline, etc.

subdirectory Any directory other than the root directory.

subhead(ing) Any heading for the division of a chapter.

subject *(rep.)* The term used to describe any single image which is to be reproduced or originated.

submenu A menu attached to a main menu item, which appears as the result of selecting that item. It is normally indicated by a (▶).

subscriber → publish and subscribe.

subscript → inferior character.

subsidiaries → end matter.

subtractive colors The primary colors used in printing – cyan, magenta, and yellow. → primary colors; process color.

Suggested Memory Size Information provided via the Get Info dialog box (File menu) regarding the minimum amount of memory that an application needs to be able to run, as suggested by its author or producer. This is the portion of RAM that will be set aside for use exclusively by that application. A box is provided for you to modify the amount of memory allocated to the application, and you may need to increase it if you are working on very long, complex, or graphics-intensive documents. To alter the memory size, you must first

quit the application.
→ Application Memory Size.

suitcase (file) A file, represented by an icon of a suitcase – thence its name – which may be either a desk accessory or a screen font.

Suitcase *(util.)* 75, 88, 89, 98

SuperCard *(app.)* 72, 76–7

SuperDrive → floppy disk drive.

superior The term used to describe figures or letters that are smaller than text size, the top of which is aligned with the cap height of the text as in (²), as distinct from superscript, which appears above the cap height.

superscript The term used to describe figures or letters that are smaller than text size, and which are raised above the cap height as in (²), as distinct from superior.

support The term used to describe after-sales help, provided by the producer of a product or by its sales representative.

surface mapping → texture/surface mapping.

surface mount SIMM Alternative term for a "low-profile" SIMM.

surge suppressor An essential item for protecting hardware from damaging fluctuations in power supply. Various forms are available, such as in-line units or power strips. Also called "spike suppressors" and "power cleaners."

surprinting → overprint.

swatch A color sample.

swelled dash/rule A rule that prints as a thick line in the center, tapering at both ends.

Swivel 3D Professional *(app.)* 70, 71

SYLK *abb:* symbolic link, a file format for transferring spreadsheet data between applications. 128

symbol A letter, figure, or drawn sign that represents or identifies an object, process, or activity, although not necessarily pictorially.

synchronous communication A communications protocol by which data is transmitted, in chunks, between rigid timing signals. As distinct from asynchronous communication.

sysop *abb:* system operator, a person who operates a bulletin-board system.

system A complete set of connected things, organized to achieve an objective.

system disk A disk containing (at the very least) a System and Finder file. If you use it when you boot up, it becomes the startup disk.

system error → bomb.

system extension A file, stored in the Extensions folder, that adds enhancements to the system software.

System file The file used to provide, with the Finder and software residing in ROM, the Mac's operating system. The System file also contains fonts, sounds, and keyboard files. 22

system folder A folder that contains the System and Finder files and any other files that are run as part of the system. It is distinguishable from other folders by an icon of a Mac on its front. Also called a "blessed folder."

system heap The part of RAM set aside for use by the System. The size of the heap is determined at startup.

system operator → sysop.

system software The term that describes all the programs that contribute toward the operating infrastructure of your Mac. It includes, in addition to the System and Finder files, all the RAM-based files – control panel devices, inits, desk accessories, utilities, fonts, and resources – in your system folder.

System Tools The name given to describe a collection of concurrent versions of system files.

T

tab-delimit To separate data elements such as records or fields by using the Tab key.

Tab key The key that moves the insertion point to the next tab stop or, in dialog boxes, databases and spreadsheets comprising fields, from one box (field) to the next.

tablet → digitizing pad/tablet.

tab stop The place at which

the text insertion point stops when the Tab key is pressed.

tabular work Type matter set in columns.

tabulate To arrange text or figures in the form of a columnar table, according to fixed measures.

tail The bottom edge of a book.

tail margin The margin at the bottom of a page, also called a "foot margin."

take back *(typ.)* An instruction, marked on a proof, to take back characters, words, or lines to the preceding line, column, or page.

take in *(typ.)* An instruction, marked on a proof, to include extra copy supplied.

take over *(typ.)* An instruction, marked on a proof, to take over characters, words, or lines to the following line, column, or page.

tape drives *37*

taper Of gradated tones and colors, the progression of one tone or color to the next. Gradations may be in equal increments or may be logarithmic (the increments of tones or colors increase from one end of the gradation to the other).

taper angle The direction of gradated tones or colors.

target Used of files, folders, and disks to mean the one something is going to, as distinct from the source, the one where it came from.

target printer The device that a document is sent to for printing.

TCP/IP *abb:* Transmission Control Protocol/Internet Protocol. Communication format for contact between computers on the Internet.

TeachText *obs.* → Simple Text

tear-off menu In some applications, a menu that, when it pops down from the menu bar, can be "torn" off by dragging it away from the menu bar onto the desktop, where it can be moved around as you need it.

technical support → support.

temp file A temporary file, used by the application that created it.

template (1) A shape, or sheet with cutout shapes, used as a drawing aid. **(2)** A document or page created

with page, paragraph, and text formats to be used as a basis for repeated use in other documents.

terminal emulation Software that allows one computer to mimic another by acting as a terminal for its "host."

terminating resistor/terminator → SCSI terminator.

text (1) Information presented as readable characters. **(2)** Typeset matter forming the main body of a publication.

text box/field (1) In frame-based applications, a box, created with a text tool, for entering and working with text. **(2)** A field, such as in a dialog box, into which you enter text.

text by modem *117*

text chain A set of linked text boxes, with text flowing from one to another.

text editor Any program which you use to enter and edit text. → word processor.

text file A file containing only text bits, without any formatting. → ASCII.

text input *116–18*

text insertion bar The blinking bar in a text box that indicates the insertion point.

text insertion point The place, indicated by the text insertion bar, where the next character will be positioned.

text marker In word processors, a symbol positioned in the text to provide a reference marker so that you can return to it instantly (by using the Find command). Also called a "wildcard."

text on disk *117*

text reflow → reflow.

text tool → I-beam pointer.

text type/matter *(typ.)* Any typeface of a suitable size for printing a body of text, usually in a range of 8pt to 14pt.

text wrap → runaround.

texture/surface mapping A graphic technique of wrapping a two-dimensional image around a three-dimensional object.

thick *(typ.)* The term sometimes used to describe a word space measuring one-third of an em.

thin *(typ.)* The term sometimes used to describe a word space measuring one-

fifth of an em.

third-party A term sometimes used to describe an item, whether hardware or software, not made by the manufacturer of the item it is designed to be used with.

three-dimensional modeling *65, 70–1*

throughput A unit of time measured as the period elapsing between start and finish of a particular job.

Thumb Design Partnership, *case study 110–12*

thumbnail (1) Rough, miniature layouts of a proposed design or publication, showing a variety of treatments or the order of chapters, etc. **(2)** In some applications, the facility to view and print pages together on a sheet at a reduced size.

tied letter → ligature.

TIFF *abb:* tagged image file format, a standard and popular graphics file format used for scanned, high-resolution, bitmapped images. *128*

tight A term referring to a design, or to text, that is very closely-packed and includes little blank space.

tiling (1) The term used to describe copying an item and repeating it in all directions, thus creating a pattern. **(2)** The term used to describe the method of printing a document page that is too large to fit onto a single sheet by breaking it into overlapping portions which, when assembled, form the whole page.

time-slicing → multitasking.

tint (1) The effect of the admixture of white to a solid color. **(2)** The effect achieved by breaking up a solid color into dots and allowing white paper to show through. Tints are specified in percentages of the solid color. *130*

tissues → layout.

title bar The bar at the top of an open window which contains its name and, when active, six horizontal rules. The window can be moved around the desktop by clicking and dragging its title bar. The title bar may or may not contain a close box and/or a zoom box.

title page The page, normally a right-hand page, at the front of a book which bears the title, name(s) of the author(s), the publisher, and any other relevant information.

title verso (T/V) The verso of the title page of a book, usually containing copyright information. → verso.

toggle Of menus and check-boxes, those that turn from off to on (or from a positive command to a negative one), or vice versa, each time you select or check it.

tonal value The relative densities of tones in an image. → color value.

tone-line process *(rep.)* A technique of producing line art from a continuous tone original by combining a negative and positive film image.

tool A feature of most graphics applications, consisting of a device (tool) which, when selected, turns the pointer into a shape representing that tool, which you then use to perform the designated task; i.e., you use a box tool for creating boxes.

Toolbox The part of the software written into the Macintosh ROM that allows software developers to take advantage of the Mac user interface. The Toolbox Managers handle such things as dialog boxes, windows, fonts, mouse, keyboard, and so on. In fact, it is the Toolbox that sets the Macintosh computer apart from other computers. *23*

Toolbox Managers → Toolbox.

tool palette/box In those applications that feature special tools, the window, usually floating, on which they are displayed for selection. → palette.

TPD *abb:* → two (or twin) - page display.

tps *abb:* → trimmed page size.

track (**1** *pri.*) The printing line from the front edge of a plate to the back. Items imposed in track will all be subject to the same inking adjustments on press. (**2**) The term describing the concentric "rings" circumscribing a disk, in which data is stored. Each track is divided into sectors. → disk; sector.

trackball A device for moving the pointer, resembling

an upturned mouse – i.e. with the mouse ball on top rather than underneath. You move the pointer by fondling the ball. Because the device remains stationary, it occupies less desk space than the conventional mouse.

trackpad small rectangular pad used as pointing device on portable Macs. The pad is sensitive to very small finger movements.

tracking A term describing the adjustment of space between the characters in a selected piece of text. As distinct from kerning, which only involves pairs of characters.

tracking values, *table 102–3*

training *108*
in software 52–3

transformation tools The name sometimes given to tools that change the location or appearance of an item.

transient font An automatically downloaded font that only lasts in a laser printer's memory until the document currently being printed has finished printing. As distinct from a so-called "permanent" font, which lasts in memory until the printer is switched off.

transition Visual effect that occurs between two different movie frames.

transitional A classification of typefaces that are neither old face nor modern, such as Baskerville and Fournier.

translator The term describing data required by Apple File Exchange so that it can translate a document created on one operating system into a document that can be used on another.

transparent A term used to describe any software item that operates without any interaction on your part – apart from installing it in the first place.

transpose To swap the positions of any two items of text, or two images, either by design or because they are wrongly ordered.

trapping *(rep./pri.)* The slight overlap of two colors to eliminate gaps that may occur between them due to the normal fluctuations of registration during printing.

→ choke; fatty. *119*

Trash The garbage can icon, which performs like a folder, in the bottom right-hand corner of your desktop where you put files as a prelude to deleting them. Dragging the icon of a disk to the Trash both ejects the disk and removes its icon from the desktop.

trim *(fin.)* To cut printed sheets to the required size.

trim marks → corner marks.

trimmed page size A term used to describe the size of a printed and bound book, referring to the page size rather than the size including the binding.

troubleshooting *137–40*

trs *abb:* → transpose.

TrueType Apple's outline font format produced as an alternative to PostScript. A single TrueType file is used both for printing and for screen rendering – unlike PostScript fonts, which require a screen font file as well as the printer font file. → outline font. *84, 88, 94, 97*

turning off → shut down.

T/V *abb:* → title verso.

tween Contraction of "between." Traditionally, in cel animation, the creation of art between key frames, ensuring smooth transition of shape and position.

twenty-four-/24 bit color The allocation of 24 bits of memory to each pixel, giving a possible screen display of 16.7 million colors (a row of 24 bits can be written in 16.7 million different combinations of 0s and 1s). → four-bit color; eight-bit color.

twice up Artwork prepared at twice the size at which it will be reproduced.

two-page display (TPD) Name given to a 21in. monitor (measured diagonally). → monitor.

Type 1 font The Adobe PostScript outline font format containing hints. Type 1 fonts were formerly encrypted, meaning that you could not alter them, but Adobe has now made the format available to all in response to the introduction of the open format of TrueType. Type 1 fonts come as two files: an outline printer file and a bitmapped screen file. → Adobe Type Manager; hinting; encryption; outline font. *91, 94*

Type 3 font *obs.* A PostScript font format which, not being encrypted, was introduced as an alternative to the encrypted Type 1 font format. → hinting; encryption. *73, 91, 94*

type area The area of a page designed to contain the main body of text, thus creating margins.

type design, *and the computer 73*
software 80–1

type effect The modification of type characters to create a special effect, such as outline, zoom, etc.

typeface The term describing a type design, including variations on that design such as italic and bold, but excluding all the other related designs, as distinct from type family.

type family A term describing all the variations related to a basic type design, such as Goudy Old Style, Goudy Catalogue, Goudy Handtooled, etc., as distinct from a typeface.

type mark-up → mark-up.
type measurements *85–6*
type scale/gauge A rule marked with a scale of line measurements in varying increments of point size.

type series → font series.
typesetting (**1** *typ.*) The process of converting text into a recognized font and producing it in a form suitable for printing. (**2** *typ.*) The text item produced by (**1**).

typesetting, *by computer 124*

type specifications The characteristics of type used in a design, such as font, size, measure, etc.
→ mark-up.

type style → style.
type synopsis/specimen sheet A printed sample of a font showing the full character set.

typo (*typ.*) *abb:* typographic error. An error occuring during typesetting, such as the wrong font or size, as distinct from a literal, such as a spelling mistake, which may also be an error in a manuscript.

typographer (**1**) A person

whose occupation is typography. (**2**) → compositor.
typography The art, and arrangement, of type. *84–104*

typography, *and the image-setter 127, 129*
horizontal scaling 104
justification methods 100–1
special sorts 96
tracking values 102–3

U

UC *abb:* → upper case.
UCR *abb:* → under-color removal.
u/lc *abb:* upper and lower case, an instruction for type to be set in both upper and lower case, as appropriate.
umlaut → accent.
under-color removal (UCR) *(rep.)* The technique of removing unwanted color from scanned color separations either to reduce the amount of ink or because the colors cancel each other out, such as removing the magenta and yellow dots when there is enough black and cyan to cover.

underline/underscore A rule printed beneath a word or portion of text.

Undo (Edit menu) A standard command, found in most applications, that allows you to revert to the last text or format change. Some applications allow several levels of "Undo."

ungroup To "Undo" a group.
UniQorn *(app.) 58*
unit system A system of type design in which character widths conform to unit measurements associated with the set of the character. → set.

Universal Copyright Convention An international assembly that, in 1952, agreed protection for the originator of an "intellectual work" – a text, photograph, illustration, etc. – to prevent the use of that work without permission from its creator or copyright owner. The work must carry the copyright mark ©, the name of the owner of the copyright, and the date of its first publication. → copyright.

Universal Product Code (UPC) → bar code.
UNIX The AT&T operating system devised to be multitasking, and portable from

one computer type to another. Apple's UNIX system is called A/UX.

unjustified Lines of type which do not align with both left and right margins, as does justified type. Unjustified type may be ranged left or right, or it may be centered. The appearance of unjustified type is also called free line fall.

unlock → lock; locked file; write-protect.

unmount To remove a volume from the desktop or eject a disk.

unsharp masking The technique of enhancing the details in a scanned image by exaggerating the density of pixels at the edges of a color change (the image is first blurred, hence the term "unsharp").

upgrade (**1**) To modify or enhance a computer. You can upgrade your Mac by changing the logic board to one that gives the Mac greater capabilities, or by simply installing a later version of the system software. (**2**) A newer, enhanced (often merely by debugging it) issue of a program, sometimes in the form of a "patch," and as distinct from a completely new version. Upgrades can be identified by a decimalized figure – 1 being the original, 1.2 and 1.3 being upgrades, and 2.0 being a rewrite, or new version. *53–4*

upload To send data to a distant computer. Opposite of download.

upper case The capital letters of a type font.
upright → portrait.
user A person who uses hardware and software, as distinct from someone who makes or writes it.

URL *abb:* Uniform Resource Locator. Unique address of a file on the Internet. Comprises three elements: the protocol (such as HTTP), the host name, then the directory with its file name.
Usenet Network of newsgroups.
user group A group of people who share experiences, knowledge, problems, software, etc., relating to a specific type of computer. A Macintosh user group can

often be recognized by the initials MUG as part of its name.

user interface → GUI; interface.

user-specified defaults Program defaults that have been specified or modified by the user.

utility A program that enhances or supports the use of your Mac generally, or applications specifically. Typical utilities are backup programs, font management programs, file-finding programs, defragmentation programs, file recovery programs, etc. 74–5

V

value → color value; tonal value.

VDU/VDT abb: visual display unit/terminal. → monitor.

vector → object-oriented.

velox → photomechanical transfer.

Ventura Publisher (app.) 58

verification A term used to describe the process of testing the integrity of the data blocks on a disk drive by writing and reading data which is checked many times for accuracy.

verso The left-hand page of a book or, more precisely, the other side of a leaf from a recto (right-hand page).

vertical alignment The placement of lines of text in relation to the top and bottom of a page, column, or box.

vertical bar pointer → I-beam pointer.

vertical blanking interval → blanking interval.

vertical justification The spacing out of a block of text so that it vertically fills a page, column, or box.

very low frequency (VLF) → ELF.

Video A QuickTime setting which compresses image sequences with little or no degradation of quality and is suitable for playback from both hard disks and CD-ROMs, although it is limited to 16-bit color depth. → QuickTime.

video A Latin term meaning "I see," now used in reference to all television-based products.

video card A plug-in board that controls an external monitor. → board. 34

video digitizer → digitizer.

video port 31

video RAM The portion of RAM reserved for monitor display. → RAM. 29, 31

View The Finder menu that allows you to choose your preferred form of viewing the contents of a window, such as by Label, by Date, by Icon.

virtual Computer jargon for "imaginary" or "conceptual," or something that seems as though it exists, but really it doesn't – or at least it does, but only until the software that created it doesn't! So "virtual reality" is an imagined reality, indistinguishable from real life provided the environment that created it is in operation. "Virtual memory" is a technique of making memory seem larger than it really is by using whatever memory space, other than in its own RAM, may be available elsewhere for holding data, such as on a hard disk, and loading it into main memory in such a way that it appears as if it were in main memory all the time. This means that you can work with as much memory as you have disk space, but the price you pay for this luxury is speed – virtual memory is only as fast as the access time of your disk, although if you have plenty of RAM, the memory exchanges between RAM and disk should be almost transparent. 25, 27, 28

virus A computer program that is deliberately written to alter the normal operation of a computer. These virus programs are spread from computer to computer across networks or when disks are copied in one and used in another. Viruses may infect some files, but not others (say, applications, but not documents), and they manifest themselves in different ways, sometimes by crashing your computer, or by simply beeping, displaying a message, or causing strange behavior such as bouncing the pointer around the screen or altering font styles. Although very few

viruses cause malicious damage, some may create serious problems. In any event, all Macs should have virus protection software installed. 75, 138

virus protection program A utility program designed, at least, to alert you to the fact that a disk or file is infected and, at best, to eradicate the virus and prevent any other possible infections. There are many such utilities available, both commercial and shareware.

visual → rough.

visual interface → GUI.

VLF abb: very low frequency → ELF.

volume A device or a partition where data is stored. → disk; partitioning.

volume bitmap A record of the used (represented by an "on" bit) and unused (off) blocks on a volume.

volume directory → directory.

W

WAN abb: wide area network. A network spread over a large area and which may use satellite or land-based telecommunications links. As distinct from a local area network (LAN), two or more of which may connected to each other by a WAN.

warm boot To restart your Mac without recourse to the power switch. You can reboot your Mac by selecting the Restart command (Special menu) or by using the reset button on the front of the CPU.

web authoring Creating documents suitable for (publishing on) the internet. 73, 78

weight The degree of boldness of a typeface.

w.f. (typ.) abb: wrong font, a mark used in proof correction to indicate type set in a different font from the one specified.

white line A space between lines of type equivalent to the type size, including leading.

white space Page areas with no text or images. → working white.

wide area network → WAN.

widget A colloquial term for any unspecified device.

widow Strictly speaking, a short line at the end of a paragraph that falls at the top of a column or page, but the term is often used to describe a single word at the end of any paragraph.

wildcard → text marker.

WIMPs *abb:* Windows, icon, mouse (or menus), and pointer – the acronym for the graphical user interface of the Mac. *17, 19*

window An area on the screen that displays the contents of a disk, folder, or document. Windows can be opened or closed, moved around the desktop, and you can sometimes change their size or scroll through them. *18, 20–1*

Windows/Windows 95/ Windows NT Forms of the Microsoft PC operating system that partially emulate the Macintosh user interface. Software and/or hardware solutions allow the system to run on Macs as well.

word A term used to describe a given number of bits.

Word *(app.)* 74

word break → hyphenation.

WordPerfect *(app.)* 74

word processor An application that provides text editing features such as spelling checkers, indexing, sorting, etc. *74*

word space The space between whole words, based on the width of characters of the typeset size.

word underline → underline.

word wrap The automatic flow of text from one line to the next as you enter it, without the need to press the Return key.

working methods, *case study 110–12*

working white (ww) A term describing white space in a design or layout which contains no text or images, but which forms an integral part of the design.

worksheet A term sometimes used to describe a spreadsheet template.

workstation A term used to describe the physical location and immediate environment of computer input – in other words, the place where you work on your computer.

WORM *abb:* write once read many, a large-capacity data storage device utilizing optical disks onto which data can be written only once and which can then never be erased → CD-ROM

wristwatch pointer The shape the pointer usually assumes to advise you that data is being processed. → pointer.

write-enable The opposite of write-protect.

write once read many → WORM.

write-protect To protect a disk from erasure, accidental or otherwise, or from contamination by viruses, by preventing any data from being written to it or deleted from it, although the contents can still be read.

writing head → read/write head.

wrong reading *(rep./pri.)* The term used to describe copy or film that reads backwards when viewed with the emulsion on the desired side.

ww *abb:* → working white.

WWW *abb:* World Wide Web. Web sites can display styled text, graphics, and video.

WYSIWYG (pron: wizzywig) An acronym for "what you see is what you get," referring to the accuracy of on-screen rendering relative to printed output. *39*

X

XCMD *abb:* → external command.

x-height The height, or "mean-line," of a lower-case letter, without ascenders or descenders.

xerography A dry copying process in which electrostatically charged powder is bonded to paper.

XFCN *abb:* → external function.

XON/XOFF A "handshaking" protocol used by computers when communicating via modems.

XRes *(app.)* 65

YZ

Y *abb:* yellow → process yellow.

zapping the PRAM The term used to describe the re-setting of a Mac's parameter RAM to its original default settings, if and when it becomes corrupted. You do this by holding down the Option-Command-P-R keys while restarting your computer. Date and time settings will not be affected.

zero point → origin.

zone One part of two or more connected networks.

zoom box The box at the right of some window title bars that, when clicked, expands the window to display all of its contents (if possible). Clicking it again reduces it to its original size.

CREDITS

p.56–7, p.62–3, p.66–7, p.68–9, 76–7, p.78–9: Digital Wisdom; p.110, p.111, p.112: Thumb Design Partnership; p.113: Steve Caplin; p.134: (top) Quarto (photographer David Burch).